■■ A YEAR IN THE LIFE ■■ OF AN ESL STUDENT

IDIOMS AND VOCABULARY YOU CAN'T LIVE WITHOUT

EDWARD J. FRANCIS

Order this book online at www.trafford.com/03-2482
or email orders@trafford.com

Most Trafford titles are also available at major online book retailers.
© Copyright 2008 Edward Francis.

Editors: David G. Tycho, Kim Rogerson

Typography and Illustrations by Arthur Mak
www.arthurmak.com

Cover design by: Art Department Design
www.artdepartmentdesign.com

First Edition, 2004

Note for Librarians: A cataloguing record for this book is available from Library
and Archives Canada at www.collectionscanada.ca/amicus/index-e.html

Printed in Victoria, BC, Canada.

ISBN: 978-1-4120-2003-9

*We at Trafford believe that it is the responsibility of us all, as both individuals
and corporations, to make choices that are environmentally and socially sound.
You, in turn, are supporting this responsible conduct each time you purchase a
Trafford book, or make use of our publishing services. To find out how you are
helping, please visit www.trafford.com/responsiblepublishing.html*

*Our mission is to efficiently provide the world's finest, most comprehensive
book publishing service, enabling every author to experience success.
To find out how to publish your book, your way, and have it available
worldwide, visit us online at www.trafford.com/10510*

www.trafford.com

North America & international
toll-free: 1 888 232 4444 (USA & Canada)
phone: 250 383 6864 ♦ fax: 250 383 6804
email: info@trafford.com

The United Kingdom & Europe
phone: +44 (0)1865 487 395 ♦ local rate: 0845 230 9601
facsimile: +44 (0)1865 481 507 ♦ email: info.uk@trafford.com

10 9 8 7

To Mom and Dad,

For everything you've done for me
both past and present

Love, Ward

ACKNOWLEDGMENTS

I would like to express my gratitude to the following people whose support and advice were invaluable in writing this textbook.

David Tycho
Kim Rogerson
Elaini Gardiner
Illean Madrid
Joel Murray
Richard Martynowski

I also wish to thank many of the teachers and students at **Pacific Language Institute** for their helpful comments and encouragement.

Finally, I would like to recognize **Arthur Mak** who was responsible for both the typography and illustrations. His artistic ability and technical skills were crucial to the design of this textbook. Feel free to e-mail him at **artmak@ymail.com**

TABLE OF CONTENTS

INTRODUCTION

PREFACE

After years of study, every student of English as a Second Language invariably asks the following questions:

"Why can't I understand my English speaking friends once they start chatting with one another?"

"Why did everyone else in the movie theater laugh at a particular line of dialogue, but I didn't?"

"Why don't I feel like my English is improving anymore?"

Students often feel frustrated by their inability to understand 'English outside of the classroom' despite having spent countless hours studying endless grammar structures. The comprehension and usage of idioms becomes crucial at this point in a student's English language development.

Learning idioms one by one and in isolation is an almost impossible endeavor. Context is the key to making the daunting task of understanding and using idiomatic English not only possible, but enjoyable too.

A Year In The Life Of An ESL Student gives a context to idioms by presenting them in lively dialogues that revolve around the experiences that international students actually have while studying English in North America.

This book makes an impression because it is written about and speaks directly to the very people who are studying it. Students will recall the language that is presented because it relates to their current learning environment, and will continue to be relevant as long as they speak English.

OVERVIEW

A Year in the Life of an ESL Student can be used by:

- Teachers as a supplementary text for advanced-level adult ESL students
- Students who want to improve their comprehension and usage of idioms and advanced vocabulary found in daily conversations, movies, TV shows, and radio broadcasts
- Students who need to refine their understanding and usage of social register
- Students who are currently studying English at a language school in North America
- Students who are preparing to study English abroad or those who desire further study once they have returned to their country

Each of the 16 chapters in the book consist of:

- Dialogues that use the idioms and vocabulary in a realistic manner and deal with the experiences and challenges that an ESL student is likely to have while studying in North America
- Clearly written definitions complete with sample sentences
- A wide range of exercises that reinforce the idioms and vocabulary that are covered in the dialogues (i.e. matching, cloze, crossword, word search, and scrambled sentences)
- Thoughtful comprehension questions that assess a student's understanding of the dialogue
- Engaging discussion questions that push the students to use the idioms and vocabulary to talk about their own life experiences
- Interesting extension exercises that draw a student's attention to one specific aspect of the dialogue

The final section of the book contains:

- A list of websites related to the topics discussed in each of the chapters
- An easy-to-use and concise answer key
- A glossary that includes all of the idioms and vocabulary covered in the dialogues

SYNOPSIS

A Year In The Life Of An ESL Student is an essential addition to the advanced level ESL classroom. By studying the varied and interesting dialogues and completing the challenging exercises, students will dramatically improve their comprehension and usage of everyday idioms and advanced level vocabulary.

The book follows Andre, a student from Switzerland, as he spends a year completing his English studies at a private language school in North America: from his arrival at the airport, to getting around the city, to attending school, to hanging out with his classmates. All of the situations and corresponding language are real and directly relevant to adult ESL students.

So join Andre on his one-year adventure. It's about to begin just outside the airport terminal.

▪▪ CHARACTERS ▪▪

MAIN CHARACTER:
ANDRE
FROM GENEVA,
SWITZERLAND

ANDRE'S CLASSMATE
CLAUDIA
FROM SANTOS,
BRAZIL

ANDRE'S ROOMMATE:
HANS
FROM STUTTGART,
GERMANY

ANDRE'S CLASSMATE
HIRO
FROM SAPPORO,
JAPAN

ANDRE'S CLASSMATE
MIN-JUNG
FROM SEOUL,
KOREA

ANDRE'S CLASSMATE
JOSE
FROM GUADALAJARA,
MEXICO

A YEAR IN THE LIFE OF AN ESL STUDENT
WEBSITE ADDRESS: www.ayearinthelife.net

▪▪ CHAPTER ONE ▪▪

ARRIVING IN THE COUNTRY

Hans picks up his friend at the airport terminal

Hans   How was the flight?

Andre   Don't ask!

Hans   Come on, what happened? **Fill me In**.

Andre   I was sitting in the window seat when this **humongous** football player sat down next to me. I'm not exaggerating; the guy took up a seat and a half. I was literally **pinned up against** the window for the whole flight.

Hans   Oh, man. That sounds terrible!

Andre   No kidding! I decided it was probably best to try and get some sleep, but I couldn't because he kept **blabbering** on and on. The only way I could escape him was to get up and **stretch my legs** for a few minutes. The moment I'd sit back down, he'd start **running off at the mouth** again.

Hans   What a nightmare! No wonder you look so tired.

Andre   Hold on. I'm just getting started. He kept ordering more and more **booze**. He was constantly **pestering** the flight attendants for scotch until finally he was completely **bombed**. He didn't stop **gulping down** drinks until we were at least half way through the flight. Oh and I almost forgot, he had the worst **B.O.** God, it was **appalling**.

Hans   Well, **on the bright side**, at least you got here **safe and sound**.

Andre   I'm still not finished yet. There was this young couple and their son sitting across the aisle. What a **spoiled brat** that kid was! When he wasn't running up and down the aisle, he was **flinging** food all over the place. When somebody finally told him to **settle down**, he **burst into tears**.

Hans	That's unbelievable! You're going to need at least a week to recover from that flight, never mind the **jetlag**.
Andre	Hopefully I'll **get over** everything faster than that.
Hans	Here's the car. Why don't we put your bags in the trunk? Let me help you. They look pretty heavy.
Andre	Thanks. ....What's the apartment you found for us like? I hope it's not **a dive**.
Hans	I think you'll like it. It's right downtown. The apartment building is fairly new so everything is clean. It even has a nice swimming pool that we'll be able to use in the summer. It took me a while to **come across** an affordable two-bedroom that we'd be comfortable in.
Andre	Thanks for finding it for us. It sounds great. I'm sure that I'll **feel right at home**. I can't wait to get there and **put that flight behind me**.
Hans	OK. Let's get in the car.
Andre	Will it take long to get to the apartment?
Hans	Don't worry. We'll be there **in no time**.

DEFINITIONS

adj. – adjective	*exclam.* – exclamation	*n.* – noun
adv. – adverb	*i.* – idiom, phrasal verb	*v.* – verb

fill me in (to) *i.* – give me the details
I want to know what happened on your date last night. Fill me in.

humongous *adj.* – enormous, gigantic, huge, immense
You'd better study hard because the final exam is going to be humongous.

pin someone up against something (to) *i.* – push someone up against something
The hockey player pinned his opponent up against the boards.

blabber (to) *v.* – talk too much, gab, yak, yap
The drunk guy I met in the bar blabbered on and on about his ex-wife.

stretch one's legs (to) *i.* – exercise one's legs after a period of inactivity
I really needed to stretch my legs after sitting on the bus for five hours.

run off at the mouth (to) *i.* – talk too much, gab, yak, yap
She was running off at the mouth about her new boyfriend for the entire evening.

booze *n.* – alcohol, liquor
Don't forget we have to buy some booze for the party tonight.

pester someone (to) *v.* – constantly harass/bother someone
The young boy kept pestering his mother to buy him the expensive toy.

bombed *adj.* – hammered, loaded, smashed, very drunk
She got bombed on New Year's Eve because she drank too much champagne.

gulp down something (to) *i.* – drink something quickly
He gulped down the orange juice after playing tennis in the hot summer sun.

B.O. *n.* – bad body odor (a hygiene problem)
He had terrible B.O. because he hadn't taken a shower in three days.

appalling *adj.* – awful, dreadful, terrible
The appalling behavior of the teenagers shocked the older married couple.

on the bright side *i.* – on the positive side
He crashed the car, but on the bright side nobody got hurt.

safe and sound *i.* – safely
We arrived home safe and sound even though we had to drive through the blizzard.

spoiled *adj.* – pampered, get anything one wants
That child was spoiled rotten because his parents never disciplined him.

brat *n.* – terrible child
Someone should tell that brat to sit down and be quiet until the movie is finished.

fling something (to) *v.* – throw something
The infant didn't eat the food. She was more interested in flinging it all over the place.

settle down (to) *i.* – calm down
The teacher finally had to tell the noisy students to settle down.

burst into tears (to) *i.* – start to cry suddenly and loudly
She burst into tears when she found out that her husband had died in the car accident.

jetlag *n.* – fatigue caused by air travel
I can't stay awake in class because I still have jetlag.

get over something/someone (to) *i.* – recover from something/someone
It took me almost two weeks to get over my cold.

dive (a) *n.* – a terrible, old, dirty place
That bar was disgusting. I'm never going back to that dive again.

come across something (to) *i.* – find something by accident
I came across an old high school picture while I was cleaning up my room.

feel at home (to) *i.* – feel comfortable in a new place
I'm starting to feel at home after living here for several weeks.

put something behind someone (to) *i.* – forget about a bad experience
I'm going to have to put that awful experience behind me.

in no time *i.* – quickly, soon
He finished his homework in no time because he wanted to go to the movies.

__H__	1 booze	A	soon
____	2 safe and sound	B	exercise legs after inactivity
____	3 fling something	C	forget a bad experience
____	4 spoiled	D	push someone against something
____	5 in no time	E	safely
____	6 humongous	F	recover from something
____	7 settle down	G	drink something quickly
____	8 bombed	H	alcohol
____	9 stretch one's legs	I	awful
____	10 pester someone	J	on the positive side
____	11 fill me in	K	calm down
____	12 B.O.	L	terrible child
____	13 gulp down something	M	give me the details
____	14 put something behind someone	N	throw something
____	15 brat	O	very drunk
____	16 appalling	P	start crying suddenly
____	17 pin someone up against something	Q	enormous
____	18 on the bright side	R	bad body odor
____	19 get over something	S	harass/bother someone
____	20 burst into tears	T	pampered

EXERCISE 2

USE THE WORDS/IDIOMS BELOW TO COMPLETE EACH OF THE FOLLOWING SENTENCES.

brat	gulped down	safe and sound
fill me in	running off at the mouth	jetlag
dive	get over	bombed
pester	pinned up against	burst into tears
B.O.	stretch my legs	came across

1 The basketball player _____ the whole bottle of water in a flash.

2 I really needed to _____ after sitting in the car for more than three hours.

3 The young girl _____ when her mother left her at pre-school for the first time.

4 I don't want to go over to his apartment again because it's a _____.

5 He just arrived in the country, so I think he's still suffering from _____.

6 I was _____ the window because there were too many people in the car.

7 The customer continued to _____ the waitress until she brought him the bill.

8 The student kept _____ even though the teacher had told him to be quiet.

9 He's a _____ because his parents have never disciplined him.

10 I _____ a $100 bill while I was vacuuming my car this morning.

11 What happened when you went for an interview at that company? _____.

12 He was _____ after he spent most of the evening in the bar with his friend.

13 The man who sat next to me on the bus had _____. The smell was terrible.

14 It took him a long time to _____ his divorce.

15 She arrived home _____ even though she almost got hit in the crosswalk.

EXERCISE 3

COMPLETE THE FOLLOWING CROSSWORD PUZZLE
USING WORDS/IDIOMS FROM THE DIALOGUE.

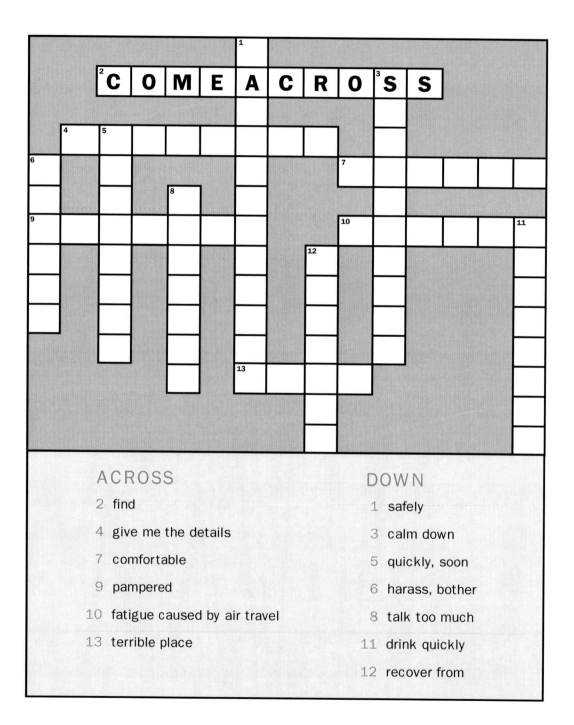

ACROSS

2 find

4 give me the details

7 comfortable

9 pampered

10 fatigue caused by air travel

13 terrible place

DOWN

1 safely

3 calm down

5 quickly, soon

6 harass, bother

8 talk too much

11 drink quickly

12 recover from

EXERCISE 4

1 After the game, he **gulped down** the entire bottle of Coke **in no time**.
   a After the game, he sipped the Coke for a while.
   b After the game, he drank the Coke in a flash.

2 It was difficult for him to **put that frightening experience behind him**.
   a He couldn't remember the frightening experience he'd had.
   b He couldn't forget about the frightening experience he'd had.

3 I couldn't wait to **stretch my legs** after the long drive was finally finished.
   a I needed to get out of the car and walk around.
   b I wanted to get into the car after walking around for a while.

4 The young man was **bombed** after he drank too much beer.
   a He certainly wasn't sober after drinking so much.
   b He was still fairly sober after drinking a lot of beer.

5 The mistake that the student made in front of the class was **humongous**.
   a The student made an insignificant mistake in front of the class.
   b The mistake the student made in front of the class was enormous.

6 The teenager kept **pestering** his mother until she finally let him have the car.
   a His mother let him have the car after being asked many times.
   b The teenager didn't get the car because he annoyed his mother.

7 She was so excited that we couldn't stop her from **running off at the mouth**.
   a She was so excited that we couldn't understand what she said.
   b She was so excited that we couldn't get her to stop talking.

8 That man had such bad **B.O.** that I had to hold my breath until I got off the bus.
   a The man who smelled really bad was breathtaking.
   b I couldn't wait to get off the bus because that man had such bad B.O.

9 The **spoiled brat** had a temper tantrum when he didn't get what he wanted.
   a The terrible child acted poorly when he got what he wanted.
   b The terrible child misbehaved when he couldn't get what he wanted.

10 The teacher told the class that if they didn't **settle down**, they'd all get a detention.
   a The teacher told the class they'd be staying late if they didn't behave themselves.
   b The teacher told the class they wouldn't have to stay late if the noise continued.

EXERCISE 5

UNSCRAMBLE THE FOLLOWING SENTENCES, ADDING PUNCTUATION WHEN NEEDED. THE BEGINNING AND END OF EACH SENTENCE HAVE ALREADY BEEN DONE FOR YOU. HINT: IT'S HELPFUL TO IDENTIFY THE WORD/IDIOM FROM THE DIALOGUE IN EACH SENTENCE.

1 **The passenger** is / stretching / to / his / bus / the / forward / legs / when / looking / **ride is over.**

   The passenger is looking forward to stretching his legs when the bus ride is over   .

2 **She asked him** / to / he / because / running / had / be / off / at / the / quiet / been / **mouth for hours.**

   _____.

3 **The boy was** / the / up / six / there / pinned / backseat / in / because / the / children / window / were / against / **of the car.**

   _____.

4 **My father told** / when / I / his / during / too / much / to / me / made / noise / down / settle / **favorite TV program.**

   _____.

5 **We arrived at** / safe / the / and / airport / sound / even / plane / though / the / **had engine trouble.**

   _____.

6 **The young girl** / she / when / saw / burst / brother / her / toy / tears / into / favorite / her / break / **into many pieces.**

   _____.

7 **He could not** / the / over / fact / get / sister / won / a / had / that / his / medal / gold / **at the Olympics.**

   _____.

8 **The teacher was** / using / to / language / the / the / hear / students / were / appalled / foul / **in the classroom.**

   _____.

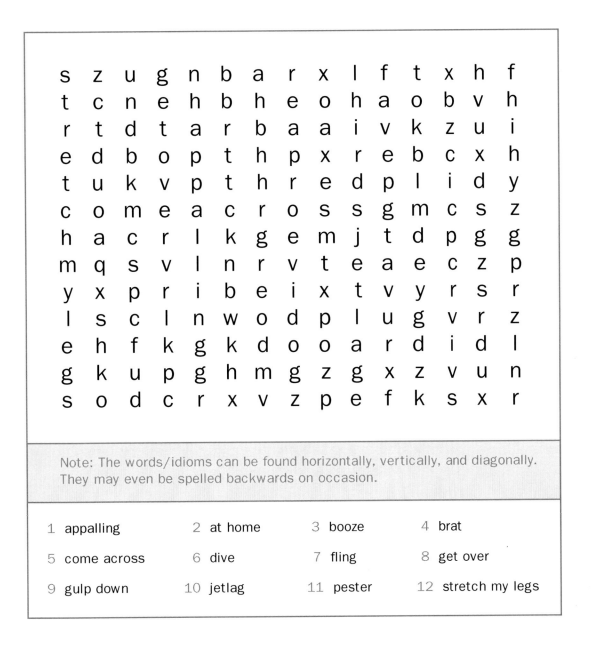

```
s  z  u  g  n  b  a  r  x  l  f  t  x  h  f
t  c  n  e  h  b  h  e  o  h  a  o  b  v  h
r  t  d  t  a  r  b  a  a  i  v  k  z  u  i
e  d  b  o  p  t  h  p  x  r  e  b  c  x  h
t  u  k  v  p  t  h  r  e  d  p  l  i  d  y
c  o  m  e  a  c  r  o  s  s  g  m  c  s  z
h  a  c  r  l  k  g  e  m  j  t  d  p  g  g
m  q  s  v  l  n  r  v  t  e  a  e  c  z  p
y  x  p  r  i  b  e  i  x  t  v  y  r  s  r
l  s  c  l  n  w  o  d  p  l  u  g  v  r  z
e  h  f  k  g  k  d  o  o  a  r  d  i  d  l
g  k  u  p  g  h  m  g  z  g  x  z  v  u  n
s  o  d  c  r  x  v  z  p  e  f  k  s  x  r
```

Note: The words/idioms can be found horizontally, vertically, and diagonally.
They may even be spelled backwards on occasion.

1 appalling	2 at home	3 booze	4 brat
5 come across	6 dive	7 fling	8 get over
9 gulp down	10 jetlag	11 pester	12 stretch my legs

Hans picks up his friend at the airport terminal

Hans   How was the flight?

Andre   Don't ask!

Hans   Come on, what happened? F_____ me in.

Andre   I was sitting in the window seat when this h_____ football player sat down
next to me. I'm not exaggerating; the guy took up a seat and a half. I was literally
p_____ up a_____ the window for the whole flight.

Hans   Oh, man. That sounds terrible!

Andre   No kidding! I decided it was probably best to try and get some sleep, but I couldn't
because he kept b_____ on and on. The only way I could escape him was to
get up and s_____ my legs for a few minutes. The moment I'd sit back down,
he'd start r_____ o_____ at the mouth again.

Hans   What a nightmare! No wonder you look so tired.

Andre   Hold on. I'm just getting started. He kept ordering more and more b_____. He
was constantly p_____ the flight attendants for scotch until finally he was
completely b_____. He didn't stop g_____ d_____ drinks until
we were at least half way through the flight. Oh and I almost forgot, he had the
worst B.O. God, it was a_____.

Hans   Well, on the b_____ s_____, at least you got here s_____ and
s_____.

Andre   I'm still not finished yet. There was this young couple and their son sitting across the
aisle. What a s_____ b_____ that kid was! When he wasn't running up
and down the aisle, he was f_____ food all over the place. When somebody
finally told him to s_____ d_____, he b_____ into
t_____.

Hans	That's unbelievable! You're going to need at least a week to recover from that flight, never mind the j_____.
Andre	Hopefully I'll g_____ o_____ everything faster than that.
Hans	Here's the car. Why don't we put your bags in the trunk? Let me help you. They look pretty heavy.
Andre	Thanks. ....What's the apartment you found for us like? I hope it's not a d_____.
Hans	I think you'll like it. It's right downtown. The apartment building is fairly new so everything is clean. It even has a nice swimming pool that we'll be able to use in the summer. It took me a while to c_____ a_____ an affordable two-bedroom that we'd be comfortable in.
Andre	Thanks for finding it for us. It sounds great. I'm sure that I'll feel right at h_____. I can't wait to get there and put that flight b_____ me.
Hans	OK. Let's get in the car.
Andre	Will it take long to get to the apartment?
Hans	Don't worry. We'll be there in n_____ t_____.

COMPREHENSION QUESTIONS

TRY TO ANSWER THE FOLLOWING QUESTIONS WITHOUT LOOKING AT THE DIALOGUE. ONCE YOU'VE FINISHED THE QUESTIONS, YOU CAN REFER TO THE DIALOGUE TO CHECK YOUR ANSWERS.

1   Who picked Andre up at the airport?

2   Do you think Andre looked relaxed after his flight? If not, how did he look?

3   Why did Andre feel uncomfortable when the passenger next to him sat down?

4   Why couldn't Andre get any sleep during the flight?

5   What was the only way Andre could get away from the passenger next to him?

6   Why was the passenger always pestering the flight attendants?

7   What hygiene problem did the passenger have?

8   Why was the young boy across the aisle annoying?

9   What happened when someone told the young boy to settle down?

10   What two things will Andre have to recover from?

11   Describe the apartment that Hans found for himself and Andre.

12   How long did it take Hans to find the apartment?

13   What did Andre want to put behind him?

14   How will they get from the airport to the apartment?

15   How long will it take to get to the apartment?

DISCUSSION QUESTIONS

DISCUSS THE FOLLOWING QUESTIONS WITH YOUR PARTNER.

PART A: General Discussion Questions

1 Who took you to the airport when you left your country? Were there any problems at the airport?

2 How did you pass the time during the flight?

3 How was the food the airline served you? What did you eat?

4 Were you able to sleep during the flight? Why? Why not?

5 Who picked you up at the airport once you arrived here? What was your first impression of him/her/them?

PART B: Idiomatic Discussion Questions

1 Did you phone your family to let them know you arrived **safe and sound**? Was it a long or short conversation? What was said?

2 How long did it take you to **get over** your **jetlag**?

3 How long did it take until you **felt at home** here?

4 Did you buy any duty-free perfume, cigarettes or **booze** on the flight here? Will you buy anything on the flight home?

5 Have you ever noticed a passenger whose behavior was **appalling**? What did he/she do?

6 Have you ever had to **pester** a flight attendant or check-in clerk in order to get something you wanted? What was it?

7 Have you ever sat next to a passenger who **ran off at the mouth**? What did he/she talk about?

GIVE IT A SHOT

IN THE DIALOGUE, THE PASSENGER SITTING NEXT TO ANDRE ON THE PLANE HAD A HYGIENE PROBLEM. TRY TO IDENTIFY WHAT'S WRONG WITH THE GENTLEMAN IN THE CHART BELOW.

PART A

G   1   Bob's running shoes are five years old.   A   He's going bald.

___   2   Bob's underwear is showing.   B   He has sleep in his eyes.

___   3   Bob hasn't taken a bath in days.   C   He has bad breath.

___   4   Bob hasn't brushed his teeth in weeks.   D   His fly is open.

___   5   Bob has been eating too much chocolate.   E   He belches after every meal.

___   6   Bob makes noise after he eats.   F   He has dandruff.

___   7   Bob's hairline is receding.   G   His running shoes reek.

___   8   Bob has white stuff on his shoulders.   H   He has zits on his face.

___   9   Bob can't open his eyes in the morning.   I   He has terrible B.O.

PART B

B   1   Bob never cleans his ears.   A   He has hay fever.

___   2   Bob's pillow has saliva on it.   B   He has earwax.

___   3   Bob always removes stuff from his nose.   C   He always snores.

___   4   Bob makes noise when he sleeps.   D   He drools while sleeping.

___   5   Bob hasn't washed his feet in days.   E   His pants are always wrinkled.

___   6   Bob eats a lot of beans.   F   He's hungover today.

___   7   Bob has itchy red eyes.   G   He has toe-jam.

___   8   Bob drank too much last night.   H   He farts a lot.

___   9   Bob never irons his pants.   I   He picks his nose constantly.

••CHAPTER TWO••

WANDERING AROUND THE CITY

Andre and Min-Jung leave school after their English placement test

Andre   So how'd your placement test go?

Min-Jung   All right I guess. I was a **bundle of nerves** during the test; I'd be amazed if I managed to answer many of the questions correctly. I could just **kick myself** for getting so anxious.

Andre   I'm sure you did fine. I was a little **keyed up** too. For some reason I had **a knot in my stomach** while the instructor was assessing me. I should've just relaxed. There really wasn't anything to get tense about.

Min-Jung   How about **a change of pace**? Do you want to **wander** through downtown with me?

Andre   Yeah I'd like to do that. I don't **know my way around** yet. It'll give me a chance to explore the city.

Min-Jung   Great! We can **take in the sights** together. Have you gone in that direction before? I wonder what's down that way?

Andre   I think we should go up the street. My roommate told me that the neighborhood to the east of the school is kind of **down-and-out**. We don't want to end up on **the wrong side of the tracks**.

Min-Jung   That's good to know. Let's **play it safe** today.

Andre   **As far as I know**, the shopping district is up this way. Let's go there. That way, if we **get off the beaten path**, we won't get ourselves into trouble.

They walk around the shopping district for an hour

Min-Jung	There sure is a lot to see. I don't think I'll **run out of** things to do in my free time. I'll have to be careful, though.
Andre	What do you mean?
Min-Jung	I could easily spend **a bundle** in some of these stores. I'd hate to **wipe out** my savings on **a shopping spree**.
Andre	You should try to keep your spending **in check**. You don't want to **run up a huge bill** while you're here. **Take it from me**, paying off a big credit card debt is such **a drag**. I had to do it once before. I never want to do that again. .... Hey, did you notice the park that we passed a few minutes ago?
Min-Jung	You mean the one across the street from the train station?
Andre	No, the big park that was **kitty-corner** to the hotel.
Min-Jung	Oh that one. Yeah, it looked beautiful. Why? Do you want to get away from all these shoppers for a while?
Andre	Yeah. I wouldn't mind **taking a break** from the crowds. Let's go see what that park has to offer.
Min-Jung	OK. Why don't we **stroll** through the park and then **check out** what's on the other side? I don't think we've been over there.
Andre	Sounds like a plan. Wow! We're **covering a lot of ground** this afternoon.
Min-Jung	That's for sure. I'll **know downtown like the back of my hand** by the time we're finished today.

DEFINITIONS

adj. – adjective	*exclam.* – exclamation	*n.* – noun
adv. – adverb	*i.* – idiom, phrasal verb	*v.* – verb

bundle of nerves (a) *i.* – very nervous
I was a bundle of nerves before I took the TOEFL exam.

kick oneself (to) *i.* – regret doing something
I could just kick myself for leaving my wallet in the restaurant last night.

keyed up *i.* – very nervous
The tennis player was keyed up while he waited for his match to begin.

knot in one's stomach (a) *i.* – a nervous feeling in the stomach
I had a knot in my stomach when I asked that beautiful girl for a date.

change of pace (a) *i.* – a change from one activity to something different
I'm tired of studying. How about a change of pace? Why don't we go for coffee?

wander (to) *v.* – walk slowly, saunter, stroll
Would you like to wander through the shopping mall this afternoon?

know one's way around (to) *i.* – be familiar with a particular area
I've never been to this part of town before. Do you know your way around?

take in the sights (to) *i.* – sightsee
I'd like to take in the sights after we check into the hotel.

down-and-out *i.* – destitute, very poor
The unshaven man in the dirty clothes looks down-and-out.

wrong side of the tracks (the) *i.* – the bad section of a city
She became a millionaire even though she grew up on the wrong side of the tracks.

play it safe (to) *i.* – be careful
I think you've had too much to drink. Let's play it safe and take a taxi home.

as far as someone knows *i.* – to the best of one's knowledge
As far as I know, there's a bank right around the next corner.

get off the beaten path (to) *i.* – go to an area not visited by most people
He was completely lost for two hours after he got off the beaten path.

run out of something (to) *i.* – use up all of something
I ran out of things to do in my free time while I was living in that small town.

bundle (a) *n.* – a lot of money
I spent a bundle when I bought a jacket at that designer clothing store.

wipe out something (to) *i.* – destroy something
The hurricane wiped out at least half of the town.

shopping spree (a) *n.* – a shopping binge, shop a lot
He went on a huge shopping spree after he won the state lottery.

in check *adv.* – under control
I'll have to try to keep my smoking in check.

run up a bill (to) *i.* – get into debt, spend a lot of money
I ran up a large bill at the hotel while I was there on vacation.

take it from me (to) *i.* – trust me
Take it from me, that movie is unbelievably boring.

drag (a) *n.* – a bore
The advanced accounting course I took at college was such a drag.

kitty-corner *adj.* – diagonal in location
The post office you're looking for is kitty-corner to the high school.

take a break (to) *i.* – take a rest
I think we've worked long enough. What do you say we take a break from studying?

stroll (to) *v.* – walk slowly, saunter, wander
I'd like to stroll along that beautiful white sand beach after lunch.

check out something/someone (to) *i.* – look at something/someone
Check out that convertible sports car. It must be really expensive.

cover a lot of ground (to) *i.* – travel a great distance
We've been walking for over an hour. We've certainly covered a lot of ground.

know something like the back of one's hand (to) *i.* – be very familiar with something
I know this area like the back of my hand because I've lived here all my life.

_S_	1 wander	A	very nervous
___	2 down-and-out	B	a shopping binge
___	3 play it safe	C	go into debt
___	4 kick oneself	D	destitute
___	5 a drag	E	use up all of something
___	6 check out something	F	to the best of one's knowledge
___	7 cover a lot of ground	G	be familiar with an area
___	8 take it from me	H	a change of activity
___	9 a shopping spree	I	destroy something
___	10 run out of something	J	regret doing something
___	11 keyed up	K	be careful
___	12 take in the sights	L	diagonal in location
___	13 a change of pace	M	sightsee
___	14 the wrong side of the tracks	N	look at something
___	15 as far as someone knows	O	a lot of money
___	16 run up a bill	P	trust me
___	17 kitty-corner	Q	the bad section of a city
___	18 wipe out something	R	travel a great distance
___	19 a bundle	S	stroll
___	20 know one's way around	T	a bore

EXERCISE 2

USE THE WORDS/IDIOMS BELOW TO COMPLETE
EACH OF THE FOLLOWING SENTENCES.

shopping spree	a drag	kitty-corner
take it from me	a bundle	ran out of
like the back of his hand	take in the sights	kick myself
wrong side of the tracks	to wander	wiped out
check out	a knot in my stomach	a change of pace

1 We were only in the city for one day, so we didn't have a chance to _____ .

2 You should _____ that beautiful girl over there. I think she likes you.

3 We had to walk home because the car _____ gas on the highway.

4 I don't want to study with that teacher because I heard his class is _____ .

5 He knows that town _____ because he went to high school there.

6 She went on a _____ after she got her first paycheck from that job.

7 I'm bored. Why don't we go to the amusement park for _____ ?

8 I was a little scared when I realized that I was on the _____ .

9 I like _____ along my favorite street and look in the store windows.

10 She spent _____ while on a two-week vacation in the south of France.

11 I had _____ when I took a university exam for the first time.

12 I could just _____ for forgetting my girlfriend's birthday.

13 The beautiful park you are looking for is _____ to the public library.

14 _____ , you don't want to eat dinner in that restaurant.

15 The underground gas explosion _____ a whole block of the city.

EXERCISE 3

WHAT WORD/IDIOM FROM THE DIALOGUE MATCHES THE FOLLOWING
DEFINITIONS? WHEN THE EXERCISE HAS BEEN COMPLETED, THE IDIOM
FOR 'THE BAD SECTION OF A CITY' WILL BE SPELLED VERTICALLY.

1   a nervous feeling in my stomach   a knot in my s(t)omach
2   sightsee   _ _ _ _ _ _ _(_)_ _ _ _ _ _
3   look at   _ _(_)_ _ _ _ _

4   destroy   (_)_ _ _ _ _ _
5   a bore   _ _(_)_ _
6   a shopping binge   _ _ _(_)_ _ _ _ _ _ _ _ _
7   get into debt   _ _(_) _ _ _ _ _ _ _
8   travel a great distance   _ _ _ _ _ _ _ _ _ _ _ (_)_ _ _ _

9   walk slowly   (_)_ _ _ _ _
10 diagonal in location   _(_)_ _ - _ _ _ _ _ _
11 a lot of money   _ _ _ _(_)_ _
12 take a rest   _ _ _(_) _ _ _ _ _ _ _ _

13 use up everything   _ _ _ (_)_ _ _ _
14 to the best of my knowledge   _ _ (_)_ _ _ _ _ _ _ _ _

15 be careful   _ _ _ _ _(_) _ _ _ _
16 a change from one activity to another _ _(_)_ _ _ _ _ _ _ _ _ _
17 walk slowly   _ _ _(_)_

18 destitute   _ _ _ _ - _ _ _ - _ _(_)
19 very nervous   _ _ _ _ _ _ _ _ _ _ _(_)_ _ _
20 an area not commonly visited   _ _ _ _ _ _ _ _(_)_ _ _ _ _ _ _
21 under control   _ _ _ _ _(_)_
22 be very familiar with   _ _ _ _ _ _ _ _ _ _ _ _ _(_) _ _ _ _ _ _ _ _
23 I regret   _ _ _ _ _ _(_)_ _ _

Unscramble the following words/idioms from the dialogue.

24 wkons ish ywa rudnao   _ _ _ _ _ _ _ _ _ _ _ _ _ _ _ _ _
25 etak ti mfor em   _ _ _ _ _ _ _ _ _ _ _ _
26 vcreo a tlo fo drnugo   _ _ _ _ _ _ _ _ _ _ _ _ _ _ _ _

EXERCISE 4

REWRITE THE FOLLOWING SENTENCES USING
A WORD/IDIOM FROM THE DIALOGUE.

1 To the best of my knowledge, the park is four blocks down the street and on the right.

   _As far as I know, the park is four blocks down the street and on the right_____.

2 I'd like to go sightseeing as soon as we finish breakfast this morning.

   _____.

3 I had a nervous feeling in my stomach when I saw my ex-girlfriend on the street.

   _____.

4 The tidal wave completely destroyed the small fishing village 20 miles down the coast.

   _____.

5 Look at that handsome guy standing in front of the vending machine.

   _____.

6 I spent a lot of money on that state-of-the-art computer I bought yesterday.

   _____.

7 The store you're looking for is diagonal to the gas station in the next block.

   _____.

8 They might get into trouble if they end up in the bad part of town.

   _____.

9 That subject is such a bore that I'm considering changing classes.

   _____.

10 We can't make pancakes this morning because we've used up all of the milk.

   _____.

EXERCISE 5

UNSCRAMBLE THE FOLLOWING SENTENCES, ADDING PUNCTUATION WHEN NEEDED. THE BEGINNING AND END OF EACH SENTENCE HAVE ALREADY BEEN DONE FOR YOU. HINT: IT'S HELPFUL TO IDENTIFY THE WORD/IDIOM FROM THE DIALOGUE IN EACH SENTENCE.

1 **I think it's** / here/ from / safe / play / walk / too / and / it / so / late / home / let's / to / **take a taxi.**

   I think it's too late to walk home from here, so let's play it safe and take a taxi   .

2 **I'm going to** / scuba / goes / wife / ocean / sights / take / my / in / in / the / diving / while / the / **with her friend.**

   _____ .

3 **She had a** / give / had / she / a / stomach / when / knot / to / speech / her / in / front / in / **of 200 people.**

   _____ .

4 **I don't really** / here / around / city / because / know / only / I've / my / way / this / been / yet / **for two days.**

   _____ .

5 **The muscular sprinter** / bundle / a / the / before / at / final / 100–meter / nerves / was / of / **the track meet.**

   _____ .

6 **She exceeded her** / credit / she / when / shopping / on / went / a / three-day / limit / spree / card / **in New York.**

   _____ .

7 **The elderly couple** / through / garden / colorful / a / on / the / flower / strolled / **sunny Friday afternoon.**

   _____ .

8 **The group of** / the / the / they / when / boys / of / side / on / wrong / up / ended / got / nervous / tracks / **late at night.**

   _____ .

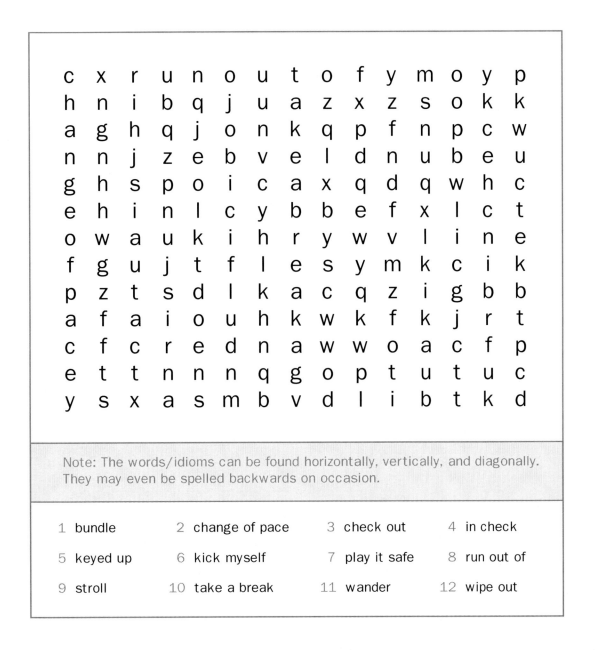

```
c  x  r  u  n  o  u  t  o  f  y  m  o  y  p
h  n  i  b  q  j  u  a  z  x  z  s  o  k  k
a  g  h  q  j  o  n  k  q  p  f  n  p  c  w
n  n  j  z  e  b  v  e  l  d  n  u  b  e  u
g  h  s  p  o  i  c  a  x  q  d  q  w  h  c
e  h  i  n  l  c  y  b  b  e  f  x  l  c  t
o  w  a  u  k  i  h  r  y  w  v  l  i  n  e
f  g  u  j  t  f  l  e  s  y  m  k  c  i  k
p  z  t  s  d  l  k  a  c  q  z  i  g  b  b
a  f  a  i  o  u  h  k  w  f  k  j  r  t
c  f  c  r  e  d  n  a  w  w  o  a  c  f  p
e  t  t  n  n  n  q  g  o  p  t  u  t  u  c
y  s  x  a  s  m  b  v  d  l  i  b  t  k  d
```

Note: The words/idioms can be found horizontally, vertically, and diagonally.
They may even be spelled backwards on occasion.

1 bundle	2 change of pace	3 check out	4 in check
5 keyed up	6 kick myself	7 play it safe	8 run out of
9 stroll	10 take a break	11 wander	12 wipe out

EXERCISE 7

Andre and Min-Jung leave school after their English placement test

Andre So how'd your placement test go?

Min-Jung All right I guess. I was a b_____ of n_____ during the test; I'd be amazed if I managed to answer many of the questions correctly. I could just k_____ myself for getting so anxious.

Andre I'm sure you did fine. I was a little k_____ u_____ too. For some reason I had a k_____ in my s_____ while the instructor was assessing me. I should've just relaxed. There really wasn't anything to get tense about.

Min-Jung How about a c_____ of p_____? Do you want to w_____ through downtown with me?

Andre Yeah I'd like to do that. I don't k_____ my way a_____ yet. It'll give me a chance to explore the city.

Min-Jung Great! We can t_____ in the s_____ together. Have you gone in that direction before? I wonder what's down that way?

Andre I think we should go up the street. My roommate told me that the neighborhood to the east of the school is kind of d_____-and-o_____. We don't want to end up on the w_____ side of the t_____.

Min-Jung That's good to know. Let's p_____ it s_____ today.

Andre As f_____ as I k_____, the shopping district is up this way. Let's go there. That way, if we get off the b_____ p_____, we won't get ourselves into trouble.

They walk around the shopping district for an hour

Min-Jung There sure is a lot to see. I don't think I'll r_____ o_____ of things to do in my free time. I'll have to be careful, though.

Andre What do you mean?

Min-Jung I could easily spend a b_____ in some of these stores. I'd hate to w_____ o_____ my savings on a s_____ s_____.

Andre You should try to keep your spending i_____ c_____. You don't want to r_____ u_____ a huge bill while you're here. T_____ it from me, paying off a big credit card debt is such a d_____. I had to do it once before. I never want to do that again. .... Hey, did you notice the park that we past a few minutes ago?

Min-Jung You mean the one across the street from the train station?

Andre No, the big park that was k_____-c_____ to the hotel.

Min-Jung Oh that one. Yeah, it looked beautiful. Why? Do you want to get away from all these shoppers for a while?

Andre Yeah. I wouldn't mind t_____ a b_____ from the crowds. Let's go see what that park has to offer.

Min-Jung OK. Why don't we s_____ through the park and then c_____ out what's on the other side? I don't think we've been over there.

Andre Sounds like a plan. Wow! We're c_____ a lot of g_____ this afternoon.

Min-Jung That's for sure. I'll know downtown like the b_____ of my h_____ by the time we're finished today.

COMPREHENSION QUESTIONS

1. How did Min-Jung's placement test go?

2. How did she feel during the test?

3. Why did she say, "I could just kick myself"?

4. What expressions did Andre use to describe how he felt during his test?

5. What did Min-Jung suggest as a change of pace?

6. Did Andre know his way around the city?

7. What did Andre's roommate tell him about the neighborhood to the east of the school?

8. What part of town did they end up going to?

9. What would happen if they got off the beaten path in the shopping district?

10. Why was Min-Jung worried about spending money?

11. Has Andre been in debt before? What was his advice to Min-Jung?

12. Which park did Andre want to go to?

13. Why did he want to go there?

14. What did Min-Jung want to check out after they strolled through the park?

15. What will Min-Jung know like the back of her hand by the end of the day?

DISCUSSION QUESTIONS

DISCUSS THE FOLLOWING QUESTIONS WITH YOUR PARTNER.

PART A: General Discussion Questions

1 Tell me about the first time you walked around this city. What was your first impression of the city?

2 What's your favorite street in this city? Why do you like it?

3 Did you have any difficulty finding the school the first time you came here?

4 How long did it take you to become familiar with the public transportation system here?

5 How does the shopping in this city compare with your hometown?

PART B: Idiomatic Discussion Questions

1 Have you **taken in most of the sights** in this area? Name something you haven't seen yet. What other nearby city would you like to visit? Why do you want to go there?

2 Do you think that you'll **run out of** things to do in your free time while you're here?

3 Have you ever ended up **on the wrong side of the tracks** while **wandering** around this city? Tell me about it.

4 What would you like to do for **a change of pace** this weekend?

5 If you could go on a $1,000 **shopping spree** in just one store, where would you go?

6 Tell me about the last time you spent **a bundle** on something. Do you think it was worth the money you spent on it?

7 Were you **keyed up** during your English placement test? How did it go? Do you think the teacher who assessed you placed you at an appropriate level?

GIVE IT A SHOT

IN THE DIALOGUE, ANDRE AND MIN-JUNG WANDER THROUGH DOWNTOWN TOGETHER. HAVE YOUR TEACHER EXPLAIN/ DEMONSTRATE THE FOLLOWING WALKING STYLES.

Leisurely	Meander–Mosey–Saunter–Stroll–Wander
Slowly	Edge–Shuffle
Quickly	Hurry–Stride
Gracefully	Parade–Prance–Strut–Swagger
Uniformly	March–Pace
Heavily	Lumber–Plod–Slog–Stomp–Trudge
Secretly	Creep–Sneak–Tiptoe
Childlike	Toddle–Totter
Awkwardly	Limp–Lurch–Hobble–Stagger–Stumble–Trip

Choose the correct answer to complete the following sentences

1. The romantic couple (marched/strolled) along the beautiful beach at sunset.

2. The teenager (sneaked/hobbled) out of the house even though he had been grounded.

3. The drunk (staggered/tiptoed) out of the bar and down the street towards his house.

4. The rugby player (pranced/limped) off the field after being tackled by three players.

5. The gorgeous model (strutted/shuffled) up and down the runway in her slinky outfit.

6. The marines (sauntered/marched) down the street in the 'Fourth of July' parade.

7. The girl dropped her books when she (paced/stumbled) over a rock on the sidewalk.

8. The baby (toddled/strode) out of the yard and toward a busy street.

9. The handsome man (shuffled/swaggered) up to the woman and asked her to dance.

10. The man (stomped/edged) out of the living room after he had a fight with his wife.

▪▪CHAPTER THREE▪▪

SITTING IN THE STUDENT LOUNGE

SITTING IN THE STUDENT LOUNGE

Andre joins Claudia at a table in the lounge

Andre   Hi. What's with all the papers everywhere?

Claudia   I just finished **a pile** of homework I had to do for my next class.

Andre   How's that class going? I've heard that the material in that course is kind of **run of the mill**.

Claudia   Actually, the course material is pretty good, but the teacher certainly isn't **the cream of the crop**. I'm sure **his days are numbered**.

Andre   It's a shame you didn't get the other instructor who's teaching that class. I've heard she's really interesting. Do you have to continue with the same teacher next month?

Claudia   I hope not. I won't know for sure until the schedule for next month is posted. I'll **keep my fingers crossed**. How're things going with you?

Andre   So far so good, but I'm going to have to **knuckle down**. **My first crack at** the TOEFL exam is coming up soon. If I start **slacking off** now, I'll have to **cram** for the entire week before the exam. I really need to get a good score if I hope to go to graduate school in the States some day.

Claudia   When do you take the exam?

Andre   It's **slated** for the middle of next month. I've forgotten the exact date. I'll have to **look into it**.

Claudia   Well, don't get too **stressed out** about it.

Andre   I promise I won't **lose any sleep over it**.

Claudia   What are you **up to** this weekend?

Andre	I plan on **hooking up with** this cute girl I met at that new club that just opened. There's only one **hitch**. My friend wants to join us.
Claudia	Oh no! That could be a problem. **Two's company, three's a crowd**, wouldn't you say?
Andre	Exactly. I get the feeling my friend likes her too. Maybe I'll just **ditch him** at the library before the date.
Claudia	Really?
Andre	No. I'm just **pulling your leg**. To tell the truth, I'm not sure what to do. I'll have to **sleep on it**, I guess. What've you got planned for the weekend?
Claudia	Not too much. I'll probably just run a few **errands**.
Andre	That's it?
Claudia	Well, it's my homestay mother's birthday on Sunday. I should probably buy her a gift of some kind. She said that she doesn't want us to **make a fuss over it**, but she'd be **crushed** if everyone forgot her big day.
Andre	How old is she?
Claudia	I'm not sure, but she's **getting on**. Maybe sixty something. She's still **young at heart**, though. She jogs four times a week, plays tennis in the summer, and even skis every winter.
Andre	That's impressive. Look at the time! I have to **run**. I'll talk to you again at coffee break. See you.

DEFINITIONS

adj. – adjective	*exclam.* – exclamation	*n.* – noun
adv. – adverb	*i.* – idiom, phrasal verb	*v.* – verb

pile (a) *n.* – a bunch, a load, a lot, a stack, a ton
I have a pile of laundry that I have to wash this morning.

run of the mill *i.* – average, ordinary
The speech he gave to the college students was just run of the mill

cream of the crop (the) *i.* – the best of the group
The cream of the crop study at Harvard University.

one's days are numbered *i.* – someone is going to die or get fired soon
I think his days are numbered because of his poor performance at work.

keep one's fingers crossed (to) *i.* – hope for a positive result
I hope your team wins the game this afternoon. I'll keep my fingers crossed.

knuckle down (to) *i.* – become serious about one's work
I'm going to have to knuckle down if I hope to pass that difficult course.

one's first crack at something *i.* – one's first attempt at something
Today he's going to take his first crack at ballroom dancing.

slack off (to) *i.* – reduce the amount of work one does
Most of the students slacked off after they wrote the midterm exam.

cram (to) *v.* – study hard
She has to spend tonight cramming for the final exam.

slate (to) *v.* – schedule
He said that the quiz is slated for the day after tomorrow.

look into something (to) *i.* – investigate something
I don't know the answer to your question. I'll have to look into it.

stressed out *i.* – more stress than someone can handle
She's stressed out over the presentation she has to give to the class tomorrow.

lose sleep over something (to) *i.* – worry about something
I'm sure your audition will go well. Don't lose any sleep over it.

up to *adj.* – doing, occupied with
What are you up to after school today?

hook up with someone (to) *i.* – meet someone
She's going to hook up with her friends at the club tonight.

hitch *n.* – problem
I'd like to go to the movies with you. There's just one hitch. I don't have any money.

two's company, three's a crowd *i.* – a third person isn't welcome
I don't want your sister to come with us on our date. Two's company, three's a crowd.

ditch someone (to) *v.* – lose someone on purpose
We ditched him at the bar when he went to the bathroom.

pull one's leg (to) *i.* – joke, kid
I'm not serious. I'm just pulling your leg.

sleep on something (to) *i.* – consider something overnight
That's a big decision. I'm afraid that I'll have to sleep on it.

errand *n.* – a short trip to buy groceries, do banking, etc.
I'll be back in about thirty minutes because I need to run a few errands.

make a fuss over something (to) *i.* – overreact, go over the top
My friends really made a fuss over my 21st birthday.

crushed *adj.* – devastated, emotionally destroyed
The little boy was crushed when his dog got run over by a car.

getting on *i.* – getting old
I realized that my parents are getting on the last time I went home for a visit.

young at heart *i.* – have a youthful attitude
My grandmother is 75 years old, but she's still young at heart.

run (to) *v.* – leave
I have to run or I'll be late for my next business appointment.

K	1 up to	A	joke
___	2 run	B	a lot of something
___	3 two's company, three's a crowd	C	problem
___	4 young at heart	D	consider something overnight
___	5 a pile of something	E	investigate something
___	6 run of the mill	F	become serious about one's work
___	7 hook up with someone	G	getting old
___	8 hitch	H	average
___	9 look into something	I	overreact
___	10 slated for	J	lose someone on purpose
___	11 the cream of the crop	K	doing
___	12 keep one's fingers crossed	L	more stress than one can handle
___	13 knuckle down	M	devastated
___	14 pull one's leg	N	the best of the group
___	15 ditch someone	O	a third person isn't welcome
___	16 sleep on something	P	leave
___	17 getting on	Q	hope for a positive result
___	18 crushed	R	have a youthful attitude
___	19 make a fuss over something	S	meet someone
___	20 stressed out	T	scheduled for

EXERCISE 2

USE THE WORDS/IDIOMS BELOW TO COMPLETE
EACH OF THE FOLLOWING SENTENCES.

run a few errands	slated for	hook up with
cream of the crop	sleep on it	slacked off
two's company, three's a crowd	young at heart	made a fuss
his days are numbered	cram	crushed
lose any sleep over it	up to	run

1 You have to be the _____ if you plan on attending that famous university.

2 I almost failed the mid-term because I _____ the week before the exam.

3 The election date is _____ the first Monday in October.

4 You can't come with my girlfriend and me tonight. Sorry, _____.

5 The customer _____ when the waiter spilled coffee all over the table.

6 The graduate student was _____ when he received a failing mark on his thesis.

7 Even though my grandfather is 79 years old, he's still _____.

8 She's not at home right now because she had to _____ this morning.

9 I can't go out with you tonight because I have to _____ for tomorrow's exam.

10 I was surprised that I didn't see you last weekend. What were you _____?

11 That employee's performance has been terrible. I'm sure _____.

12 We should _____ or we'll never make it to the airport in time for the flight.

13 He'd like to _____ you at the coffee shop on the corner this afternoon.

14 I'm sorry, I can't make that decision right away. I'll have to _____.

15 I'm sure that you'll do fine at your new job. You shouldn't _____.

EXERCISE 3

COMPLETE THE FOLLOWING CROSSWORD PUZZLE
USING WORDS/IDIOMS FROM THE DIALOGUE.

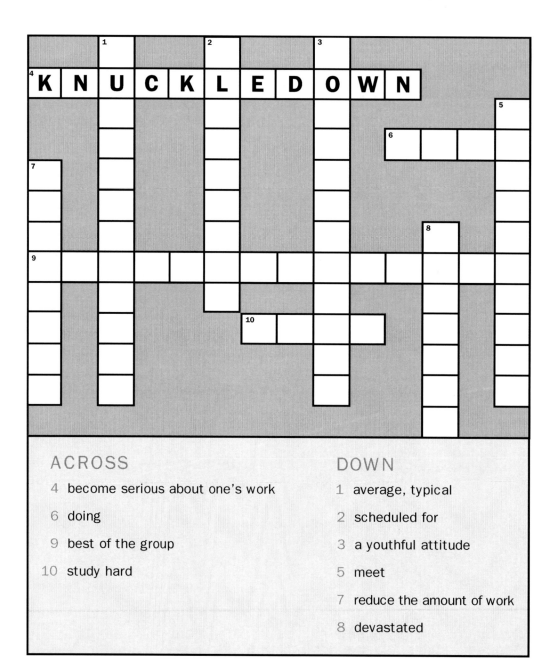

ACROSS

4 become serious about one's work

6 doing

9 best of the group

10 study hard

DOWN

1 average, typical

2 scheduled for

3 a youthful attitude

5 meet

7 reduce the amount of work

8 devastated

1 His **days are numbered** because he never shows up for work on time.
   a It's only a matter of time before he gets fired because he's always late for work.
   b He won't be let go because he almost never shows up late for work.

2 She is **stressed out** because she has way too much work to do today.
   a She is tense because she has done way too much work today.
   b She is uptight because she has way too much work to do today.

3 The customer **made a fuss** because the soup he ordered for lunch was cold.
   a There was a commotion because the customer didn't like his soup.
   b The customer complimented the waiter about the cold soup.

4 I'm going to **hook up with** my best friend at the gym after lunch.
   a I'm going to meet my friend for lunch after I work out at the gym.
   b I'm going to get together with my best friend at the gym this afternoon.

5 I won't be able to see you this afternoon because I have to run some **errands**.
   a I have to go out so I won't be able to see you this afternoon.
   b I can't see you this afternoon because I have to do some work at home.

6 My grandmother is still **young at heart** even though she's well over 70 years old.
   a My grandma has a youthful attitude even though she is almost 70 years old.
   b Even though my grandmother is more than 70 years old, she still has a youthful attitude.

7 You have to be the **cream of the crop** if you want to get hired by that company.
   a You have to be extremely talented if you want to work for that company.
   b That company only hires young and inexperienced workers.

8 I don't think that he'll be able to pass the course because he's been **slacking off**.
   a He won't be able to pass the course because he hasn't been doing enough work.
   b He'll probably fail the course because the material is too difficult for him.

9 He was **crushed** when he got the news that he had been kicked off the soccer team.
   a He was ecstatic when he found out that he wouldn't be on the team any more.
   b He was devastated when he heard that he had been cut from the soccer team.

10 I didn't do enough work this term, so I'm going to have to **cram** for the final exam.
   a I'm not ready for the final exam, so I want to cheat off you during the test.
   b I have to study very hard tonight because I'm not ready for the final exam.

EXERCISE 5

UNSCRAMBLE THE FOLLOWING SENTENCES, ADDING PUNCTUATION WHEN NEEDED. THE BEGINNING AND END OF EACH SENTENCE HAVE ALREADY BEEN DONE FOR YOU. HINT: IT'S HELPFUL TO IDENTIFY THE WORD/IDIOM FROM THE DIALOGUE IN EACH SENTENCE.

1 **His days are** / because / been / for / numbered / work / late / he's / **too many times.**

   His days are numbered because he's been late for work too many times   .

2 **I have to** / a / errands / afternoon / I / won't / run / so / this / be / probably / few / **back until 5:00.**

   _____ .

3 **The young man** / a / when / store / let / fuss / wouldn't / the / him / made / **return the computer.**

   _____ .

4 **My father is** / he / young / even / at / heart / though / still / celebrated / just / **his 70th birthday.**

   _____ .

5 **I'll be sure** /my / crossed / you / for / keep / interview / fingers / to / with / an / when / go / **that new company.**

   _____ .

6 **We're going to** / up / our / at / café / across / hook / the / with / that's / friends / the / **street from here.**

   _____ .

7 **I'm going to** / have / down / or / to / math / fail / soon / I / knuckle / could / the / **course I'm taking.**

   _____ .

8 **My younger sister** / stressed / has / she / been / out / too / because / spending / much / is / **time at work.**

   _____ .

EXERCISE 6

WHAT WORD/IDIOM FROM THE DIALOGUE MATCHES THE FOLLOWING DEFINITIONS? WHEN THE EXERCISE HAS BEEN COMPLETED, THE IDIOM FOR 'BEST OF THE GROUP' WILL BE SPELLED VERTICALLY.

1	average	r u n o f (t) h e m i l l
2	problem	(_) _ _ _ _
3	a lot of	_ _ _ _(_) _ _
4	study hard	(_) _ _ _
5	more stress than one can handle	_ _(_) _ _ _ _ _ _ _ _
6	become serious about one's work	_ _ _ _ _ _(_) _ _ _ _
7	scheduled for	_ _(_) _ _ _ _ _ _
8	he will be fired soon	_ _ _ _ _ _ _ _ _ _ _ _(_) _ _ _
9	a youthful attitude	_(_) _ _ _ _ _ _ _ _ _ _
10	overreact	_ _ _ _ _ (_) _ _ _ _ _ _
11	doing	_ _ (_) _
12	devastated	_ _ _ _(_) _ _
13	getting old	_(_) _ _ _ _ _ _ _
14	reduce the amount of work one does	_ _ _(_) _ _ _ _
15	leave	(_) _ _
16	meet	_ _(_) _ _ _ _ _ _ _
17	worry about	_ _ _ _ _ _ _ _(_) _ _ _ _

Unscramble the following words/idioms from the dialogue.		
18	epke reh igrfnes dsescor	_ _ _ _ _ _ _ _ _ _ _ _ _ _ _ _ _ _ _ _
19	nru fo eht ilml	_ _ _ _ _ _ _ _ _ _ _ _
20	unr osem rdsnrae	_ _ _ _ _ _ _ _ _ _ _ _ _ _
21	koho pu twhi	_ _ _ _ _ _ _ _ _ _
22	ekam a sfsu rvoe	_ _ _ _ _ _ _ _ _ _ _ _ _

EXERCISE 7

FILL IN THE WORDS/IDIOMS THAT ARE MISSING FROM THE DIALOGUE.

Andre joins Claudia at a table in the lounge

Andre   Hi. What's with all the papers everywhere?

Claudia   I just finished a p_____ of homework I had to do for my next class.

Andre   How's that class going? I've heard that the material in that course is kind of
r_____ of the m_____.

Claudia   Actually, the course material is pretty good, but the teacher certainly isn't the
c_____ of the c_____. I'm sure his d_____ are n_____.

Andre   It's a shame you didn't get the other instructor who's teaching that class. I've
heard she's really interesting. Do you have to continue with the same teacher next
month?

Claudia   I hope not. I won't know for sure until the schedule for next month is posted. I'll
k_____ my f_____ crossed. How're things going with you?

Andre   So far so good, but I'm going to have to k_____ down. My first c_____
at the TOEFL exam is coming up soon. If I start s_____ o_____ now,
I'll have to c_____ for the entire week before the exam. I really need to get
a good score if I hope to go to graduate school in the States some day.

Claudia   When do you take the exam?

Andre   It's s_____ f_____ the middle of next month. I've forgotten the exact
date. I'll have to l_____ i_____ it.

Claudia   Well, don't get too s_____ o_____ about it.

Andre   I promise I won't l_____ any s_____ over it.

Claudia   What are you u_____ t_____ this weekend?

Andre   I plan on h_____ u_____ with this cute girl I met at that new club that just opened. There's only one h_____. My friend wants to join us.

Claudia   Oh no! That could be a problem. Two's c_____, three's a c_____, wouldn't you say?

Andre   Exactly. I get the feeling my friend likes her too. Maybe I'll just d_____ him at the library before the date.

Claudia   Really?

Andre   No. I'm just p_____ your l_____. To tell the truth, I'm not sure what to do. I'll have to s_____ on it, I guess. What've you got planned for the weekend?

Claudia   Not too much. I'll probably just r_____ a few e_____.

Andre   That's it?

Claudia   Well, it's my homestay mother's birthday on Sunday. I should probably buy her a gift of some kind. She said that she doesn't want us to m_____ a f_____ over it, but she'd be c_____ if everyone forgot her big day.

Andre   How old is she?

Claudia   I'm not sure, but she's g_____ o_____. Maybe sixty something. She's still y_____ at h_____, though. She jogs four times a week, plays tennis in the summer, and even skis every winter.

Andre   That's impressive. Look at the time! I have to r_____. I'll talk to you again at coffee break. See you.

COMPREHENSION QUESTIONS

TRY TO ANSWER THE FOLLOWING QUESTIONS WITHOUT LOOKING AT THE DIALOGUE. ONCE YOU'VE FINISHED THE QUESTIONS, YOU CAN REFER TO THE DIALOGUE TO CHECK YOUR ANSWERS.

1. What had Claudia just finished doing when Andre approached her in the student lounge?

2. What did Claudia say about her teacher?

3. Does Claudia have to continue with the same teacher next month?

4. Why does Andre have to knuckle down soon?

5. What will happen if he starts to slack off now?

6. Where does Andre hope to go to graduate school?

7. What is Andre up to this weekend?

8. What did Claudia mean when she said, "Two's company, three's a crowd"?

9. Why did Andre say, "I'll have to sleep on it"?

10. Whose birthday is on Sunday?

11. Has Claudia decided on the gift she will buy as a birthday present?

12. How old is the homestay mother?

13. What did Claudia say about her homestay mother's attitude?

14. What kinds of sports does the homestay mother participate in?

15. When will Andre have a chance to talk to Claudia again?

DISCUSSION QUESTIONS

DISCUSS THE FOLLOWING QUESTIONS WITH YOUR PARTNER.

PART A: General Discussion Questions

1 Are you usually prepared for class when you get to school?

2 What course have you enjoyed the most while studying here?

3 Do you have to take any exams at school in the near future? Are you prepared?

4 How do you like to spend your weekends here?

5 Have you celebrated a special occasion with your homestay family/roommate? What was it? Did you enjoy yourself?

PART B: Idiomatic Discussion Questions

1 What universities do **the cream of the crop** go to in your country? Do you know anyone who attends one of these institutions?

2 Have you been **knuckling down** or **slacking off** at school recently? Why?

3 Tell me about something you'd like to **take a crack at** while you're here.

4 What **stresses you out** about living in your hometown? How about here?

5 Tell me about the last time somebody **made a fuss over you**.

6 Describe a big decision that you **had to sleep on**. What did you finally decide?

7 Describe a time in your life when you felt **crushed**.

GIVE IT A SHOT

WHO WAS THE CREAM OF THE CROP? CAN YOU NAME THE LAST
PERSON, TEAM, OR COUNTRY TO WIN EACH OF THE FOLLOWING?

Nobel Peace Prize
Winner's Name:
Find the answer at: **http://en.wikipedia.org/wiki/Nobel_Peace_Prize_Winner**

Oscars
Best Actor:
Best Actress:
Find the answers at: **http://en.wikipedia.org/wiki/Academy_awards**

Olympic 100 meters (Track)
Male Athlete's Name:
Female Athlete's Name:
Find the answers at: **http://en.wikipedia.org/wiki/Lists_of_Olympic_medalists**

Super Bowl (Football)
Team's Name:
Find the answer at: **http://en.wikipedia.org/wiki/Super_Bowl_champions**

NBA Championship (Basketball)
Team's Name:
Find the answer at: **http://en.wikipedia.org/wiki/Nba_champions**

World Series (Baseball)
Team's Name:
Find the answer at: **http://en.wikipedia.org/wiki/World_Series**

Stanley Cup (Hockey)
Team's Name:
Find the answer at: **http://en.wikipedia.org/wiki/Stanley_Cup_champions**

World Cup (Soccer)
Country's Name:
Find the answer at: **http://en.wikipedia.org/wiki/FIFA_World_Cup**

••CHAPTER FOUR••

ATTENDING A TOEFL CLASS

ATTENDING A TOEFL CLASS

Jose sees Andre in class before the lesson starts

Jose   Hi there. I see you're **hitting the books** as usual.

Andre   I didn't have a chance to **go over the material** we studied yesterday. I tell you, I'm almost **at the end of my rope**. I can't remember the grammar points we covered yesterday, never mind all the vocabulary we're supposed to know. You've got **a mind like a steel trap**. What's the expression we studied that means to think something over? It's right **on the tip of my tongue**.

Jose   I think you mean **mull something over**, don't you?

Andre   Yeah that's it. Thanks. I've been **hung up on** this question for a while now.

Jose   Hey, did you notice **what's-his-face** in the hallway? You know, that guy who falls asleep in class sometimes.

Andre   No. I can't say I did. How come?

Jose   You should have seen it. Mrs. Jones was **coming down hard on** him again. That guy was really **catching hell**.

Andre   Why was the teacher **telling him off** this time?

Jose   I think she was **chewing him out** because he didn't hand in the last two homework assignments. I also heard that she caught him **badmouthing** some of the other students.

Andre   I think she **has it in for** him. He isn't the only one that does those kinds of things.

Jose   You're right about that. .... Have you **run into** Alex today?

Andre	No. I haven't. Why do you ask?
Jose	He asked us to **cover for** him tomorrow because he's going horseback riding with that **new flame** of his. If the teachers ask us where he is we're supposed to say that he's **come down with** the flu.
Andre	I'll cover for him as long as he does the same for us next week.
Jose	I'm sure he'll **come up with** a good excuse for us when we go sailing. He has a pretty **vivid** imagination.
Andre	Do you happen to know what we're studying today?
Jose	It's Tuesday so we'll probably study gerunds and infinitives from that new textbook we've been using.
Andre	All right. I like studying from that book. It's really great practice.
Jose	It is pretty helpful.
Andre	How's the presentation you have to do in our other class **coming along**?
Jose	I've only just **made a dent in** it so far. I have to go to the computer lab this afternoon to **surf the net** for some more information on my topic. You must be relieved that you've already got it out of the way.
Andre	Sure. It's **a huge weight off my shoulders**. Here's the teacher. I guess we better pay attention.

hit the books (to) *i.* – study
We should hit the books tonight because we have a quiz tomorrow.

go over something (to) *i.* – review something
She wants to go over her notes before she gives her speech to the audience.

at the end of one's rope *i.* – frustrated, stressed out
I'm almost at the end of my rope because my lazy co-worker never helps me.

mind/memory like a steel trap (a) *i.* – a great memory
She never forgets a name. She has a mind like a steel trap.

on the tip of one's tongue *i.* – on the verge of remembering something
What's the name of that small town we went to? It's right on the tip of my tongue.

mull something over (to) *i.* – consider, think something over
I'll have to mull it over for a while before I make a decision.

hung up on something/someone *i.* – stuck on something/someone, unable to continue
I can't stop thinking about that beautiful woman. I'm really hung up on her.

what's-(his/her)-face *i.* – used when a person's name can't be remembered
Could you please give this book to what's-her-face the next time you see her.

come down hard on someone (to) *i.* – reprimand someone harshly
The boss came down hard on the salesman who fell asleep during the meeting.

catch hell (to) *i.* – get reprimanded harshly
The teenage boy caught hell because he didn't come home last night.

tell someone off (to) *i.* – reprimand someone harshly
He told his girlfriend off because she forgot his birthday for the second time.

chew someone out (to) *i.* – reprimand someone harshly
She chewed her brother out after he broke her CD player.

badmouth someone (to) *i.* – say negative things about someone
That guy never says anything positive about anyone. He's always badmouthing people.

have it in for someone (to) *i.* – get even with someone, seek revenge
I've had it in for him ever since I found out that he stole my wallet.

run into someone (to) *i.* – meet someone by accident
I ran into some friends from school while I was at the library on Sunday.

cover for someone (to) *i.* – provide an alibi for someone
I'll cover for you if you skip class and go to the beach instead.

new flame *i.* – new lover
She's very happy because her new flame is handsome and charming.

come down with something (to) *i.* – get a cold/the flu
I came down with the flu just before my vacation started.

come up with something (to) *i.* – think of something
Have you come up with something to do on Friday night?

vivid *adj.* – colorful, dramatic, vibrant
The vivid colors in that painting of the sunset are very interesting.

coming along *v.* – progressing
How's the essay that you're writing coming along?

make a dent in something (to) *i.* – make little progress in something
I've only made a dent in the essay that I have to write.

surf the net (to) *i.* – use the internet
I usually surf the net on my new computer when I get home from school.

weight off one's shoulders (a) *i.* – a relief
It was a weight off his shoulders when he finally got accepted to law school.

_D_	1	have it in for someone	A	get reprimanded harshly
___	2	surf the net	B	make little progress in something
___	3	go over something	C	think of something
___	4	catch hell	D	seek revenge
___	5	chew someone out	E	say negative things about a person
___	6	at the end of one's rope	F	a relief
___	7	badmouth someone	G	progressing
___	8	hit the books	H	use the internet
___	9	run into someone	I	consider, think something over
___	10	make a dent in something	J	a great memory
___	11	cover for someone	K	study
___	12	on the tip of one's tongue	L	get a cold
___	13	a weight off one's shoulders	M	reprimand someone harshly
___	14	hung up on something	N	new lover
___	15	coming along	O	provide an alibi for someone
___	16	come down with something	P	meet someone by accident
___	17	come up with something	Q	unable to continue
___	18	new flame	R	review something
___	19	mind like a steel trap	S	on the verge of remembering
___	20	mull something over	T	stressed out

EXERCISE 2

USE THE WORDS/IDIOMS BELOW TO COMPLETE
EACH OF THE FOLLOWING SENTENCES.

on the tip of my tongue	hung up on	coming down with
mind like a steel trap	at the end of his rope	badmouth
hits the books	new flame	vivid
weight off my shoulders	mull it over	chews her out
has it in for	made a dent in	go over

1 That guy is really angry about what happened last night. I think he _____ you.

2 I can't remember her name. What is it? It's right _____.

3 We have a big test tomorrow. We should _____ the material this evening.

4 It was a huge _____ when I found out that I had passed the entrance exam.

5 I've got a stuffy nose and I'm running a fever. I think I'm _____ the flu.

6 I haven't even _____ the pile of homework I have to do this evening.

7 He's always talking about the girl he met last weekend. He's really _____ her.

8 The teacher is really angry at her. I bet he _____ when she arrives for class.

9 That's a big decision you have to make. You should _____ for a few days.

10 She has a fantastic memory. She never forgets anything. She has a _____.

11 Her friend always gossips about other people. She loves to _____ everyone.

12 He's stressed out about the final exam. He looks like he's _____.

13 She decided to paint her daughter's bedroom a _____ yellow color.

14 He always goes to the library after school and _____ with his girlfriend.

15 I'm looking forward to tonight because I'm having dinner with my _____.

EXERCISE 3

COMPLETE THE FOLLOWING CROSSWORD PUZZLE USING WORDS/IDIOMS FROM THE DIALOGUE.

2 Across: C O M I N G A L O N G

ACROSS

2 progressing

5 seek revenge

6 provide an alibi

7 new lover

8 use the internet

DOWN

1 study

2 get reprimanded

3 meet by chance

4 think of

EXERCISE 4

1 I was stressed out after spending the whole day trying to fix my car.

   <u>I was at the end of my rope after spending the whole day trying to fix my car</u>.

2 She's going to review her notes at the library before she takes the final exam.

   _____.

3 I needed some more time to think over the purchase of that brand-new sports car.

   _____.

4 It was a big relief when he finally found a job that was in his field.

   _____.

5 The cop reprimanded the driver because he had sped through a school zone.

   _____.

6 He said that he met his new girlfriend on a blind date last weekend.

   _____.

7 That guy always gets high marks at school because he never forgets anything.

   _____.

8 She was stuck on that question because she hadn't listened to the teacher's instructions.

   _____.

9 I've only made a little progress on the work I have to do for tomorrow's class.

   _____.

10 I don't like the way her boyfriend is always saying bad things about our friends.

   _____.

EXERCISE 5

1 **It was a** / weight / I / when / my / off / out / shoulders / that / huge / found / **I wasn't pregnant.**

It was a huge weight off my shoulders when I found out that I wasn't pregnant   .

2 **I have had** / for / in / about / lied / it / my / ever / he / since / car / using / him / **without my knowledge.**

_____ .

3 **I don't like** / boyfriend / badmouthing / he's / new / your / always / because / my / **friends and me.**

_____ .

4 **I have been** / while / still / mulling / I'm / over / a / for / not / decision / but / sure / this / **what to do.**

_____ .

5 **The young woman** / ex-boyfriend / was / up / on / though / cheated / even / her / he / hung / had / on / **her many times.**

_____ .

6 **I spent over** / trying / net / hours / the / to / more / find / surfing / three / information / **for my presentation.**

_____ .

7 **I'm going to** / studying / I / because / hit / been / have / to / haven't / books / the / **nearly enough recently.**

_____ .

8 **The teenaged boy** / him / saw / when / hell / the / father / caught / smoking / park / in / his / really / **with his friends.**

_____ .

EXERCISE 6

FIND THE WORDS/IDIOMS LISTED BELOW
IN THE WORD SEARCH GAME.

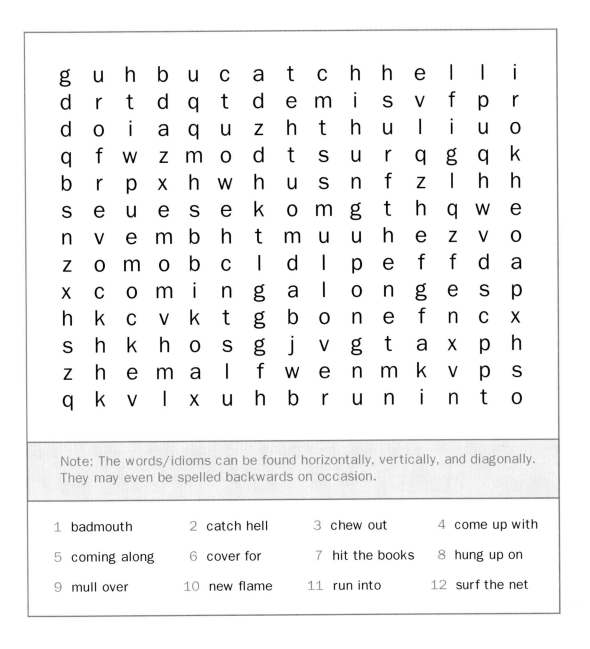

```
g u h b u c a t c h h e l l i
d r t d q t d e m i s v f p r
d o i a q u z h t h u l i u o
q f w z m o d t s u r q g q k
b r p x h w h u s n f z l h h
s e u e s e k o m g t h q w e
n v e m b h t m u u h e z v o
z o m o b c l d l p e f f d a
x c o m i n g a l o n g e s p
h k c v k t g b o n e f n c x
s h k h o s g j v g t a x p h
z h e m a l f w e n m k v p s
q k v l x u h b r u n i n t o
```

Note: The words/idioms can be found horizontally, vertically, and diagonally.
They may even be spelled backwards on occasion.

1 badmouth	2 catch hell	3 chew out	4 come up with
5 coming along	6 cover for	7 hit the books	8 hung up on
9 mull over	10 new flame	11 run into	12 surf the net

EXERCISE 7

FILL IN THE WORDS/IDIOMS THAT ARE
MISSING FROM THE DIALOGUE.

Jose sees Andre in class before the lesson starts

Jose   Hi there. I see you're h_____ the b_____ as usual.

Andre   I didn't have a chance to g_____ o_____ the material we studied
yesterday. I tell you, I'm almost at the e_____ of my r_____. I can't
remember the grammar points we covered yesterday, never mind all the vocabulary
we're supposed to know. You've got a m_____ like a s_____
t_____. What's the expression we studied that means to think something
over? It's right on the t_____ of my t_____.

Jose   I think you mean m_____ something o_____, don't you?

Andre   Yeah that's it. Thanks. I've been h_____ up o_____ this question for a
while now.

Jose   Hey, did you notice w_____-his-f_____ in the hallway? You know, that
guy who falls asleep in class sometimes.

Andre   No. I can't say I did. How come?

Jose   You should have seen it. Mrs. Jones was c_____ down h_____ on him
again. That guy was really c_____ hell.

Andre   Why was the teacher t_____ him o_____ this time?

Jose   I think she was c_____ him o_____ because he didn't hand in the last
two homework assignments. I also heard that she caught him b_____ some
of the other students.

Andre   I think she h_____ it i_____ for him. He isn't the only one that does
those kinds of things.

Jose   You're right about that. .... Have you r_____ i_____ Alex today?

Andre	No. I haven't. Why do you ask?
Jose	He asked us to c_____ for him tomorrow because he's going horseback riding with that n_____ f_____ of his. If the teachers ask us where he is we're supposed to say that he's c_____ d_____ with the flu.
Andre	I'll cover for him as long as he does the same for us next week.
Jose	I'm sure he'll c_____ u_____ with a good excuse for us when we go sailing. He has a pretty v_____ imagination.
Andre	Do you happen to know what we're studying today?
Jose	It's Tuesday so we'll probably gerunds and infinitives from that new textbook we've been using.
Andre	All right. I like studying from that book. It's really great practice.
Jose	It is pretty helpful.
Andre	How's the presentation you have to do in our other class c_____ a_____?
Jose	I've only just m_____ a d_____ in it so far. I have to go to the computer lab this afternoon to s_____ the n_____ for some more information on my topic. You must be relieved that you've already got it out of the way.
Andre	Sure. It's a huge w_____ off my s_____. Here's the teacher. I guess we better pay attention.

COMPREHENSION QUESTIONS

TRY TO ANSWER THE FOLLOWING QUESTIONS WITHOUT LOOKING AT THE DIALOGUE. ONCE YOU'VE FINISHED THE QUESTIONS, YOU CAN REFER TO THE DIALOGUE TO CHECK YOUR ANSWERS.

1   Where was Andre reviewing his notes?

2   Why was Andre almost at the end of his rope?

3   Who has a mind like a steel trap?

4   What expression was Andre trying to remember?

5   Who was catching hell in the hallway before the class started?

6   Why was the teacher telling him off?

7   Why did Andre think the teacher had it in for the student in the hall?

8   Why won't Alex be at school tomorrow? What are Andre and Jose supposed to do for him?

9   What will Andre and Jose do next week? How will Alex help them?

10   What topic are they probably going to study today?

11   Do they like studying from the new textbook the teacher uses?

12   How was Jose's presentation coming along?

13   How is Jose going to get some more information for his presentation?

14   What was Andre talking about when he said, "It's a huge weight off my shoulders"?

15   Why did Andre and Jose have to stop talking to each other?

DISCUSSION QUESTIONS

DISCUSS THE FOLLOWING QUESTIONS WITH YOUR PARTNER.

PART A: General Discussion Questions

1 What is the best time of day for you to study? How about the worst?

2 Where do you do your best studying?

3 Do you prefer to study in silence or with the stereo/TV on?

4 What teacher at this school has a reputation for giving a lot of homework?

5 Are you studying more or less than you did in your country?

PART B: Idiomatic Discussion Questions

1 Tell me about the last time a teacher / coach / parent / sibling **chewed you out**. Did you deserve it?

2 Did you **run into** anyone from the school over the weekend? Where were you? What were they doing?

3 How much time do you spend **surfing the net** each day? What are some of your favorite sites? Have you ever used the internet for your studies? How?

4 Do you have a **memory like a steel trap**? a sieve?

5 Have you ever **covered for** another student at school? What did they do? What did you say?

6 Have you been **at the end of your rope** while living here? How come?

7 Have you ever been **hung up on** someone? What did you do about it? Has anyone ever been hung up on you? Were you attracted to them?

GIVE IT A SHOT

IN THE DIALOGUE, MRS. JONES GOT VERY ANGRY AT A STUDENT IN THE HALLWAY BEFORE THE CLASS BEGAN. HAVE YOUR TEACHER EXPLAIN/DEMONSTRATE THE FOLLOWING DEGREES OF ANGER.

Less Angry:	He/she was	annoyed miffed peeved	He/she	made a fuss
Angry:	He/she was	angry mad pissed off teed off ticked off	He/she	made a scene
More Angry:	He/she was	enraged fuming (mad) furious incensed infuriated irate livid	He/she	blew a fuse flew off the handle hit the roof went ballistic went postal

Choose the correct answer to complete the following sentences.

1 The teacher *(mad/hit the roof)* because so many students skipped the test.

2 My father was *(miffed/furious)* when I destroyed his vintage sports car.

3 My mother was *(annoyed/infuriated)* when I forgot to make my bed this morning.

4 She *(enraged/flew off the handle)* when her husband forgot their wedding anniversary.

5 The customer *(made a fuss/peeved)* when the waiter forgot to bring a glass of water.

6 My girlfriend *(furious/went ballistic)* when she saw me flirting with a cute cheerleader.

7 The young man *(made a scene/irate)* when the police gave him a ticket for speeding.

8 He was *(flew off the handle/livid)* when he got fired from his job for no reason.

9 She was *(teed off/went postal)* because her parents wouldn't let her go to the dance.

10 He was *(miffed/incensed)* when his girlfriend arrived 10 minutes late for their date.

••CHAPTER FIVE••

EATING DINNER WITH A ROOMMATE

Hans comes home to find Andre making dinner

Hans   This pasta **doesn't look half bad**. Did you make this, or did it come out of a can?

Andre   It better be good. I **made it from scratch**. I've been working in the kitchen for at least an hour now. Which reminds me, it's your turn to make dinner tomorrow night. You should remember to **thaw out** the meat that's in the freezer. I'd like to **chow down** on some steak for a change.

Hans   Umm. **I don't know how to break this to you**, but I do volunteer work at the community center tomorrow afternoon. I don't think I'll be back in time to have dinner ready by 6:00. We could go out for supper **on me**. How does that sound?

Andre   Where? Not McDonald's again!

Hans   Of course not. You'll **never let me live that down**, will you? Why don't we try that popular German restaurant on the corner?

Andre   OK. I'll **let you off the hook** this time, but you're **fixing dinner** on Thursday night for sure. No excuses.

Hans   I promise I won't **let you down**. Hey, is the microwave still **on the fritz**?

Andre   No. I had a repairman come by and take a look at it this afternoon.

Hans   What did the repairs **come to**? Did he **rip us off**?

Andre   No, not at all. In fact, the guy lives in the building. He's sort of a **jack-of-all-trades**. He works cheaply. It only cost $15 to have the work done. He said that other than a couple of loose wires, our microwave is **in mint condition**.

Hans	I think I know the guy you're talking about. My girlfriend said that he kind of **gives her the creeps**.
Andre	Oh, that's because when he was here to fix the toilet a few weeks ago, he walked into **the can** and almost saw her standing there **in the buff**. She should try locking the door in the future.
Hans	I wonder why she never mentioned anything about that to me?
Andre	It probably just **slipped her mind**. You should have seen the repairman. He **turned beet red** and couldn't stop apologizing. He came back about an hour after your girlfriend had left and fixed the toilet for free. We should probably **stay on his good side**. **In the long run**, it could save us a lot of **dough**.
Hans	I suppose you're right.
Andre	Why does she take a shower here in the middle of the day anyway?
Hans	She comes here after she **works out** at the fitness club that's in our neighborhood.
Andre	I see. Is she still going to **drop in on** us after dinner tonight?
Hans	I think she's planning to **pop by** on her way home from her friend's apartment. She said that she'd bring us something **decadent** from that cake shop up the street.
Andre	There's the phone. Why don't you set the table while I answer this call?
Hans	Sure. It's the least I can do. After all, you made dinner.

DEFINITIONS

doesn't look half bad *i.* – looks pretty good
The meal you prepared for us tonight doesn't look half bad.

make something from scratch (to) *i.* – make something by oneself, not store bought
I'm proud of this tasty dessert because I made it from scratch.

thaw out something (to) *i.* – defrost something
Do you want me to thaw out the lasagna for dinner tonight?

chow down on something (to) *i.* – eat something
I'm really hungry. I want to chow down on some pizza for lunch.

I don't know how to break this to you *i.* – I don't know how to tell this to you
I don't know how to break this to you, but you didn't get the job.

something is on me *i.* – I'll pay for you
Would you like to go out for supper tonight? It's on me.

never let someone live something down (to) *i.* – never let someone forget something
I went to school once with my zipper open. My friends never let me live that down.

let someone off the hook (to) *i.* – let someone avoid punishment
My father let my sister off the hook after she broke the living room window.

fix breakfast/lunch/dinner (to) *v.* – make/prepare/cook a meal
Could you fix breakfast for me this morning?

let someone down (to) *i.* – disappoint someone
My friend let me down when he forgot to help me move into my new apartment.

on the fritz *i.* – broken, on the blink
The television has been on the fritz for the last three days.

come to *i.* – cost, the total bill
What did the repairs to the fridge come to?

rip someone off (to) *i.* – overcharge someone
The mechanic ripped me off when I had him fix my car's transmission.

jack-of-all-trades (a) *i.* – a multitalented laborer
It seems as though you can repair anything. You're a jack-of-all-trades.

in mint condition *i.* – in perfect condition
The antique table I bought at the auction was in mint condition.

give someone the creeps (to) *i.* – scare or disgust someone
That scary-looking guy over there gives me the creeps.

can (the) *n.* – the bathroom/washroom
Are you finished yet? You've been in the can for over an hour.

in the buff *i.* – in the nude, in the raw, in one's birthday suit, naked
The baby was running around the kitchen in the buff.

slip one's mind (to) *i.* – forget something
I'm really sorry I forgot your birthday. It completely slipped my mind.

turn beet red (to) *i.* – blush
He turned beet red once he realized that he had a piece of spinach on his tooth.

stay on one's good side (to) *i.* – make someone have a favorable opinion of you
You should stay on your father's good side if you want to use his car.

in the long run *i.* – in the long term, over a long period of time
You ought to get some regular exercise. You'll be healthier in the long run.

dough *n.* – cash, money
She must have spent a lot of dough on that beautiful wedding dress.

work out (to) *i.* – exercise
I try to work out at the fitness club at least three times a week.

drop in on someone (to) *i.* – visit someone
I was happy when my friend dropped in on me this afternoon.

pop by somewhere (to) *i.* – visit somewhere
I want to pop by the supermarket on our way home.

decadent *adj.* – indulgent
That famous actor is very rich. I'm sure he has a decadent lifestyle.

EXERCISE 1

F	1 make something from scratch	A	the washroom
___	2 on the fritz	B	scare someone
___	3 the can	C	forget something
___	4 dough	D	never let you forget something
___	5 drop in on	E	exercise
___	6 in the long run	F	make something by oneself
___	7 slip one's mind	G	in perfect condition
___	8 a jack-of-all-trades	H	blush
___	9 in mint condition	I	let someone avoid punishment
___	10 chow down on something	J	I'll pay for you
___	11 work out	K	indulgent
___	12 turn beet red	L	visit someone
___	13 decadent	M	a multitalented laborer
___	14 in the buff	N	broken
___	15 pop by	O	looks pretty good
___	16 something is on me	P	naked
___	17 never let you live something down	Q	visit somewhere
___	18 let someone off the hook	R	eat something
___	19 doesn't look half bad	S	money
___	20 give someone the creeps	T	over a long period of time

EXERCISE 2

USE THE WORDS/IDIOMS BELOW TO COMPLETE
EACH OF THE FOLLOWING SENTENCES.

in the long run	on the fritz	let her down
gives me the creeps	in the buff	thaw out
popped by	in mint condition	chow down
drop in on	made it from scratch	let him off the hook
the teacher's good side	jack-of-all-trades	turned beet red

1 That strange man _____ because he keeps staring at me.

2 I'd like to _____ on a deluxe hamburger and fries for lunch today.

3 We can't watch the playoff baseball game tonight because the TV is _____.

4 She _____ the office to say goodbye on her way to the airport.

5 It saves money _____ if you keep your car well maintained.

6 He has worked in the construction industry for many years. He's a _____.

7 Be sure to take the meat out of the freezer so it can _____ by supper.

8 If you want a high mark in this class, you'll have to stay on _____.

9 He _____ when he didn't recommend her for the job opening at that company.

10 The used car I bought from him was wonderful. It was _____.

11 He _____ when he realized that he was wearing his shirt inside out.

12 The meal we had at her house was fantastic because she _____.

13 I'm going to _____ my friend after I finish shopping at the mall.

14 The baby boy was running around on the beach _____.

15 Most people think he is guilty of murder, but the judge _____.

EXERCISE 3

COMPLETE THE FOLLOWING CROSSWORD PUZZLE
USING WORDS/IDIOMS FROM THE DIALOGUE.

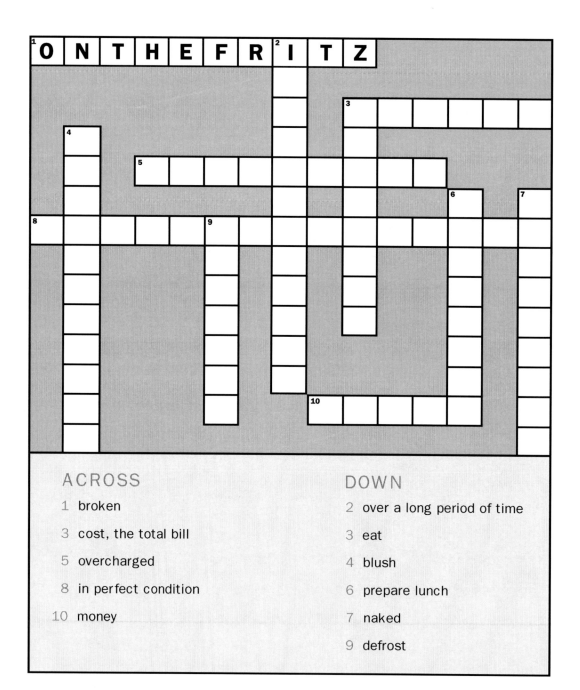

ACROSS

1 broken

3 cost, the total bill

5 overcharged

8 in perfect condition

10 money

DOWN

2 over a long period of time

3 eat

4 blush

6 prepare lunch

7 naked

9 defrost

EXERCISE 4

REWRITE THE FOLLOWING SENTENCES USING
A WORD/IDIOM FROM THE DIALOGUE.

1　I'm going to visit my friend on my way home from the swimming pool.

　I'm going to drop in on my friend on my way home from the swimming pool _____.

2　The washing machine has been broken ever since you tried to wash those blankets.

　_____.

3　I just want you to relax. I'm going to prepare dinner for you tonight.

　_____.

4　My mother's desserts are always delicious because she takes care when baking them.

　_____.

5　I don't like shopping in that area because the merchants usually overcharge me.

　_____.

6　My friends will probably visit the bank before they come here.

　_____.

7　You're going to have to start exercising if you want to lose some weight.

　_____.

8　He really blushed when I told him that his zipper was wide open.

　_____.

9　She said that I disappointed her when I forgot to water the plants while she was away.

　_____.

10　I was awfully surprised when I saw that woman suntanning naked on the beach.

　_____.

1 **I'd like to** / friend / haven't / I / because / my / in / on / drop / a / in / her / seen / **very long time.**

I'd like to drop in on my friend because I haven't seen her in a very long time   .

2 **You'll have a** / long / little / money / more / in / the / if / run / save /you / lot / a / **bit each month.**

_____ .

3 **The computer is** / again / take / fritz / so / have / we'll / the / to / to / the / on / it / **repair shop tomorrow.**

_____ .

4 **I told him** / the / was / he / let / that / when / hook / professor / him / off / lucky / the / **for missing class.**

_____ .

5 **The beautiful antique** / was / mint / in / to / so / I / table / decided / condition / **buy it yesterday.**

_____ .

6 **My stupid boyfriend** / down / didn't / for / up / let / date / show / our / he / when / me / **on Friday night.**

_____ .

7 **The big dog** / the / yard / me / creeps / because / in / he / that / gives / always / **snarls at me.**

_____ .

8 **I really got** / pair / when / off / I / ripped / this / of / sunglasses / at / bought / **the mall today**

_____ .

EXERCISE 6

WHAT WORD/IDIOM FROM THE DIALOGUE MATCHES THE FOLLOWING DEFINITIONS? WHEN THE EXERCISE HAS BEEN COMPLETED, THE IDIOM FOR 'MAKE IT BY ONESELF' WILL BE SPELLED VERTICALLY.

1   I'll pay for you   o n (m)e
2   defrost   _ _(_)_
3   a multitalented laborer   _   _ _(_) - _ _ - _ _ _ - _ _ _ _ _
4   in the nude   _ _   _ _(_)   _ _ _ _

5   in perfect condition   _ _   _(_)_ _   _ _ _ _ _ _ _ _
6   blush   _ _ _ _   _ _(_)   _ _ _

7   broken   _ _   _ _ _   (_)_ _ _ _
8   visit someone   _(_)_ _   _ _   _ _
9   in the long term   _ _   _ _ _   _(_)_   _ _ _
10 disappoint him   _ _ _   _ _(_)   _ _ _ _

11 looks pretty good   _ _(_)_' _   _ _ _ _   _ _ _ _   _ _ _
12 cost, the total bill   (_)_ _ _   _ _
13 overcharge me   (_)_ _   _ _   _ _ _
14 indulgent   _ _ _(_)_ _ _ _
15 exercise   _ _ _ _   _ _(_)
16 the bathroom   _ _ _   (_)_ _
17 money   _ _ _ _(_)

Unscramble the following words/idioms from the dialogue.

18 tle ihm fof eht okho   _ _ _   _ _ _   _ _ _   _ _ _   _ _ _ _
19 wohc ndwo   _ _ _ _   _ _ _ _
20 ysat no shi oodg sdei   _ _ _ _   _ _   _ _ _   _ _ _ _   _ _ _ _
21 dslppie reh dmni   _ _ _ _ _ _ _   _ _ _   _ _ _ _
22 ni het fubf   _ _   _ _ _   _ _ _ _

Hans comes home to find Andre making dinner

Hans This pasta doesn't l_____ half b_____. Did you make this, or did it come out of a can?

Andre It better be good. I m_____ it from s_____. I've been working in the kitchen for at least an hour now. Which reminds me, it's your turn to make dinner tomorrow night. You should remember to t_____ o_____ the meat that's in the freezer. I'd like to c_____ d_____ on some steak for a change.

Hans Umm. I don't k_____ how to b_____ this to you, but I do volunteer work at the community center tomorrow afternoon. I don't think I'll be back in time to have dinner ready by 6:00. We could go out for supper o_____ m_____. How does that sound?

Andre Where? Not McDonald's again!

Hans Of course not. You'll never let me l_____ that d_____, will you? Why don't we try that popular German restaurant on the corner?

Andre OK. I'll let you o_____ the h_____ this time, but you're f_____ dinner on Thursday night for sure. No excuses.

Hans I promise I won't l_____ you d_____. Hey, is the microwave still on the f_____?

Andre No. I had a repairman come by and take a look at it this afternoon.

Hans What did the repairs c_____ t_____? Did he r_____ us o_____?

Andre No, not at all. In fact, the guy lives in the building. He's sort of a j_____-of-all-t_____. He works cheaply. It only cost $15 to have the work done. He said that other than a couple of loose wires, our microwave is in m_____ c_____.

Hans   I think I know the guy you're talking about. My girlfriend said that he kind of g_____ her the c_____.

Andre   Oh, that's because when he was here to fix the toilet a few weeks ago, he walked into the c_____ and almost saw her standing there i_____ the b_____. She should try locking the door in the future.

Hans   I wonder why she never mentioned anything about that to me?

Andre   It probably just s_____ her m_____. You should have seen the repairman. He t_____ beet r_____ and couldn't stop apologizing. He came back about an hour after your girlfriend had left and fixed the toilet for free. We should probably stay on his g_____ s_____. In the l_____ r_____, it could save us a lot of d_____.

Hans   I suppose you're right.

Andre   Why does she take a shower here in the middle of the day anyway?

Hans   She comes here after she w_____ o_____ at the fitness club that's in our neighborhood.

Andre   I see. Is she still going to d_____ i_____ on us after dinner tonight?

Hans   I think she's planning to p_____ b_____ on her way home from her friend's apartment. She said that she'd bring us something d_____ from that cake shop up the street.

Andre   There's the phone. Why don't you set the table while I answer this call?

Hans   Sure. It's the least I can do. After all, you made dinner.

COMPREHENSION QUESTIONS

TRY TO ANSWER THE FOLLOWING QUESTIONS WITHOUT LOOKING AT THE DIALOGUE. ONCE YOU'VE FINISHED THE QUESTIONS, YOU CAN REFER TO THE DIALOGUE TO CHECK YOUR ANSWERS.

1   What did Andre make for dinner?

2   What does he want to eat for dinner tomorrow night?

3   Why can't Hans make dinner tomorrow night?

4   What did Hans suggest they do instead of having dinner at home tomorrow?

5   Where did Hans take Andre the last time he couldn't make dinner at home?

6   What was on the fritz in the kitchen?

7   Who fixed it? How much did it cost to have it fixed? What was wrong with it?

8   Who gives Han's girlfriend the creeps?

9   Why does she feel this way?

10   What was the repairman's reaction when he walked into the can?

11   When did he return to fix the toilet?

12   Why did Andre think they should stay on the repairman's good side?

13   Who will drop in on Andre and Hans after dinner? Where is she coming from?

14   What will she bring to the apartment?

15   Who is going to set the table for dinner?

DISCUSSION QUESTIONS

DISCUSS THE FOLLOWING QUESTIONS WITH YOUR PARTNER.

PART A: General Discussion Questions

1 Do you enjoy cooking for yourself? How often do you do it?

2 Do you usually eat three square meals a day? If not, why?

3 What's the biggest difference between the food you eat here and in your country?

4 What's the most important meal of the day in your country? How about here?

5 What's your favorite food to snack on?

PART B: Idiomatic Discussion Questions

1 Describe a delicious meal that you can **make from scratch**.

2 What would you really like to **chow down on** for dinner tonight?

3 What's the most **decadent** thing you've bought for yourself or someone else?

4 Tell me about something you did that your friends/family have **never let you live down**.

5 Describe the last person or thing that **gave you the creeps**.

6 Do you remember something you did that made you **turn beet red**?

7 Has anyone **let you down** while you've been living here? How?

GIVE IT A SHOT

IN THE DIALOGUE, ANDRE SAYS THAT HE'D LIKE TO 'CHOW DOWN ON SOME STEAK'. HAVE THE TEACHER EXPLAIN/DEMONSTRATE THE FOLLOWING WAYS TO EAT OR DRINK SOMETHING.

	Eat:	Drink:
Slowly	nibble on something pick at s/t	sip something
Neutral	eat s/t have s/t	drink s/t have s/t
Quickly	chow down on s/t devour s/t gobble down s/t pig out on s/t wolf down s/t	down s/t gulp down s/t guzzle down s/t knock back s/t swig back s/t

Choose the answer that completes the following sentences.

1   She was (sipping/gulping down) the piping hot coffee she had just poured for herself.

2   After skiing all day, she (picked at/devoured) a large pizza and some chicken wings.

3   He wasn't very hungry, so he just (gobbled down/nibbled on) a piece of cheese.

4   She (downed/wolfed down) a bottle of Gatorade after she finished her 30-minute run.

5   He got very drunk after he (picked at/knocked back) 4 shots of tequila in 10 minutes.

6   I'm stuffed after eating that meal. I think I'll just (devour/nibble on) some fruit for dessert.

7   He poured himself a short glass of whiskey and then slowly (sipped it/swigged it back).

8   I'm starving. Why don't we (have/guzzle down) a burger and fries at Wendy's.

9   She (picked at/wolfed down) lunch because she had to go straight back to school.

10 The soccer players (drank/pigged out on) orange juice during half-time at the game.

11 He (gulped down/sipped) the expensive cognac after he finished dinner.

12 He was so hungry that he (swigged back/gobbled down) two heaping plates of pasta.

••CHAPTER SIX••

SHOPPING FOR CLOTHES IN A MALL

SHOPPING FOR CLOTHES IN A MALL

Andre and Claudia are wandering past the store windows

Andre What store do you feel like **hitting** next? We haven't had much luck so far.

Claudia I don't know. How about this store? I heard they're having a huge sale today. Everything is supposed to be **marked way down**.

Andre I'll believe it when I see it, but it's certainly worth a look. I'd like to buy some clothes today, but I don't want to **break the bank** doing it.

Claudia Here it is. Let's go inside.

Andre Sure.

They enter the crowded store

Claudia Wow! This place is **jam-packed**. From the looks of it, most of the bargains have already been **snapped up**. Wait a minute. What about this pair of pants? They're **right up your alley**, don't you think?

Andre Let me see them. Actually, I don't mind them at all. I'd have to have them **taken in**, though. Is there a smaller size?

Claudia Unfortunately that's the last pair. How much do they **run**?

Andre $149!

Claudia That seems pretty **steep** to me.

Andre No kidding! I'm not **shelling out** that kind of **cash** on pants that don't even fit properly. Could you put them back on the **rack** for me?

Claudia   Sure. Let me have them.

Andre   It's too bad we didn't get here **first thing in the morning**. I saw a sweater in here last week that **had my name on it**. It's **long gone** now that everything is on sale.

Claudia   That's too bad. .... **Get a load of** that saleswoman over there. Can you believe what's she's wearing? You'd think that somebody who works in a clothing store would know that pink and green **clash**.

Andre   Hey, **there's no accounting for taste**. The funny thing is that she looks so **full of herself**. I bet she thinks she's **dressed to kill** in that outfit.

Claudia   I wouldn't wear something like that even as **a last resort**. I should probably stop **shooting my mouth off**. I'm not exactly **dressed to the nines** myself this afternoon.

Andre   Oh, come on. Don't **sell yourself short**. You're really good-looking.

Claudia   Thanks. I think I've had enough of shopping **for the time being**. How about you? What do you say we drop by that chocolate store on the lower level of the mall?

Andre   You mean Godiva Chocolates?

Claudia   That's the one. Something sweet would really **hit the spot** right about now. I'm telling you, their truffles **melt in your mouth**.

Andre   Sounds like a great idea. Lead the way.

DEFINITIONS

adj. – adjective	*exclam.* – exclamation	*n.* – noun
adv. – adverb	*i.* – idiom, phrasal verb	*v.* – verb

hit somewhere (to) *v.* – visit somewhere
Why don't we hit the library after we finish school today?

mark down (to) *i.* – reduce in price
They're having a sale. All of their tennis shoes are supposed to be marked (way) down.

break the bank (to) *i.* – spend all of one's savings
I'd like to buy a new suit today, but I don't want to break the bank doing it.

jam-packed *adj.* – crowded, mobbed
The subway was jam-packed during rush hour this morning.

snap up something (to) *i.* – buy/take something quickly
The customers snapped up the sale merchandise in less than 15 minutes.

right up one's alley *i.* – perfectly suited to someone
I think the beautiful blouse you found in that store is right up your alley.

take in (to) *i.* – reduce the waist size of one's pants/skirt
These pants are too big. I'm going to ask the tailor to take them in.

run (to) *v.* – cost
How much does that flashy sports car run?

steep *adj.* – expensive
I can't afford to buy a house in that district because the prices are really steep.

shell out (to) *i.* – fork out, spend
He shelled out a lot of money when he redecorated his entire apartment.

cash *n.* – dough, money
How much cash did you spend on dinner at that Italian restaurant?

rack *n.* – a stand used to display clothes
Could you please put this coat back on the rack for me?

first thing in the morning *i.* – very early in the morning
If we're going skiing tomorrow, we'll have to leave first thing in the morning.

have one's name on it (to) *i.* – perfectly suited to someone
It's too bad they didn't have my size because that shirt had my name on it.

long gone *i.* – bought/left/taken a long time ago
I'm sure our friends are long gone now that the concert's over.

get a load of something/someone (to) *i.* – look at something/someone
Get a load of the view from this apartment. It's unbelievable.

clash (to) *v.* – do not match in color or design
Do you think this shirt clashes with the pants I'm wearing?

there's no accounting for taste *i.* – there's no explaining someone's style
I can't believe what he's wearing. There's certainly no accounting for taste.

full of oneself *i.* – arrogant, conceited, smug, snobby
I don't like her because she always looks so full of herself.

dressed to kill *i.* – dressed up
She was dressed to kill when she went to her high-school graduation party.

last resort (a) *i.* – a final option
I wouldn't go to that terrible restaurant even as a last resort.

shoot one's mouth off (to) *i.* – speak in an inappropriate manner
That student often gets into trouble because he shoots his mouth off in class.

dressed to the nines *i.* – dressed up
She was dressed to the nines when she went out on her big date.

sell oneself short (to) *i.* – underestimate oneself
You have plenty of ability and experience. Don't sell yourself short.

for the time being *i.* – for now
What do you say we just relax in the park for the time being?

hit the spot (to) *i.* – satisfying
A hot cup of coffee would really hit the spot right now.

melt in one's mouth (to) *i.* – food that easily dissolves in one's mouth
This steak is so tender that it almost melts in your mouth.

EXERCISE 1

__M__	1 steep	A	spend all of one's savings
___	2 have one's name on it	B	crowded
___	3 rack	C	look at something
___	4 break the bank	D	arrogant
___	5 long gone	E	food that dissolves in one's mouth
___	6 dressed to the nines	F	perfectly suited to someone
___	7 melt in one's mouth	G	very early in the morning
___	8 shoot one's mouth off	H	cost
___	9 first thing in the morning	I	a final option
___	10 mark down	J	taken a long time ago
___	11 clash	K	reduce in price
___	12 full of oneself	L	for now
___	13 hit the spot	M	expensive
___	14 a last resort	N	visit somewhere
___	15 run	O	satisfying
___	16 jam-packed	P	a stand used to display clothes
___	17 cash	Q	don't match in color or design
___	18 for the time being	R	speak in an inappropriate manner
___	19 get a load of something	S	money
___	20 hit somewhere	T	dressed up

EXERCISE 2

USE THE WORDS/IDIOMS BELOW TO COMPLETE
EACH OF THE FOLLOWING SENTENCES.

shell out	clashes	jam-packed
first thing in the morning	take in	dressed to the nines
shot his mouth off at	hit the spot	cash
long gone	mark down	a last resort
get a load of	had her name on it	full of herself

1 The elevator I took this morning was so _____ that I could barely move.

2 I've lost a lot of weight, so I'll have to get a tailor to_____ these pants.

3 When I go fishing with my father we always leave home_____.

4 The robber was _____ by the time the police showed up at the jewelry store.

5 You will need a lot of _____ if you want to buy a Gucci watch at that store.

6 The store will _____ the price of that DVD player on Boxing Day.

7 He got fired from his job because he _____ the annual meeting in Chicago.

8 She said that she couldn't resist buying that sweater because it _____.

9 How much did you _____ on that gorgeous silk tie?

10 I really didn't like that woman's arrogant attitude. She was so _____.

11 An ice-cold bottle of imported beer would really _____ right about now.

12 I wouldn't go on a date with that disgusting guy even as _____.

13 We'll have to get _____ if we're going to that New Year's Eve party.

14 Do you think this pink shirt _____ with my brown pants?

15 _____ that beautiful sports car that's turning down our street.

EXERCISE 3

COMPLETE THE FOLLOWING CROSSWORD PUZZLE
USING WORDS/IDIOMS FROM THE DIALOGUE.

ACROSS

1 reduced in price

4 spend all of one's savings

7 visit

8 expensive

9 reduce the waist size

11 a stand used to display clothes

12 spend

DOWN

2 dressed up

3 bought quickly

5 satisfying

6 money

10 don't match

EXERCISE 4

1 I could just barely get on the subway this morning because it was so **jam-packed**.
   a I couldn't get on the subway this morning because it was really crowded.
   b The subway was so full that I had difficulty getting on it this morning.

2 The sunglasses I saw at the mall this afternoon **had my name on them**.
   a I wasn't crazy about the pair of sunglasses I looked at this afternoon.
   b The sunglasses I saw at the mall today were perfectly suited to me.

3 A cold glass of lemonade would really **hit the spot** now that we've finished the game.
   a A cold drink of lemonade would be really satisfying now that we've finished.
   b I'd rather not have a cold glass of lemonade after the game is finished.

4 I think the blouse you're wearing **clashes** with the skirt you have on.
   a The blouse you're wearing doesn't match the skirt you have on
   b The blouse you're wearing goes well with the skirt you have on.

5 I **shelled out** a lot of money on the diamond engagement ring that I bought for her.
   a I spent as little as possible on the engagement ring I bought for her.
   b The diamond engagement ring I bought for her was very pricey.

6 All of the merchandise was **snapped up** in the first fifteen minutes of the sale.
   a The merchandise was purchased quickly by the customers in the store.
   b There was still some merchandise left fifteen minutes after the sale had begun.

7 She takes her dog for a walk around the neighborhood **first thing in the morning**.
   a The dog takes her for a walk around the neighborhood early in the morning.
   b She takes her dog for a walk around the neighborhood right after she wakes up.

8 If you don't stop **shooting your mouth** off, somebody's going to beat you up.
   a If you don't stop speaking in an impolite manner, you're going to get beaten up.
   b If you don't stop speaking in a rude manner, you'll have to beat someone up.

9 The steak I ate last night was so tender that it almost **melted in my mouth**.
   a The steak I ate last night was so small that it was gone after a few bites.
   b The steak I ate last night was so tender that I hardly had to chew it.

10 Your ex-girlfriend was **dressed to kill** at the party I went to last night.
   a When I met your ex-girlfriend, she told me that she wants to kill you.
   b Your ex-girlfriend looked very attractive when I saw her last night.

EXERCISE 5

UNSCRAMBLE THE FOLLOWING SENTENCES, ADDING PUNCTUATION WHEN NEEDED. THE BEGINNING AND END OF EACH SENTENCE HAVE ALREADY BEEN DONE FOR YOU. HINT: IT'S HELPFUL TO IDENTIFY THE WORD/IDIOM FROM THE DIALOGUE IN EACH SENTENCE.

1 **I'm going to** / for / though / being / keep / job / my / even / I / time / the / **don't like it.**

I'm going to keep my job for the time being, even though I don't like it   .

2 **The young women** / dressed / to / when / went / were / hottest / club / the / to / in / kill / they / **town last night.**

_____.

3 **We'll have to** / thing / get / to / want / leave / the / in / if / morning / you / first / **there by lunchtime.**

_____.

4 **He said that** / of / cold / really / doing / after / hit / would / juice / a / the / spot / glass / **all that exercise.**

_____.

5 **After he won** / competition / was / full / people / that / started / the / he / himself / of / so / **to dislike him.**

_____.

6 **I hope he** / annual / his / the / at / off / meeting / the / mouth / shoot / during / doesn't / **head office today.**

_____.

7 **You really shouldn't** / and / short / you / experience / the / have / because / education / to / sell / yourself / **do that job.**

_____.

8 **How much would** / to / you / out / apartment / for / willing / be / a / brand-new / shell / **in that area?**

_____.

FIND THE WORDS/IDIOMS LISTED BELOW
IN THE WORD SEARCH GAME.

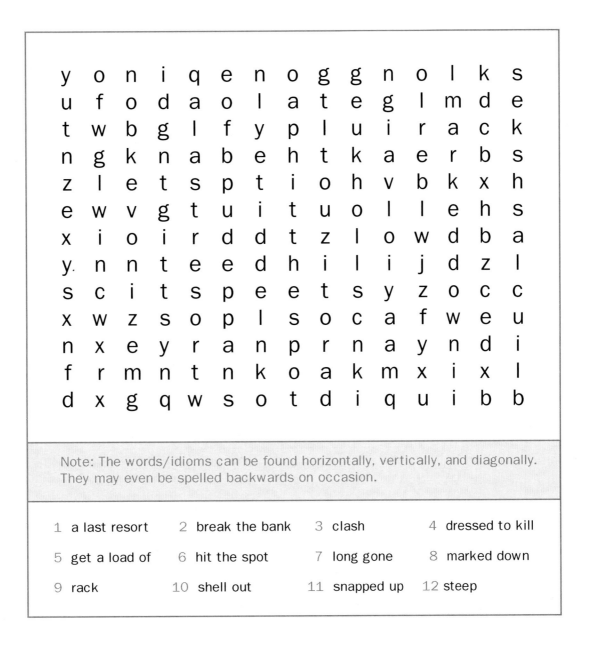

```
y  o  n  i  q  e  n  o  g  g  n  o  l  k  s
u  f  o  d  a  o  l  a  t  e  g  l  m  d  e
t  w  b  g  l  f  y  p  l  u  i  r  a  c  k
n  g  k  n  a  b  e  h  t  k  a  e  r  b  s
z  l  e  t  s  p  t  i  o  h  v  b  k  x  h
e  w  v  g  t  u  i  t  u  o  l  l  e  h  s
x  i  o  i  r  d  d  t  z  l  o  w  d  b  a
y. n  n  t  e  e  d  h  i  l  i  j  d  z  l
s  c  i  t  s  p  e  e  t  s  y  z  o  c  c
x  w  z  s  o  p  l  s  o  c  a  f  w  e  u
n  x  e  y  r  a  n  p  r  n  a  y  n  d  i
f  r  m  n  t  n  k  o  a  k  m  x  i  x  l
d  x  g  q  w  s  o  t  d  i  q  u  i  b  b
```

Note: The words/idioms can be found horizontally, vertically, and diagonally.
They may even be spelled backwards on occasion.

1 a last resort	2 break the bank	3 clash	4 dressed to kill
5 get a load of	6 hit the spot	7 long gone	8 marked down
9 rack	10 shell out	11 snapped up	12 steep

EXERCISE 7

Andre and Claudia are wandering past the store windows

Andre   What store do you feel like h_____ next? We haven't had much luck so far.

Claudia   I don't know. How about this store? I heard they're having a huge sale today. Everything is supposed to be m_____ way d_____.

Andre   I'll believe it when I see it, but it's certainly worth a look. I'd like to buy some clothes today, but I don't want to b_____ the b_____ doing it.

Claudia   Here it is. Let's go inside.

Andre   Sure.

They enter the crowded store

Claudia   Wow! This place is j_____-p_____. From the looks of it, most of the bargains have already been s_____ u_____. Wait a minute. What about this pair of pants? They're r_____ up your a_____, don't you think?

Andre   Let me see them. Actually, I don't mind them at all. I'd have to have them t_____ i_____, though. Is there a smaller size?

Claudia   Unfortunately that's the last pair. How much do they r_____?

Andre $149!

Claudia   That seems pretty s_____ to me.

Andre   No kidding! I'm not s_____ o_____ that kind of c_____ on pants that don't even fit properly. Could you put them back on the r_____ for me?

Claudia   Sure. Let me have them.

Andre   It's too bad we didn't get here first t_____ in the m_____. I saw a sweater in here last week that h_____ my n_____ on it. It's l_____ g_____ now that everything is on sale.

Claudia   That's too bad. .... G_____ a l_____ of that saleswoman over there. Can you believe what's she's wearing? You'd think that somebody who works in a clothing store would know that pink and green c_____.

Andre   Hey, there's no a_____ for t_____. The funny thing is that she looks so f_____ of h_____. I bet she thinks she's d_____ to k_____ in that outfit.

Claudia   I wouldn't wear something like that even as a l_____ r_____. I should probably stop s_____ my m_____ off. I'm not exactly d_____ to the n_____ myself this afternoon.

Andre   Oh, come on. Don't s_____ yourself s_____. You're really good-looking.

Claudia   Thanks. I think I've had enough of shopping for the t_____ b_____. How about you? What do you say we drop by that chocolate store on the lower level of the mall?

Andre   You mean Godiva Chocolates?

Claudia   That's the one. Something sweet would really h_____ the s_____ right about now. I'm telling you, their truffles m_____ in your m_____.

Andre   Sounds like a great idea. Lead the way.

COMPREHENSION QUESTIONS

TRY TO ANSWER THE FOLLOWING QUESTIONS WITHOUT LOOKING AT THE DIALOGUE. ONCE YOU'VE FINISHED THE QUESTIONS, YOU CAN REFER TO THE DIALOGUE TO CHECK YOUR ANSWERS.

1. Why did Andre and Claudia go into the store?

2. How many customers were in the store?

3. Were there a lot of bargains to choose from? Why? Why not?

4. What did Claudia find in the store that was suitable for Andre?

5. What was wrong with the size? How much did they run?

6. Did Andre think that price was reasonable or expensive?

7. What did Andre see in the store last week that had his name on it?

8. Why didn't he buy it now that it's on sale?

9. What did they think was wrong with the saleswoman's clothes?

10. What was the saleswoman's attitude?

11. Would Claudia ever wear the same outfit as the saleswoman?

12. Why did Claudia say, "I should probably stop shooting my mouth off"?

13. Who had had enough of shopping for the time being?

14. Where did Andre and Claudia decide to go next? Who suggested it?

15. What will they probably buy at that shop?

DISCUSSION QUESTIONS

PART A: General Discussion Questions

1 What's your favorite store when shopping for clothes? CDs? chocolate? magazines?

2 In your opinion, what store has the best sales in this city?

3 Are you able to find clothes in your size when shopping here?

4 Do you prefer to shop on a long street or in a huge mall? Why?

5 Do you think the quality of the clothes here is the same as, worse than, or better than in your country?

PART B: Idiomatic Discussion Questions

1 What store would you **hit** after school if you had $100 to spend?

2 At what time of year are the stores in your country **jam-packed**? How about here?

3 How much **dough** would you **shell out** on a nice sweater? fashionable haircut? pair of running shoes? state-of-the-art computer?

4 Describe the last thing you saw that **had your name on it**. Did you buy it?

5 Tell me about an outfit you wear when you want to **dress to the nines**.

6 What would you like to do this weekend as a first choice? How about as **a last resort**?

7 What drink/food would **hit the spot** right now?

GIVE IT A SHOT

Negative: hideous / repulsive / revolting / sleazy
butt ugly / gross
ugly
unattractive

Neutral: average-looking / not bad-looking

Positive: attractive / cute / easy-on-the-eyes / good-looking / nice-looking
beautiful / handsome / lovely / striking
a babe / a hunk / breathtaking / gorgeous / hot / sexy / stunning

How many of the following celebrities do you know? How would you describe the celebrities you recognize using words/expressions from the chart above?

Male	Female
Brad Pitt	Mariah Carey
Michael Jackson	Bette Midler
Jim Carrey	Elizabeth Hurley
Marilyn Manson	Madonna
Michael Jordan	Nicole Kidman
Tom Hanks	Whoopi Goldberg
Denzel Washington	Rosey O'Donnell
Keith Richards	Beyonce
Johnny Depp	Paris Hilton

Give your opinion about who you think is attractive. Name an actor/actress not in the chart above.

1 In my opinion, _____ was handsome
                          (actor)

    in the movie _____.
                          (movie title)

2 I think _____ was gorgeous
                    (actress)

    in the movie _____.
                          (movie title)

··■CHAPTER SEVEN■··

PICKING UP A FRIEND AT THE AIRPORT

PICKING UP A FRIEND AT THE AIRPORT

Andre and Hiro have just entered the terminal

Andre   Well, we certainly arrived here with **time to spare**.

Hiro   No doubt about that. We **made great time** getting here. Usually there's **gridlock** at this time of day. The traffic was incredibly light for a Monday morning.

Andre   We sure **lucked out**. So what are we going to do now? We've got to **kill some time** before Yuka's flight arrives.

Hiro   What do you say we stroll through the airport? Maybe we can **grab a bite to eat**.

Andre   Sounds good. But I think I'll just have something hot and caffeinated. I need **a pick-me-up**.

Hiro   Hey look, there's a sandwich shop. Why don't we **take five** there?

Andre   OK. It's perfect and only **a stone's throw away** from the arrival area.

They sit down in a booth after getting their order

Hiro   This coffee is way too strong for me. I should have used some **half-and-half** instead of milk.

Andre   **That goes without saying**. Whenever I have coffee at your place, it tastes more like tea than coffee. You should have ordered the light roast. Here, swap with me; mine's lighter.

Hiro   Thanks. .... Are you still not smoking? I bet you sneak one from time to time, don't you?

Andre	No way. I **went cold turkey** a month ago and haven't had one since. You should have seen me at first. I was incredibly **grumpy**, especially in the morning. My friends couldn't **get over** how I would **go ballistic** if the slightest thing went wrong.
Hiro	I'm glad I was out of town last month. Do you still have any **cravings**?
Andre	Right now, it's not too bad. I really go crazy though when I'm having a few drinks with my buddies. Other than that, it's tolerable.
Hiro	Do you find that you're snacking a lot?
Andre	**You bet**. In fact, I'm starting to **pack on the pounds**. I'm going to have to start working out or I'll end up with quite the **spare-tire**. I'd really hate to get **chubby** again. Listen, let me use **the john** and then after you're finished, we should **head** over to the arrival area.
	After the sandwich shop, they walk over to the arrival board
Hiro	**Holy cow!**
Andre	What?
Hiro	Don't **hit the roof**. The flight's been delayed by 2 hours. I can't believe it!
Andre	**That does it**! We're going outside. I've got to have a **butt**.

time to spare *i.* – extra time
He spent an hour at the coffee shop because he had time to spare.

make great time (to) *i.* – arrive somewhere faster than expected
They made great time getting to the office this morning.

gridlock *n.* – very heavy traffic
I was late for work this morning because of the gridlock downtown.

luck out (to) *i.* – lucky
She lucked out when she picked the winning numbers for the lottery.

kill time (to) *i.* – waste time
I'm going to kill time in the student lounge until the class begins.

grab a bite to eat (to) *i.* – eat something quickly
What do you say we grab a bite (to eat) before we go to the theater?

pick-me-up (a) *i.* – coffee, coke (any caffeinated beverage)
I feel kind of tired this morning. I really need a pick-me-up.

take five (to) *i.* – take a short break
I think we deserve a break after doing all that work in the yard. Let's take five.

stone's throw away (a) *i.* – close by, near by
The stadium is only a stone's throw away from the subway station.

half-and-half *n.* – cream
Do you prefer half-and-half or milk in your coffee?

that goes without saying *i.* – that's obvious
Steve: *I don't think she likes me very much.* **Alan:** *That goes without saying.*

go cold turkey (to) *i.* – quit smoking completely
I finally decided to quit smoking. I went cold turkey two weeks ago.

grumpy *adj.* – cranky, grouchy, irritable
The boss is grumpy this morning because he didn't get any sleep last night.

get over something/someone (to) *i.* – recover from something/someone
It took Thomas several months to get over his ex-girlfriend.

go ballistic (to) *i.* – furious, livid, very angry
She went ballistic when her son spilled coffee on the expensive white sofa.

craving *n.* – desire
These days, I can't control my cravings for chocolate.

you bet *i.* – absolutely, of course
Dave: *Do you think it will rain today?* **Kate:** *You bet.*

pack on the pounds (to) *i.* – put on weight
I should go on a diet because I'm starting to pack on the pounds.

spare-tire (a) *i.* – big stomach, pot belly
That middle-aged man in the tracksuit has a spare-tire.

chubby *adj.* – chunky, fat, overweight, pudgy, tubby
If you keep eating all those fatty foods, you're going to get chubby.

john (the) *n.* – the bathroom/washroom
You'll have to ask the waiter where the john is.

head somewhere (to) *v.* – go somewhere
I think I'm going to head home after we finish watching the video.

holy cow *exclam.* – holy smoke, wow
Holy cow! That car almost hit a woman in the crosswalk.

hit the roof (to) *i.* – furious, livid, very angry
My mom hit the roof when I came home late for Christmas dinner.

that does it *exclam.* – I can't handle anymore
That does it! I'm going to tell my noisy neighbors to turn down their stereo.

butt *n.* – cigarette
My older brother likes to smoke a butt after he eats dinner.

__F__	1 holy cow	A	eat something quickly
___	2 a stone's throw away	B	extra time
___	3 luck out	C	that's obvious
___	4 hit the roof	D	cranky
___	5 head somewhere	E	cigarette
___	6 grab a bite to eat	F	wow
___	7 take five	G	the washroom
___	8 time to spare	H	near by
___	9 gridlock	I	desire
___	10 pack on the pounds	J	go somewhere
___	11 go cold turkey	K	cream
___	12 a spare-tire	L	very heavy traffic
___	13 butt	M	lucky
___	14 kill time	N	put on weight
___	15 the john	O	a big stomach
___	16 craving	P	arrive faster than expected
___	17 grumpy	Q	furious
___	18 make great time	R	quit smoking completely
___	19 half-and-half	S	waste time
___	20 that goes without saying	T	take a short break

EXERCISE 2

USE THE WORDS/IDIOMS BELOW TO COMPLETE
EACH OF THE FOLLOWING SENTENCES.

head	time to spare	to take five
went cold turkey	grab a bite	a stone's throw away
pack on the pounds	grumpy	lucked out
half-and-half	holy cow	get over
cravings for	gridlock	spare-tire

1 We'll be there soon because it's only_____ from here.

2 My wife wanted me to quit smoking, so I _____ over two weeks ago.

3 If I were you, I'd stay away from him this morning because he is very _____.

4 He found it extremely difficult to _____ the unexpected death of his father.

5 We have plenty of _____ , so let's go over to the cafeteria for a little while.

6 When my wife was pregnant, she always had _____ chocolate.

7 I started to _____ when I began eating more and exercising less.

8 He'd like to _____ to eat before we go to the lecture this afternoon.

9 There's always _____ in this part of town during rush hour.

10 I've been studying for three hours straight, so I think I'm going _____.

11 I'm going to have to start working out again because I'm getting a _____.

12 _____! Did you see that shooting star in the sky?

13 She said that she'd prefer to have some _____ in her coffee.

14 He _____ when he guessed the right answer to the professor's question.

15 She's going to _____ straight home right after we finish eating dinner.

WHAT WORD/IDIOM FROM THE DIALOGUE MATCHES THE FOLLOWING DEFINITIONS? WHEN THE EXERCISE HAS BEEN COMPLETED, THE IDIOM FOR 'THAT'S OBVIOUS' WILL BE SPELLED VERTICALLY.

1	quit smoking completely	g o c o l d (t)u r k e y
2	close by	_ _ _ _ _ _ ' _ _(_)_ _ _ _ _ _ _
3	can't handle anymore	_ _(_)_ _ _ _ _ _ _
4	lucky	_ _ _ _ _ _(_)
5	arrive faster than expected	_ _ _ _ (_)_ _ _ _ _ _ _ _
6	the bathroom	_ _ _ _(_)_ _
7	recover from	_ _ _ _ _(_)_
8	big stomach	(_)_ _ _ _ - _ _ _ _
9	wow	_ _ _ _ _ _(_)
10	eat something quickly	_ _ _ _ _ _(_)_ _ _ _ _ _ _
11	waste time	_ _ _ _ (_)_ _ _
12	go	(_)_ _ _
13	furious	_(_) _ _ _ _ _ _ _ _ _
14	absolutely	_ _(_) _ _ _
15	cigarette	_ _(_)_
16	extra time	_ _ _ _ _ _ (_)_ _ _ _
17	take a short break	_(_)_ _ _ _ _ _
18	cranky	_ _ _ _ _(_)
19	desire	_ _ _ _(_)_ _
20	put on weight	_ _ _ _ _ _ _ _ _ _ _(_)_ _
21	very heavy traffic	(_)_ _ _ _ _ _ _

Unscramble the following words/idioms from the dialogue.

22	ekma treag meit	_ _ _ _ _ _ _ _ _ _ _ _
23	cakp no eht ondpsu	_ _ _ _ _ _ _ _ _ _ _ _ _ _
24	og lclsitbia	_ _ _ _ _ _ _ _ _ _

EXERCISE 4

REWRITE THE FOLLOWING SENTENCES USING
A WORD/IDIOM FROM THE DIALOGUE.

1 Could we eat something quickly at the diner before we go to the concert?

   <u>Could we grab a bite to eat at the diner before we go to the concert?</u>   .

2 After smoking for more than 10 years, he quit completely.

   _____ .

3 We've been working for more than 4 hours. What do you say we take a short break?

   _____ .

4 My father was furious when my younger brother was arrested for vandalism.

   _____ .

5 He's got a big stomach because he overeats and never exercises.

   _____ .

6 I was up all night studying. I definitely need some coffee this morning.

   _____ .

7 The ambulance couldn't get to the accident scene because of the heavy traffic.

   _____ .

8 Do you happen to know where the washroom is?

   _____ .

9 He was really irritable this morning because he drank too much last night.

   _____ .

10 I'll be sure and go over to his house right after the basketball game finishes.

   _____ .

EXERCISE 5

UNSCRAMBLE THE FOLLOWING SENTENCES, ADDING PUNCTUATION WHEN NEEDED. THE BEGINNING AND END OF EACH SENTENCE HAVE ALREADY BEEN DONE FOR YOU. HINT: IT'S HELPFUL TO IDENTIFY THE WORD/IDIOM FROM THE DIALOGUE IN EACH SENTENCE.

1 **He really started** / pounds / to / the / on / turned / he / after / pack / **forty years old.**

He really started to pack on the pounds after he turned forty years old   .

2 **These days, there's** / in / between / 4 / always / gridlock / city / the / **and 6 o'clock.**

_____.

3 **I'd like to** / bite / a / to / at / new / opened / just / that / restaurant / that / grab / eat / **on the corner.**

_____.

4 **He was terribly** / morning / his / baby / him / because / this / newborn / grumpy / kept / **up all night.**

_____.

5 **She really hit** / when / husband / the / about / roof / forgot / her / their / completely / **tenth wedding anniversary.**

_____.

6 **The student couldn't** / fact / over / she / been / into / get / that / the / hadn't / accepted / **Harvard Law School.**

_____.

7 **We're lucky because** / throw / to / is / a / visit / the / you / want / stone's / store / only / **away from here.**

_____.

8 **I saw a** / bald / of / spare-tires / when / went / with / men / my / to / I / lot / **highschool reunion.**

_____.

EXERCISE 6

FIND THE WORDS/IDIOMS LISTED BELOW
IN THE WORD SEARCH GAME.

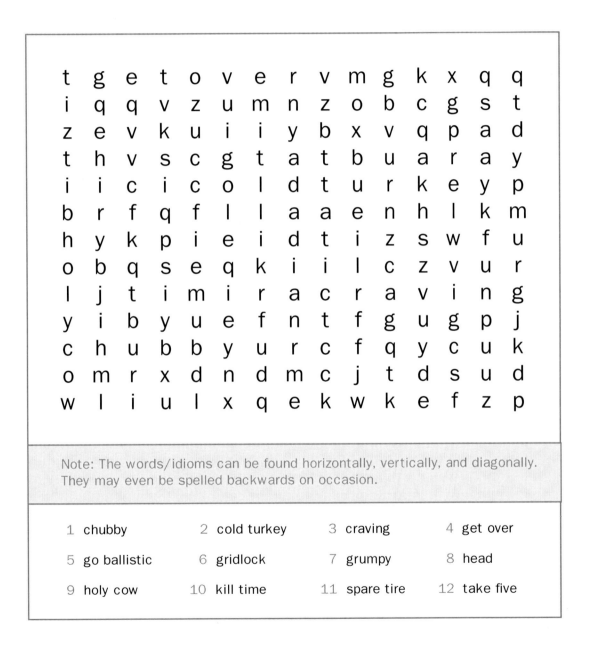

t g e t o v e r v m g k x q q
i q q v z u m n z o b c g s t
z e v k u i i y b x v q p a d
t h v s c g t a t b u a r a y
i i c i c o l d t u r k e y p
b r f q f l l a a e n h l k m
h y k p i e i d t i z s w f u
o b q s e q k i i l c z v u r
l j t i m i r a c r a v i n g
y i b y u e f n t f g u g p j
c h u b b y u r c f q y c u k
o m r x d n d m c j t d s u d
w l i u l x q e k w k e f z p

Note: The words/idioms can be found horizontally, vertically, and diagonally.
They may even be spelled backwards on occasion.

1 chubby	2 cold turkey	3 craving	4 get over
5 go ballistic	6 gridlock	7 grumpy	8 head
9 holy cow	10 kill time	11 spare tire	12 take five

EXERCISE 7

FILL IN THE WORDS/IDIOMS THAT ARE
MISSING FROM THE DIALOGUE.

Andre and Hiro have just entered the terminal

Andre   Well, we certainly arrived here with t_____ to s_____.

Hiro   No doubt about that. We m_____ great t_____ getting here. Usually there's g_____ at this time of day. The traffic was incredibly light for a Monday morning.

Andre   We sure l_____ o_____. So what are we going to do now? We've got to k_____ some t_____ before Yuka's flight arrives.

Hiro   What do you say we stroll through the airport? Maybe we can g_____ a b_____ to eat.

Andre   Sounds good. But I think I'll just have something hot and caffeinated. I need a p_____-me-u_____.

Hiro   Hey look, there's a sandwich shop. Why don't we t_____ f_____ there?

Andre   OK. It's perfect and only a s_____ throw a_____ from the arrival area.

They sit down in a booth after getting their order

Hiro   This coffee is way too strong for me. I should have used some h_____-and-h_____ instead of milk.

Andre   That g_____ without s_____. Whenever I have coffee at your place, it tastes more like tea than coffee. You should have ordered the light roast. Here, swap with me; mine's lighter.

Hiro   Thanks. .... Are you still not smoking? I bet you sneak one from time to time, don't you?

Andre No way. I w_____ cold t_____ a month ago and haven't had one since. You should have seen me at first. I was incredibly g_____, especially in the morning. My friends couldn't g_____ o_____ how I would g_____ b_____ if the slightest thing went wrong.

Hiro I'm glad I was out of town last month. Do you still have any c_____?

Andre Right now, it's not too bad. I really g_____ n_____ though when I'm having a few drinks with my buddies. Other than that, it's tolerable.

Hiro Do you find that you're snacking a lot?

Andre You b_____. In fact, I'm starting to p_____ on the p_____. I'm going to have to start working out or I'll end up with quite the s_____-t_____. I'd really hate to get c_____ again. Listen, let me use the j_____ and then after you're finished, we should h_____ over to the arrival area.

After the sandwich shop, they walk over to the arrival board

Hiro H_____ c_____!

Andre What?

Hiro Don't h_____ the r_____. The flight's been delayed by 2 hours. I can't believe it!

Andre That d_____ it! We're going outside. I've got to have a b_____.

1   Why were Andre and Hiro surprised that they made great time getting to the airport?

2   Who were they picking up at the airport?

3   How did Hiro suggest they kill time until the flight arrives?

4   What did Andre want to have at the sandwich shop?

5   Is the sandwich shop far away from the arrival area?

6   Did they sit in a booth or at a table in the sandwich shop?

7   What was wrong with the coffee Hiro was served in the sandwich shop?

8   What did Andre say about the coffee he'd had at Hiro's place?

9   What habit did Andre give up? Did he stop it gradually?

10 How did Andre feel when he first gave up the habit?

11 When does Andre really go nuts?

12 Why was Andre starting to pack on the pounds?

13 Where did they go after they finished at the sandwich shop?

14 How late was Yuka's flight going to be?

15 What did Andre want to do after he heard the bad news?

DISCUSSION QUESTIONS

PART A: General Discussion Questions

1 Have you ever had to wait for a delayed flight in an airport? Explain.

2 What problems, if any, did you have at the airport when you left your country? arrived here?

3 Have you picked up/dropped off anyone at the airport while you've been here? How did it go?

4 What's the biggest difference between the airport you departed from in your country and the one here?

5 What is the most convenient/inconvenient airport you've had to use?

PART B: Idiomatic Discussion Questions

1 What do you usually do when you arrive at the school with **time to spare**?

2 Where do you like to **grab a bite to eat** in this area?

3 Describe another place you like to go to that's only **a stone's throw away** from the school.

4 Have you **packed on the pounds** or lost weight since coming here? How do you explain this?

5 Have you **hit the roof** since arriving here? Why? If not, when was the last time you **went ballistic**?

6 At what time of day are you most likely to be **grumpy**? Why is that?

7 Would you describe the rush hour traffic in your hometown as: **gridlock**, bumper to bumper, stop and go, slow and go, heavy, or light? What city in your country has the worst traffic? How would you describe the traffic here?

GIVE IT A SHOT

IN THE DIALOGUE, ANDRE AND HIRO HAVE TO KILL SOME TIME AT THE AIRPORT. HERE ARE SOME FUNNY AIRLINE SLOGANS THAT SOME FRUSTRATED PEOPLE MUST OF THOUGHT OF WHILE WAITING FOR A DELAYED FLIGHT IN AN AIRPORT TERMINAL. INSERT THE NAME OF THE AIRLINE YOU DISLIKE THE MOST INTO THE FOLLOWING SLOGANS.

Airline Slogans that will never be used:

1   *(Airline name)*: Join our frequent miss program.

2   *(Airline name)*: Find out if there really is a God.

3   *(Airline name)*: Terrorists are afraid to fly with us.

4   *(Airline name)*: A real man lands where he wants to.

5   *(Airline name)*: Ask about our out-of-court settlements.

6   *(Airline name)*: Your kids will love our inflatable slides.

7   *(Airline name)*: We may be landing on a street near you.

8   *(Airline name)*: Complimentary champagne during free-fall.

9   *(Airline name)*: When you can't wait for the world to come to you.

10   *(Airline name)*: Watch the in-flight movie in the plane next to you.

11   *(Airline name)*: Which will fall faster, our stock price or our planes?

12   *(Airline name)*: On certain flights, every section is a smoking section.

13   *(Airline name)*: Our staff has lots of experience consoling next-of-kin.

14   *(Airline name)*: Our pilots are all terminally ill and have nothing to lose.

15   *(Airline name)*: Are the engines too noisy? Don't worry. We'll turn them off.

••CHAPTER EIGHT••

SUNTANNING ON THE BEACH

SUNTANNING ON THE BEACH

Andre and Min-Jung are sitting on their towels

Andre	Can I use some of your sunscreen?
Min-Jung	**By all means**, help yourself.
Andre	I don't see it. Where the heck is it?
Min-Jung	Oh sorry, I think it's in my bag. Let me get it for you.
Andre	Man, do you ever have **a load** of stuff in your bag. Can you find it in there?
Min-Jung	I think so. Here it is. You should probably put some sunscreen on your nose. It's getting pretty red.
Andre	Thanks; I'll slap some on right now. ....Wow! Is it ever hot out today. I'm already sweating **like crazy**. I'm afraid I can't **handle** the heat very well. You look fine. I guess you don't mind it.
Min-Jung	It doesn't **bug** me. Summers in Seoul are usually pretty hot and humid. The **heat wave** we've had recently is no problem for me. It's the cold that I don't like. As soon as the temperature dips a little bit, I have to **bundle up** or I freeze.
Andre	So what do you think? Are we going to **hang out** at the beach most of the afternoon?
Min-Jung	I wouldn't mind doing that. I feel like **kicking back** here for at least few hours. Did you have something else in mind?
Andre	No, not at all. I want to **get some sun** today. I think my tan could use a little work.
Min-Jung	Just be careful you don't get burned. .... I'm not **fishing for compliments**, but what do you think of my new swimsuit? I bought it yesterday.

Andre	I thought something was different. I like it. That color **suits you to a T**. Where'd you get it from?
Min-Jung	I **came across** it while I was shopping with Claudia in the mall. Actually, she bought **a two-piece** for herself. I wasn't quite as daring as she was, though.
Andre	What do you mean?
Min-Jung	Her suit is really **high-cut**. It's a little too **skimpy** for me. She's got a really nice figure, so she can **get away with** it.
Andre	Yeah. Claudia's got a great body. She looks so **hot** when she wears ....
Min-Jung	Oh stop it! Do all men have **a one-track mind**? I swear it's the only thing guys think about.
Andre	OK. OK. I'll **knock it off**. Have you seen the weather forecast? Is it going to be this **muggy** tomorrow?
Min-Jung	I think they're predicting a change in the weather. It's supposed to **cloud over** tonight and then **pour** tomorrow. If we're lucky, the nice weather will return by Tuesday.
Andre	I hope so. I'm playing soccer on Tuesday after school. .... I think I'm going to lie down. Do you mind if I **doze off** for a while?
Min-Jung	Sorry. Have I been **bending your ear**?
Andre	No, not at all. The heat just makes me a little sleepy.
Min-Jung	OK. While you're napping, I'm going to **take a dip** before the tide goes out.

DEFINITIONS

adj. – adjective	*exclam.* – exclamation	*n.* – noun
adv. – adverb	*i.* – idiom, phrasal verb	*v.* – verb

by all means *i.* – certainly, of course
Karen: *May I take this chair?* **Peter:** *By all means, help yourself.*

load (a) *n.* – a bunch, a lot, a pile, a stack, a ton
That student is carrying a load of books in her backpack.

like crazy *i.* – actively, fast, very much
He was studying like crazy the night before the big exam.

handle (to) *v.* – deal with, endure, tolerate
I can't handle people who pick their nose while driving a car.

bug (to) *v.* – annoy, bother
My little brother always bugs me while I'm watching my favorite TV show.

heat wave *n.* – many days of hot weather
The heat wave is expected to continue until at least the end of August.

bundle up (to) *i.* – dress warmly
It's snowing, so you should bundle up before you go outside.

hang out (to) *i.* – spend time
I think I'm going to hang out at my friend's house on Sunday afternoon.

kick back (to) *i.* – relax, take it easy
I'll probably just stay at home and kick back on Friday night.

get some sun (to) *i.* – get a suntan
Would you like go to the beach today and get some sun?

fish for compliments (to) *i.* – try to get compliments
That woman is always fishing for compliments about her wardrobe.

suit someone to a T (to) *i.* – suit someone perfectly
You look great in that new dress. It suits you to a T.

come across something (to) *i.* – find something by accident
I came across an old letter from my father while I was cleaning up the attic.

two-piece (a) *n.* – bikini, a swimsuit that has two pieces
She bought a two-piece for her trip to Cancun, Mexico.

high-cut *adj.* – a swimsuit that shows a lot of leg
Can you believe the swimsuit she's wearing? It's really high-cut.

skimpy *adj.* – scant, scarce, sparse
I think that dress is a little too skimpy for you to wear to work.

get away with doing something (to) *i.* – escape the consequences of something
The coach always lets him get away with missing the practices.

hot *adj.* – sexy, gorgeous
The famous movie actress looked hot when she arrived for the Academy Awards.

one-track mind (a) *i.* – obsession
I had a one-track mind when I was a teenager. All I thought about was soccer.

knock it off (to) *i.* – stop it
I want you guys to stop teasing me about my haircut. Knock it off!

muggy *adj.* – hot and humid
It's always muggy in New York in the summertime.

cloud over (to) *i.* – become cloudy
Do you know when it's supposed to cloud over and start raining?

pour (to) *v.* – rain heavily
Look at those dark clouds on the horizon. I think it's going to pour soon.

doze off (to) *i.* – nap, nod off, sleep, snooze
He dozed off on the sofa while watching a football game on TV.

bend one's ear (to) *i.* – talk too much
That annoying guy has been bending my ear for the last hour.

take a dip (to) *i.* – go for a swim
She took a dip in the pool as soon as she got home from school.

EXERCISE 1

MATCH THE WORD/IDIOM WITH THE CORRECT DEFINITION

_J_	1 heat wave	A	certainly
___	2 fish for compliments	B	suit someone perfectly
___	3 a two-piece	C	go for a swim
___	4 skimpy	D	become cloudy
___	5 hot	E	actively
___	6 take a dip	F	try to get compliments
___	7 high-cut	G	spend time
___	8 kick back	H	sexy
___	9 bundle up	I	relax
___	10 like crazy	J	many days of hot weather
___	11 get away with doing something	K	hot and humid
___	12 a one-track mind	L	a bikini
___	13 knock it off	M	talk too much
___	14 by all means	N	scant
___	15 cloud over	O	find something by accident
___	16 bend one's ear	P	escape the consequences
___	17 hang out	Q	an obsession
___	18 come across something	R	dress warmly
___	19 suit someone to a T	S	stop it
___	20 muggy	T	a swimsuit that shows a lot of leg

USE THE WORDS/IDIOMS BELOW TO COMPLETE
EACH OF THE FOLLOWING SENTENCES.

knock it off	one-track mind	bugs
suits you to a T	bundle up	got some sun
bending my ear	pour	can't handle
get away with	came across	hot
muggy	take a dip	like crazy

1 You should _____ before you go outside. It's freezing cold today.

2 I _____ an old family photo album while I was cleaning up the basement.

3 I can't believe how boring that guy is. He's been _____ for at least an hour.

4 I had to work _____ in order to finish the sales report by 6:00.

5 The teacher never gets angry at her for coming late. He lets her _____ it.

6 He had a _____ as a teenager. All he thought about was baseball.

7 It _____ me when she starts to talk about how rich she is.

8 It was a beautiful day, so they _____ at the beach this afternoon.

9 That new jacket you bought looks very nice on you. It really _____.

10 Stop teasing me about what happened last night. Just _____!

11 Would you like to _____ in the swimming pool before we eat lunch?

12 The golf tournament was postponed because it started to _____.

13 The model in the advertisement for Victoria's Secret looks _____.

14 I _____ people who smoke cigars while I'm eating in a restaurant.

15 They don't want to go outside today because it's so _____.

EXERCISE 3

COMPLETE THE FOLLOWING CROSSWORD PUZZLE
USING WORDS/IDIOMS FROM THE DIALOGUE.

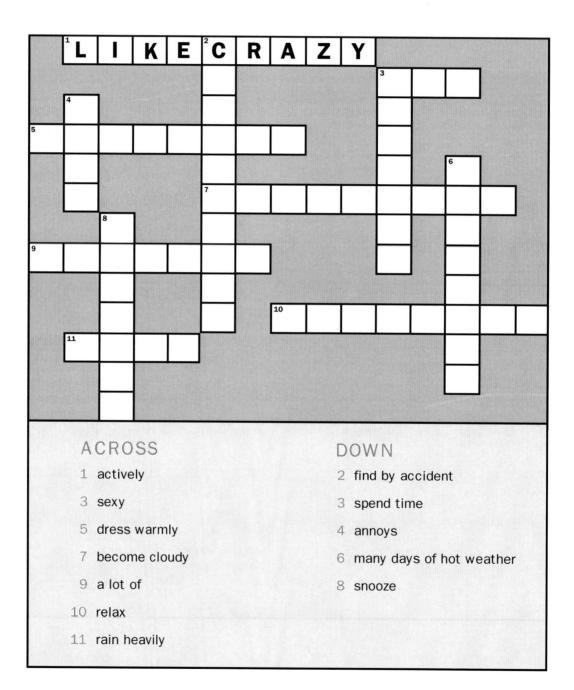

ACROSS

1 actively

3 sexy

5 dress warmly

7 become cloudy

9 a lot of

10 relax

11 rain heavily

DOWN

2 find by accident

3 spend time

4 annoys

6 many days of hot weather

8 snooze

EXERCISE 4

1 I can't stand the way his girlfriend is constantly **fishing for compliments**.
   a I hate the way his girlfriend always expects us to compliment her.
   b I don't like the way his girlfriend constantly criticizes other people.

2 My friends want to **take a dip** in the swimming pool before they go home today.
   a My friends want to go for a swim in the pool once they get home today.
   b My friends would like to go for a swim in the pool before they leave.

3 The pullover you bought at the mall this afternoon **suits you to a T**.
   a The sweater you bought at the mall is perfectly suited to you.
   b The pullover you bought at the mall doesn't match any of the clothes you have.

4 You should **bundle up** before you leave because it's very cold outside.
   a You should hurry once you get outside because it's very cold today.
   b You should dress warmly because it's cold outside today.

5 I'd like to **get some sun** at the beach before we go back to the hotel room.
   a I'd like to get my son before we go back to the hotel room.
   b I'd like to get some sun prior to going back to the hotel room.

6 I'm going to **kick back** at the coffee shop with my friend this afternoon.
   a My friend kicked me in the back at the coffee shop this afternoon.
   b I'd like to relax with my friend at the coffee shop this afternoon.

7 My boyfriend was staring at the woman who was wearing the **skimpy** swimsuit.
   a My boyfriend kept looking at the woman in the tiny swimsuit.
   b The woman in the small swimsuit was glancing at my boyfriend.

8 I **came across** a beautiful lamp while I was cleaning up the attic this morning.
   a I finally found the beautiful lamp I was looking for in the attic.
   b I found a beautiful lamp in the attic by chance this morning.

9 The student was so sleepy that he couldn't help **dozing off** during the lecture.
   a The student was sleepy, however, he managed to stay alert during the lecture.
   b The student fell asleep during the lecture because he was so sleepy.

10 I can't **handle** people who always brag about how successful they are.
   a I don't like it when people continually boast about their success.
   b I love to hear people constantly brag about how successful they are.

EXERCISE 5

UNSCRAMBLE THE FOLLOWING SENTENCES, ADDING PUNCTUATION WHEN NEEDED. THE BEGINNING AND END OF EACH SENTENCE HAVE ALREADY BEEN DONE FOR YOU. HINT: IT'S HELPFUL TO IDENTIFY THE WORD/IDIOM FROM THE DIALOGUE IN EACH SENTENCE.

1 **I think the** / ski / you / yourself / suits / for / bought / jacket / you / really / **to a T.**

   I think the ski jacket you bought for yourself really suits you to a T   .

2 **I told him** / that / are / to / out / café / at / the / he / until / going / hang / we / **joins us there.**

   _____.

3 **I can't go** / the / to / you / because / load / I / have / a / movies / homework / of / with / **to do tonight.**

   _____.

4 **She has been** / cut / she / since / at / fishing / ever / got / for / hair / her / compliments / **that trendy salon.**

   _____.

5 **He said that** / cloud / this / and / afternoon / then / to / supposed / over / it's / **start raining tonight.**

   _____.

6 **The teacher always** / class / get / with / him / skipping / lets / away / **every Friday afternoon.**

   _____.

7 **While I was** / the / through / mall / with / came / wandering / my / I / across / friend / **a beautiful blouse.**

   _____.

8 **I've been studying** / because / like / to / the / exams / crazy / have / I / final / write / two / **day after tomorrow.**

   _____.

EXERCISE 6

WHAT WORD/IDIOM FROM THE DIALOGUE MATCHES THE FOLLOWING
DEFINITIONS? WHEN THE EXERCISE HAS BEEN COMPLETED, THE IDIOM
FOR 'TRY TO GET COMPLIMENTS' WILL BE SPELLED VERTICALLY.

1	snooze	d o z e o(f)f
2	actively	_(_)_ _ _ _ _ _
3	scant	(_)_ _ _ _ _
4	tolerate	(_)_ _ _ _ _
5	stop it	_ _ _ _ _ _ _ _(_)_
6	sexy, gorgeous	_(_)_
7	rain heavily	_ _ _(_)
8	become cloudy	(_)_ _ _ _ _ _ _ _
9	a lot of	_ _(_)_ _ _ _
10	an obsession	_ _ _ _ - _ _ _ _ _ (_)_ _
11	go for a swim	_ _ _ _ _ _ _(_)
12	of course	_ _ _ _(_) _ _ _ _ _
13	relax	_(_)_ _ _ _ _ _
14	get a suntan	_ _ _ _ _(_)_ _ _ _
15	dress warmly	_ _ _ _(_) _ _
16	spend time	_ _(_)_ _ _ _
17	many days of hot weather	_ _(_) _ _ _ _
18	annoys	_ _ _(_)

Unscramble the following words/idioms from the dialogue.

19	teg meos usn	_ _ _ _ _ _ _ _ _ _
20	nedb sih rae	_ _ _ _ _ _ _ _ _ _
21	gygum	_ _ _ _ _
22	yspkmi	_ _ _ _ _ _
23	a eno-ktarc dnim	_ _ _ _ - _ _ _ _ _ _ _ _

EXERCISE 7

FILL IN THE WORDS/IDIOMS THAT ARE MISSING FROM THE DIALOGUE.

Andre and Min-Jung are sitting on their towels

Andre   Can I use some of your sunscreen?

Min-Jung   B_____ all m_____, help yourself.

Andre   I don't see it. Where the heck is it?

Min-Jung   Oh sorry, I think it's in my bag. Let me get it for you.

Andre   Man, do you ever have a l_____ of stuff in your bag. Can you find it in there?

Min-Jung   I think so. Here it is. You should probably put some sunscreen on your nose. It's getting pretty red.

Andre   Thanks; I'll slap some on right now. ....Wow! Is it ever hot out today. I'm already sweating like c_____. I'm afraid I can't h_____ the heat very well. You look fine. I guess you don't mind it.

Min-Jung   It doesn't b_____ me. Summers in Seoul are usually pretty hot and humid. The h_____ w_____ we've had recently is no problem for me. It's the cold that I don't like. As soon as the temperature dips a little bit, I have to b_____ u_____ or I freeze.

Andre   So what do you think? Are we going to h_____ o_____ at the beach most of the afternoon?

Min-Jung   I wouldn't mind doing that. I feel like k_____ b_____ here for at least few hours. Did you have something else in mind?

Andre   No, not at all. I want to g_____ some s_____ today. I think my tan could use a little work.

Min-Jung   Just be careful you don't get burned. .... I'm not f_____ for c_____, but what do you think of my new swimsuit? I bought it yesterday.

Andre   I thought something was different. I like it. That color s_____ you to a T. Where'd you get it from?

Min-Jung   I c_____ a_____ it while I was shopping with Claudia in the mall. Actually, she bought a t_____-p_____ for herself. I wasn't quite as daring as she was, though.

Andre   What do you mean?

Min-Jung   Her suit is really h_____-c_____. It's a little too s_____ for me. She's got a really nice figure, so she can g_____ away w_____ it.

Andre   Yeah. Claudia's got a great body. She looks so h_____ when she wears ....

Min-Jung   Oh stop it! Do all men have a o_____-track m_____? I swear it's the only thing guys think about.

Andre   OK. OK. I'll k_____ it o_____. Have you seen the weather forecast? Is it going to be this m_____ tomorrow?

Min-Jung   I think they're predicting a change in the weather. It's supposed to c_____ o_____ tonight and then p_____ tomorrow. If we're lucky, the nice weather will return by Tuesday.

Andre   I hope so. I'm playing soccer on Tuesday after school. .... I think I'm going to lie down. Do you mind if I d_____ o_____ for a while?

Min-Jung   Sorry. Have I been b_____ your e_____?

Andre   No, not at all. The heat just makes me a little sleepy.

Min-Jung   OK. While you're napping, I'm going to t_____ a d_____ before the tide goes out.

COMPREHENSION QUESTIONS

TRY TO ANSWER THE FOLLOWING QUESTIONS WITHOUT LOOKING AT THE DIALOGUE. ONCE YOU'VE FINISHED THE QUESTIONS, YOU CAN REFER TO THE DIALOGUE TO CHECK YOUR ANSWERS.

1 Where were Andre and Min-Jung sitting?

2 What did Andre want to borrow from Min-Jung?

3 Why did it take a moment for Min-Jung to find it?

4 Who doesn't mind the heat? Why not?

5 What does Min-Jung always do as soon as the temperature dips?

6 How long are Andre and Min-Jung going to hang out at the beach?

7 Whose tan could use a little work?

8 What did Andre say about Min-Jung's new bathing suit?

9 Where did Min-Jung buy her bathing suit? Who was she with at the time?

10 How did Min-Jung describe the bathing suit that Claudia bought for herself?

11 Who thinks Claudia looks hot?

12 What's the weather forecast for tomorrow? When will the nice weather return again?

13 What will Andre do on Tuesday afternoon?

14 What made Andre a little sleepy?

15 What will Min-Jung do while Andre dozes off?

DISCUSSION QUESTIONS

DISCUSS THE FOLLOWING QUESTIONS WITH YOUR PARTNER.

PART A: General Discussion Questions

1 Describe the best beach in your country. How often do you go there?

2 How do you usually spend time at the beach? Describe three different activities.

3 Tell me about the worst sunburn you've ever had. How long did it take to recover from it?

4 How do people in your country treat a sunburn?

5 Have you ever been to a tanning salon? Did it work? How much did it cost?

PART B: Idiomatic Discussion Questions

1 Where's your favorite place to **take a dip/get some sun** in this area?

2 Would you ever wear a **skimpy** swimsuit at the beach? What do you usually wear when you go to the seaside?

3 Describe someone you've seen at the beach who looked **hot**.

4 Where do you like to **hang out** in the summer? on the weekend? after school?

5 Can you **handle** hot or cold weather better?

6 What **bugs** you about living with your homestay family or roommate? living alone? living in this city?

7 Did you have a **one-track mind** as a teenager? What did you always think about? Do you have a one-track mind now?

GIVE IT A SHOT

Natural Disasters:

heat wave

cyclone/hurricane/typhoon

volcanic eruption

dust storm

ice storm

rain storm

snow storm

wind storm

blizzard

earthquake/tremor/aftershock

flood

cold snap

tornado/twister

brush/forest fire

land slide

mud slide

rock slide

avalanche

lightning

hail

tidal wave/tsunami

drought

Questions:

1 Have you ever been in a natural disaster? Describe what happened.

2 What are the three most common natural disasters in your country?

3 In what countries do these natural disasters occur most often?

   a earthquakes   _____

   b droughts   _____

   c avalanches   _____

   d tornados   _____

   e mud slides   _____

••CHAPTER NINE••

WAITING FOR A FIREWORKS SHOW

WAITING FOR A FIREWORKS SHOW

Andre and Hiro are at the fairgrounds just after sunset

Andre   Man, the fireworks are popular. I can't believe how **mobbed** the fairgrounds are tonight.

Hiro   You should've seen the bus I took here. It reminded me of a rush hour train in Japan. It seems like **everybody and his brother** is coming here tonight. I read in the paper that last year's fireworks were **out of this world**. I hope they don't disappoint us tonight. Do you know what time the show **kicks off**?

Andre   I think it starts in about 45 minutes. I've heard that this year's show will be the best ever. My friend told me they're going to **finish with a bang**. The finale is supposed to be **breathtaking**. I can't wait to see it!

Hiro   What time did you tell Yuka and Claudia to meet us here?

Andre   Now. Why?

Hiro   They're late again – that's **par for the course**. What's their problem?

Andre   I think Yuka is sick. She's **running a fever** or something. I doubt whether they'll even come tonight.

Hiro   Well, we better be **on the lookout for** them just in case they **show up**.

Andre   Did you **catch** that singing group that was performing over on the big stage?

Hiro   I sure did. I saw them on my way in. They were nothing special. I was **bored stiff** watching them.

Andre   They weren't very entertaining, were they?

Hiro	By the way, did you ever go out with that girl? You know, the one you were **flirting with** in the bar the other night? You told me that you **had the hots for** her.
Andre	Well, we certainly **hit it off**. She was cute, bright, and not a bad dancer either. To tell the truth, I really **have a crush on** her. I just can't **get her off my mind**.
Hiro	So have you seen her since?
Andre	I was **on the verge** of calling her last night, but I **chickened out**. I guess I'm just too shy.
Hiro	You? Too shy? I don't think so. You should **get in touch with** her.
Andre	Yeah, maybe I will. I'll have to **get up the guts** to call her. Are you hungry? What do you say we go over to the hotdog stand and **grab a bite**? That guy must be **making a killing** tonight with all these people on the fairgrounds.
Hiro	Why don't we **sit tight**? I'd rather wait and see if Yuka and Claudia show up – then we can all get something to eat together.
Andre	Hey, isn't that them over there? I guess **better late than never**.
Hiro	Let's go get them. Try not to **give them the silent treatment** just because they were late. OK?
Andre	Don't worry. I won't.

adj. – adjective	*exclam.* – exclamation	*n.* – noun
adv. – adverb	*i.* – idiom, phrasal verb	*v.* – verb

mobbed *adj.* – crowded, jam-packed
The department store was mobbed because there was a huge sale.

everybody and his brother *i.* – many people
Everybody and his brother went to the free concert in the park on Saturday.

out of this world *i.* – amazing, fantastic, great, unbelievable
I thought the pyramids in Egypt were out of this world.

kick off (to) *i.* – begin, start
The party at the community center kicks off at 7 o'clock tonight.

finish with a bang (to) *i.* – end something in a dramatic way
The band finished with a bang by playing their most popular song last.

breathtaking *adj.* – beautiful, gorgeous, stunning
I thought she was breathtaking the first time I met her.

par for the course *i.* – typical, usual
He didn't finish his homework again! That's par for the course.

run a fever (to) *i.* – have a fever/temperature
She doesn't feel very good this morning because she's running a fever.

on the lookout for someone *i.* – watch for someone
I'll be on the lookout for them just in case they arrive late.

show up (to) *i.* – arrive, come
What time will everyone show up at your house tonight?

catch (to) *v.* – see
I'd like to catch a movie tonight at the theater near your place.

bored stiff *i.* – very bored
I didn't like that class. I was bored stiff for the whole lesson.

flirt with someone (to) *i.* – show someone that you're attracted to them
I think that guy sitting alone at the bar is flirting with you.

have the hots for someone (to) *i.* – be very attracted to someone
I've had the hots for that actress since I was a teenager.

hit it off (to) *i.* – become good friends with someone quickly
She was relieved when her new boyfriend hit it off with her father.

have a crush on someone (to) *i.* – be very attracted to someone
He's had a crush on that beautiful girl for at least two years.

get someone off one's mind (to) *i.* – stop thinking about someone
I can't get her off my mind even though I only met her once.

verge (on the) *n.* – close to doing or experiencing
I was on the verge of going out, but then something interesting came on TV.

chicken out (to) *i.* – lose the courage to do something
I'd like to go skydiving, but I'm afraid that I'd chicken out.

get in touch with someone (to) *i.* – contact someone
He wants to get in touch with you before he goes back to England.

get up the guts to do something (to) *i.* – get enough courage to do something
Calvin: *Did you ask her to dance?* **Rick:** *Not yet. I have to get up the guts to talk to her.*

grab a bite to eat (to) *i.* – eat something quickly
Would you like to grab a bite (to eat) at that diner down the street?

make a killing (to) *i.* – make a lot of money
He made a killing on the new product that he invented.

sit tight (to) *i.* – wait patiently
Dave: *Do you want to wait for them a little bit longer?* **Kim:** *Yeah. Let's just sit tight.*

better late than never *i.* – better to do something late than not at all
Heather: *They finally got here.* **Blair:** *I guess better late than never.*

give someone the silent treatment (to) *i.* – ignore someone
He gave me the silent treatment because I completely forgot about his birthday.

EXERCISE 1

MATCH THE WORD/IDIOM WITH THE CORRECT DEFINITION

_E_	1 bored stiff	A	lose the courage to do something
___	2 par for the course	B	crowded
___	3 kicks off	C	be very attracted to someone
___	4 get in touch with someone	D	amazing
___	5 give someone the silent treatment	E	very bored
___	6 get someone off one's mind	F	watch for someone
___	7 sit tight	G	finish in a dramatic way
___	8 out of this world	H	become good friends quickly
___	9 catch	I	contact someone
___	10 show up	J	typical
___	11 chicken out	K	beautiful
___	12 make a killing	L	ignore someone
___	13 finish with a bang	M	wait patiently
___	14 have a crush on someone	N	arrive
___	15 grab a bite	O	close to doing or experiencing
___	16 hit it off	P	see
___	17 on the lookout for someone	Q	make a lot of money
___	18 breathtaking	R	stop thinking about someone
___	19 mobbed	S	begins
___	20 on the verge	T	eat something quickly

EXERCISE 2

USE THE WORDS/IDIOMS BELOW TO COMPLETE
EACH OF THE FOLLOWING SENTENCES.

chickened out	kicks off	on the lookout for
everybody and his brother	flirted with	out of this world
hit it off	the silent treatment	a crush
get in touch with	get up the guts	grab a bite
on the verge	bored stiff	mobbed

1 The beautiful woman who was standing at the bar _____ me all night long.

2 I think he has _____ on you. He's constantly looking in your direction.

3 He was going to ask her out on a date yesterday, but he _____.

4 I was _____ of going to the library when my best friend phoned me.

5 _____ went to the beach on that sunny Saturday afternoon.

6 She doesn't think she could ever _____ to go bungee jumping.

7 I want to speak with him before he leaves for Paris. Could you _____ him?

8 We should be _____ him because his flight just arrived at the airport.

9 I read that the huge outdoor music festival _____ at 9:00 tomorrow night.

10 I'm hungry. I'd like to _____ to eat at that donut shop across the street.

11 The department store was _____ because there was a huge sale yesterday.

12 My girlfriend gave me _____ all afternoon because she was angry at me.

13 She likes the friendly girl that moved into her dormitory room. They _____.

14 I was _____ when I went to the symphony with my mother last night.

15 The students thought the laser show they saw at the planetarium was _____.

EXERCISE 3

COMPLETE THE FOLLOWING CROSSWORD PUZZLE
USING WORDS/IDIOMS FROM THE DIALOGUE.

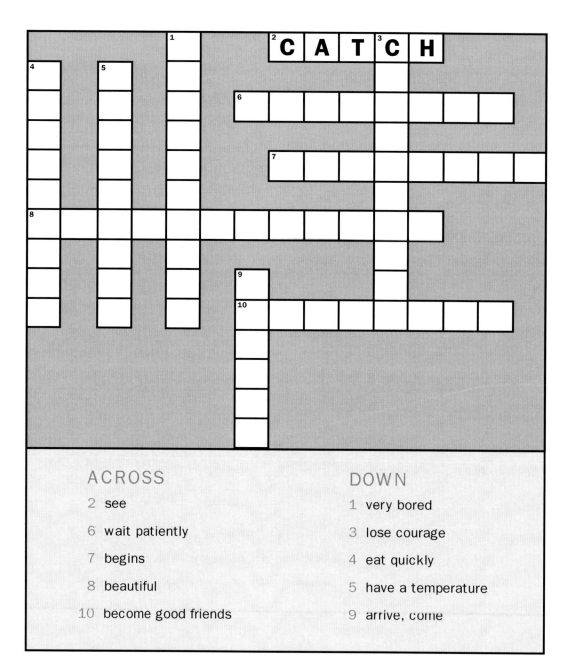

ACROSS

2 see

6 wait patiently

7 begins

8 beautiful

10 become good friends

DOWN

1 very bored

3 lose courage

4 eat quickly

5 have a temperature

9 arrive, come

EXERCISE 4

1 My boyfriend was over an hour late for our date. That's so typical.

   My boyfriend was over an hour late for our date. That's par for the course   .

2 The stores are always terribly crowded during the Christmas shopping season.

   _____.

3 My older sister made a lot of money selling real estate in San Francisco last year.

   _____.

4 He said that his friends are supposed to arrive in about 15 minutes.

   _____.

5 She has always been very attracted to that handsome guy who lives across the street.

   _____.

6 Don't worry. I'll contact you first thing tomorrow morning.

   _____.

7 She was going to ask him to dance, but then she lost the courage to do it.

   _____.

8 The summer craft fair starts at 9 o'clock tomorrow morning.

   _____.

9 Everybody went to see the new exhibition at the art gallery this weekend.

   _____.

10 His wife ignored him for three days after he forgot their wedding anniversary.

   _____.

EXERCISE 5

UNSCRAMBLE THE FOLLOWING SENTENCES, ADDING PUNCTUATION WHEN NEEDED. THE BEGINNING AND END OF EACH SENTENCE HAVE ALREADY BEEN DONE FOR YOU. HINT: IT'S HELPFUL TO IDENTIFY THE WORD/IDIOM FROM THE DIALOGUE IN EACH SENTENCE.

1 **I may have** / the / finally / ask / out / a / on / her / up / gotten / guts / to / **date this weekend.**

   I may have finally gotten up the guts to ask her out on a date this weekend.

2 **I've been waiting** / for / best / to / in / with / for / touch / friend / my / get / me / **over two hours.**

   _____

3 **The meal we** / prepared / out / this / of / ate / because / was / by / a / it / was / world / **famous European chef.**

   _____

4 **Would you like** / to / bite / eat / me / that / restaurant / at / with / a / grab / little / to / **down the street?**

   _____

5 **The professor was** / showed / when / very / not / late / up / final / pleased / the / for / she / **exam this morning.**

   _____

6 **The young woman** / mind / couldn't / the / off / get / because / he / bartender / her / so / was / **charming and handsome.**

   _____

7 **The nursing student** / it / doctor / the / she / at / off / medical / hit / with / met / interesting / the / **conference in Chicago.**

   _____

8 **The shopping mall** / the / fans / mobbed / as / from / famous / with / actress / strolled / was / **store to store.**

   _____

EXERCISE 6

FIND THE WORDS/IDIOMS LISTED BELOW IN THE WORD SEARCH GAME.

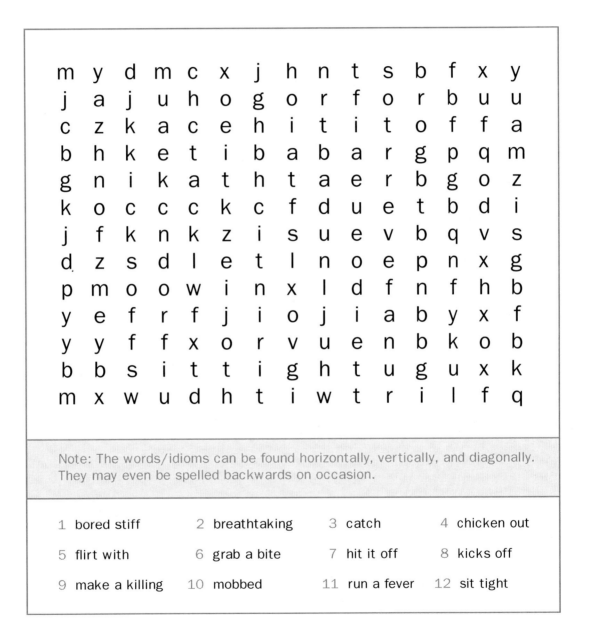

```
m  y  d  m  c  x  j  h  n  t  s  b  f  x  y
j  a  j  u  h  o  g  o  r  f  o  r  b  u  u
c  z  k  a  c  e  h  i  t  i  t  o  f  f  a
b  h  k  e  t  i  b  a  b  a  r  g  p  q  m
g  n  i  k  a  t  h  t  a  e  r  b  g  o  z
k  o  c  c  c  k  c  f  d  u  e  t  b  d  i
j  f  k  n  k  z  i  s  u  e  v  b  q  v  s
d  z  s  d  l  e  t  l  n  o  e  p  n  x  g
p  m  o  o  w  i  n  x  l  d  f  n  f  h  b
y  e  f  r  f  j  i  o  j  i  a  b  y  x  f
y  y  f  f  x  o  r  v  u  e  n  b  k  o  b
b  b  s  i  t  t  i  g  h  t  u  g  u  x  k
m  x  w  u  d  h  t  i  w  t  r  i  l  f  q
```

Note: The words/idioms can be found horizontally, vertically, and diagonally. They may even be spelled backwards on occasion.

1 bored stiff	2 breathtaking	3 catch	4 chicken out
5 flirt with	6 grab a bite	7 hit it off	8 kicks off
9 make a killing	10 mobbed	11 run a fever	12 sit tight

EXERCISE 7

FILL IN THE WORDS/IDIOMS THAT ARE
MISSING FROM THE DIALOGUE.

Andre and Hiro are at the fairgrounds just after sunset

Andre	Man, the fireworks are popular. I can't believe how m_____ the fairgrounds are tonight.
Hiro	You should've seen the bus I took here. It reminded me of a rush hour train in Japan. It seems like e_____ and his b_____ is coming here tonight. I read in the paper that last year's fireworks were o_____ of this w_____. I hope they don't disappoint us tonight. Do you know what time the show k_____ o_____?
Andre	I think it starts in about 45 minutes. I've heard that this year's show will be the best ever. My friend told me they're going to f_____ with a b_____. The finale is supposed to be b_____. I can't wait to see it!
Hiro	What time did you tell Yuka and Claudia to meet us here?
Andre	Now. Why?
Hiro	They're late again – that's p_____ for the c_____. What's their problem?
Andre	I think Yuka is sick. She's r_____ a f_____ or something. I doubt whether they'll even come tonight.
Hiro	Well, we better be on the l_____ for them just in case they s_____ up.
Andre	Did you c_____ that singing group that was performing over on the big stage?
Hiro	I sure did. I saw them on my way in. They were nothing special. I was bored s_____ watching them.
Andre	They weren't very entertaining, were they?

Hiro	By the way, did you ever go out with that girl? You know, the one you were f_____ with in the bar the other night? You told me that you h_____ the h_____ for her.
Andre	Well, we certainly h_____ it o_____. She was cute, bright, and not a bad dancer either. To tell the truth, I really h_____ a c_____ on her. I just can't g_____ her off my m_____.
Hiro	So have you seen her since?
Andre	I was o_____ the v_____ of calling her last night, but I c_____ out. I guess I'm just too shy.
Hiro	You? Too shy? I don't think so. You should g_____ in t_____ with her.
Andre	Yeah, maybe I will. I'll have to g_____ up the g_____ to call her. Are you hungry? What do you say we go over to the hotdog stand and g_____ a b_____? That guy must be m_____ a k_____ tonight with all these people on the fairgrounds.
Hiro	Why don't we s_____ t_____? I'd rather wait and see if Yuka and Claudia show up – then we can all get something to eat together.
Andre	Hey, isn't that them over there? I guess better l_____ than n_____.
Hiro	Let's go get them. Try not to give them the s_____ t_____ just because they were late. OK?
Andre	Don't worry. I won't.

COMPREHENSION QUESTIONS

TRY TO ANSWER THE FOLLOWING QUESTIONS WITHOUT LOOKING AT THE DIALOGUE. ONCE YOU'VE FINISHED THE QUESTIONS, YOU CAN REFER TO THE DIALOGUE TO CHECK YOUR ANSWERS.

1. Were the fairgrounds crowded?

2. How did Hiro describe the bus he took to come to the fairgrounds?

3. What did the newspaper say about last year's fireworks?

4. When will the show kick off?

5. What did Andre's friend say about this year's show?

6. When are Yuka and Claudia supposed to arrive?

7. What's par for the course?

8. Why did Andre doubt that Yuka and Claudia would show up?

9. What did Hiro think of the singing group that was performing on the big stage?

10. Who did Andre have the hots for?

11. What was Andre on the verge of doing last night?

12. Does Hiro think Andre is shy?

13. Who was making a killing on the fairgrounds that night?

14. Why did Hiro want to sit tight?

15. Who saw Yuka and Claudia first? Andre or Hiro?

DISCUSSION QUESTIONS

PART A: General Discussion Questions

1   Describe the best professional fireworks show you've seen.

2   When do people buy fireworks in this country? How about in your country?

3   Where can people buy fireworks in this country? What about in your country?

4   Have you ever set off fireworks to celebrate a special occasion? What was it?

5   Do you know what country invented fireworks?

PART B: Idiomatic Discussion Questions

1   Describe a place in your country that would take my breath away. Have you seen anything that was **breathtaking** in this country?

2   Who's **making a killing** in your country these days? Who's losing a fortune?

3   Tell me about something you wanted to do, but couldn't because you **chickened out**.

4   Do you remember the last time you **gave someone the silent treatment**? Why did you ignore him/her?

5   What movie star do you **have the hots for**?

6   Do you remember the very first person you **had a crush on**? Describe him/her.

7   Has anyone **flirted with** you while you've been here? Were you attracted to him/her? Have you flirted with someone recently? Did you **hit it off** with that person?

GIVE IT A SHOT

IN THE DIALOGUE, ANDRE TALKS ABOUT FLIRTING WITH A WOMAN IN THE BAR. HE MAY ALSO GIVE HIS FRIENDS THE SILENT TREATMENT BECAUSE THEY WERE LATE. HOW CAN YOU EXPRESS FEELINGS OF ATTRACTION OR ANGER WITHOUT SAYING ANYTHING? HAVE YOUR TEACHER EXPLAIN/DEMONSTRATE THE FOLLOWING WAYS TO SHOW HOW YOU FEEL.

Expressing attraction:

come on to someone

get dressed up

flirt with s/o

gaze at s/o

give s/o the eye

glance at s/o

make eyes at s/o

play footsie with s/o

run into s/o on purpose

send s/o a drink

smile at s/o

touch s/o

wear something revealing

wink at s/o

Expressing anger:

avoid someone

don't return phone calls

give s/o the cold shoulder

give s/o the finger

give s/o the silent treatment

ignore s/o

scowl at s/o

slam the door

slap s/o

sneer at s/o

stand s/o up

stare at s/o

stomp out of the room

throw an object at s/o

How do you usually express feelings of attraction or anger without saying anything?

Expressing attraction:

1 _____

2 _____

3 _____

Expressing anger:

1 _____

2 _____

3 _____

■■ CHAPTER TEN ■■

WORKING OUT AT A FITNESS CLUB

Andre and Min-Jung have just finished lifting weights

Andre   Do you feel like **working out** on the treadmills next?

Min-Jung   I guess so. I thought I was in good condition, but I'm so **out of shape**.

Andre   I know how you feel. I'm pretty **tuckered out** myself. I thought I'd get **a second wind**, but I'm finished after the treadmills. I don't think I can **stomach** doing much more than that.

Min-Jung   We really ought to do some aerobic exercise to finish our workout. It would probably **do us some good** to run for 20 minutes or so.

Andre   20 minutes? I'll be lucky if I last 15.

Min-Jung   Come on. You quit smoking, so it shouldn't be a problem. **By the way**, I think it's great that you finally **kicked the habit**.

Andre   Thanks. **Just between you and me**, I still have the occasional smoke.

Min-Jung   Shame on you!

Andre   Don't worry. I've **cleaned up my act**. I think I've only had 2 or 3 smokes in the last month. I really want to quit.

Min-Jung   You should try to stop. Look, two treadmills just **opened up**. Let's grab them.

They run on the treadmills for about 15 minutes

Andre   That's it for me. I'm **pooped**. How about you? Are you going to keep going? Don't get too **carried away**.

Min-Jung	I think I'll **call it a day** too. I'm almost **out of breath**.
Andre	Don't worry about it. We had a great workout today. If you keep exercising like this, you'll **build up** your endurance soon enough. Besides, you're **light as a feather**. You don't have to worry about losing weight.
Min-Jung	Thanks for saying that, but I still think I need to lose a couple pounds. I'd also like to improve on my strength for snowboarding this winter.
Andre	Good for you. Do you want to **hit** the change rooms now? I think a long hot shower would **do wonders for** my aching muscles. My legs are **killing me**.
Min-Jung	Why don't we go over to the weigh scales? I'd like to check my weight.
Andre	I'm almost afraid to see what I **tip the scales at**.
Min-Jung	Well, it's time to **face the music**. Are you OK? You're walking kind of strange. Are you **limping**?
Andre	I think I've got a bit of a **charley horse** in my right leg. It **hurts like the devil**.
Min-Jung	Really? It seems to be getting worse the closer we get to the scales.
Andre	You're **hilarious**.
Min-Jung	All right, here we are. Let's see if all this exercise we've been doing has **paid off**.

work out (to) *i.* – exercise
She usually works out at the gym about 3 times a week.

out of shape *i.* – poor physical condition
I was so out of shape that I couldn't even run one lap around the track.

tuckered out *i.* – exhausted, pooped, tired, wiped out, worn out
He was tuckered out after running up 10 flights of stairs.

second wind (a) *i.* – catch one's breath, recover from exercise
I got a second wind after taking a short break from the game.

stomach (to) *v.* – endure, handle, tolerate
I can't stomach doing any more exercise today.

do someone some good (to) *i.* – benefit from something
I think a nutritious meal would do me some good right about now.

by the way *i.* – incidentally
By the way, what time are you coming over to my house?

kick the habit (to) *i.* – break the habit
I've been trying to stop smoking, but I just can't kick the habit.

just between you and me *i.* – confidentially, privately
Just between you and me, I'm quitting my job at the end of next month.

clean up one's act (to) *i.* – improve one's behavior
He never pays attention in class, so the teacher told him to clean up his act.

open up (to) *i.* – become available
Look, a parking space just opened up. Let's take it before someone else does.

pooped *adj.* – exhausted, tired, tuckered out, wiped out, worn out
She was pooped because she spent the whole day working in the yard.

carried away *i.* – excited or moved to extreme action
This is our first day at the gym, so we shouldn't get too carried away.

call it a day (to) *i.* – finish work
We've been working on this project all afternoon. Let's call it a day.

out of breath *i.* – breathe heavily, winded
He is out of breath because he just finished running across the park.

build up (to) *i.* – strengthen
I'm going to build up my endurance by running for 30 minutes every day.

light as a feather *i.* – very light
This shopping bag isn't heavy. It's (as) light as a feather.

hit somewhere (to) *v.* – visit somewhere
I want to hit the washroom before we go back to the car.

do wonders for something (to) *i.* – improve the condition of something
A little rest and relaxation would do wonders for your health.

something is killing someone *i.* – something is hurting someone
I can't play tennis with you today because my back is killing me.

tip the scales at (to) *i.* – weigh
I was really surprised when I saw what I tipped the scales at.

face the music (to) *i.* – accept the unpleasant results of one's actions
The criminal has to face the music now that he has been found guilty.

limp (to) *v.* – walk in an awkward manner due to an injury to the leg
The soccer player slowly limped off the field after he twisted his ankle.

charley horse *n.* – stiffness in the leg as a result of an injury
I have a charley horse because I was kicked in the leg during the game.

hurt like the devil (to) *i.* – hurt very much
He said that his broken finger hurts like the devil.

hilarious *adj.* – very funny
I thought the movie we saw last night at the theater was hilarious.

pay off (to) *i.* – a positive result brought about by hard work
I feel healthier these days. I think the exercise I've been doing has paid off.

_C_	1 tuckered out	A	visit somewhere
___	2 kick the habit	B	very light
___	3 a second wind	C	tired
___	4 open up	D	exercise
___	5 charley horse	E	poor physical condition
___	6 by the way	F	benefit from something
___	7 stomach	G	accept the unpleasant results
___	8 work out	H	become available
___	9 hurt like the devil	I	incidentally
___	10 do one some good	J	weigh
___	11 hit somewhere	K	break the habit
___	12 limp	L	strengthen
___	13 face the music	M	moved to extreme action
___	14 call it a day	N	stiffness in the leg
___	15 tip the scales at	O	handle
___	16 build up	P	very funny
___	17 carried away	Q	catch one's breath
___	18 out of shape	R	finish work
___	19 hilarious	S	walk in an awkward manner
___	20 light as a feather	T	hurt very much

EXERCISE 2

USE THE WORDS/IDIOMS BELOW TO COMPLETE EACH OF THE FOLLOWING SENTENCES.

light as a feather	pay off	build up
clean up my act	hit	do me some good
tipped the scales	working out	stomach
kick the habit	out of breath	hilarious
call it a day	limped	open up

1 The young woman _____ down the street after twisting her ankle on the curb.

2 I was surprised to see that I _____ at well over 200 pounds.

3 It would probably _____ to study the material we covered this week.

4 I started running every morning because I want to _____ my endurance.

5 He finally managed to _____ after smoking for more than 20 years.

6 He was _____ because he had just run from the other side of the airport.

7 The boss finally told the workers that they could _____.

8 My father was angry after I failed the midterm exam. He told me to _____.

9 My younger sister is as _____ because she doesn't eat enough food.

10 My best friend loves _____ at the gym after she finishes at the office.

11 You have to see that funny movie that was just released. It's _____.

12 I'm sure that all the studying he did will _____ when he writes the final.

13 I just can't _____ spending another night listening to that idiot.

14 A great position at that company will _____ at the end of this month.

15 Would you like to _____ the sporting goods store after school today?

EXERCISE 3

COMPLETE THE FOLLOWING CROSSWORD PUZZLE
USING WORDS/IDIOMS FROM THE DIALOGUE.

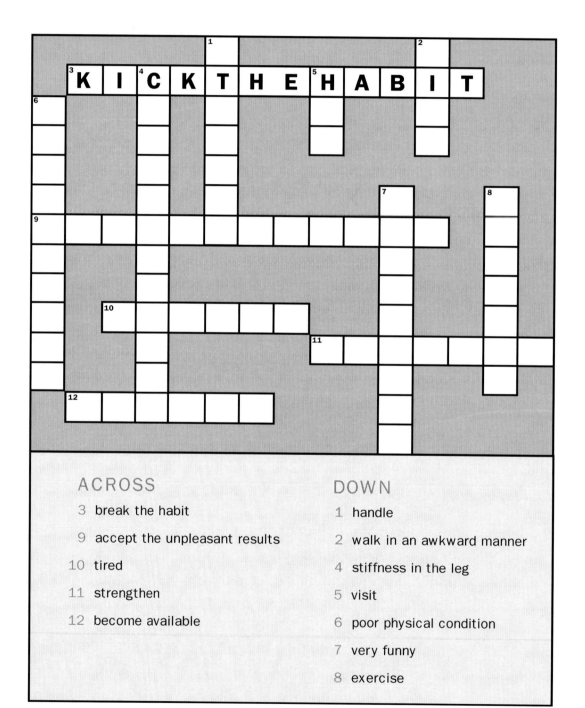

ACROSS

3 break the habit

9 accept the unpleasant results

10 tired

11 strengthen

12 become available

DOWN

1 handle

2 walk in an awkward manner

4 stiffness in the leg

5 visit

6 poor physical condition

7 very funny

8 exercise

EXERCISE 4

REWRITE THE FOLLOWING SENTENCES USING
A WORD/IDIOM FROM THE DIALOGUE.

1 The soccer coach told the player that he'd have to improve his behavior.

   The soccer coach told the player that he'd have to clean up his act   .

2 The comedian I saw at the nightclub last night was very funny.

   _____.

3 She was breathing heavily after running from one side of the campus to the other.

   _____.

4 Two seats on the bus just became available. Why don't we take them?

   _____.

5 I ate tons of food over the Christmas vacation. I'm afraid to see how much I weigh.

   _____.

6 I can't handle the way he criticizes everyone he works with at the office.

   _____.

7 I think we've done enough for one day. What do you say we finish work?

   _____.

8 We visited the shopping mall after we finished studying at the library.

   _____.

9 He's been walking in an awkward manner ever since he twisted his ankle.

   _____.

10 I don't think you've put on any weight at all. You're still very light.

   _____.

EXERCISE 5

UNSCRAMBLE THE FOLLOWING SENTENCES, ADDING PUNCTUATION WHEN NEEDED. THE BEGINNING AND END OF EACH SENTENCE HAVE ALREADY BEEN DONE FOR YOU. HINT: IT'S HELPFUL TO IDENTIFY THE WORD/IDIOM FROM THE DIALOGUE IN EACH SENTENCE.

1 **He was so** / of / that / could / run / a / only / he / shape / out / few / for / **minutes before stopping.**

He was so out of shape that he could only run for a few minutes before stopping _____.

2 **That muscular guy** / gym / always / out / 8:30 / the / at / at / works / **every Sunday morning.**

_____.

3 **The boys were** / they / spent / day / out / had / because / the / hiking / tuckered / **through the woods.**

_____.

4 **I think it** / us / good / get / of / would / sun / the / some / do / to / out / and / **into the shade.**

_____.

5 **They decided to** / it / day / they / worked / the / for / had / after / on / call / project / a / **over five hours.**

_____.

6 **My uncle decided** / after / time / act / was / it / suffering / his / clean / up / to / a / **serious heart attack.**

_____.

7 **Her arms and** / very / because / got / legs / away / the / carried / she / sore / were / fitness / at / **club last night.**

_____.

8 **She said that** / she / her / back / able / be / killing / won't / was / so / her / dancing / go / to / **with us tonight.**

_____.

EXERCISE 6

WHAT WORD/IDIOM FROM THE DIALOGUE MATCHES THE FOLLOWING
DEFINITIONS? WHEN THE EXERCISE HAS BEEN COMPLETED, THE IDIOM
FOR 'VERY LIGHT' WILL BE SPELLED VERTICALLY.

1	moved to extreme action	c a r r i e d (a)w a y
2	poor physical condition	_ _ _ _ _ (_)_ _ _ _
3	strengthen	_ _ _(_)_ _ _
4	finish work	_ _ _ _ (_)_ _ _ _ _
5	hurting me	_ _ _ _ _ _(_) _ _
6	accept the unpleasant results	_ _ _ _ _(_)_ _ _ _ _ _
7	hurt very much	_ _ _ _ _ _ _ _ (_)_ _ _ _ _ _ _
8	weigh	_ _ _ _ _ _ _ _(_)_ _ _ _ _
9	catch one's breath	_ (_)_ _ _ _ _ _ _ _ _
10	handle	_ _ _ _(_)_ _
11	a positive result	_ _ _ _(_)_
12	stiffness in the leg	_ _ _ _ _(_)_ _ _ _ _ _ _
13	incidentally	_ _ _ _ _ _(_)_
14	exercise	_ _ _ _ _ _(_)
15	break the habit	_ _ _ _ _(_)_ _ _ _ _ _
16	exhausted	_ _ _ _(_)_
17	very funny	_ _ _ _(_)_ _ _

Unscramble the following words/idioms from the dialogue.

18	tceerdku tou	_ _ _ _ _ _ _ _ _ _ _
19	uto fo arehtb	_ _ _ _ _ _ _ _ _ _
20	od su osem dogo	_ _ _ _ _ _ _ _ _ _ _ _
21	lenac pu ym cta	_ _ _ _ _ _ _ _ _ _ _ _
22	lisirhuoa	_ _ _ _ _ _ _ _ _

EXERCISE 7

FILL IN THE WORDS/IDIOMS THAT ARE MISSING FROM THE DIALOGUE.

Andre and Min-Jung have just finished lifting weights

Andre　　Do you feel like w_____ o_____ on the treadmills next?

Min-Jung　　I guess so. I thought I was in good condition, but I'm so o_____ of s_____.

Andre　　I know how you feel. I'm pretty t_____ o_____ myself. I thought I'd get a s_____ w_____, but I'm finished after the treadmills. I don't think I can s_____ doing much more than that.

Min-Jung　　We really ought to do some aerobic exercise to finish our workout. It would probably do us s_____ g_____ to run for 20 minutes or so.

Andre　　20 minutes? I'll be lucky if I last 15.

Min-Jung　　Come on. You quit smoking, so it shouldn't be a problem. B_____ the w_____, I think it's great that you finally k_____ the h_____.

Andre　　Thanks. J_____ b_____ you and me, I still have the occasional smoke.

Min-Jung　　Shame on you!

Andre　　Don't worry. I've c_____ up my a_____. I think I've only had 2 or 3 smokes in the last month. I really want to quit.

Min-Jung　　You should try to stop. Look, two treadmills just o_____ up. Let's grab them.

They run on the treadmills for about 15 minutes

Andre　　That's it for me. I'm p_____. How about you? Are you going to keep going? Don't get too c_____ a_____.

Min-Jung   I think I'll c_____ it a day too. I'm almost o_____ of b_____.

Andre   Don't worry about it. We had a great workout today. If you keep exercising like this, you'll b_____ u_____ your endurance soon enough. Besides, you're light as a f_____. You don't have to worry about losing weight.

Min-Jung   Thanks for saying that, but I still think I need to lose a couple pounds. I'd also like to improve on my strength for snowboarding this winter.

Andre   Good for you. Do you want to h_____ the change rooms now? I think a long hot shower would d_____ w_____ for my aching muscles. My legs are k_____ me.

Min-Jung   Why don't we go over to the weigh scales? I'd like to check my weight.

Andre   I'm almost afraid to see what I t_____ the s_____ at.

Min-Jung   Well, it's time to f_____ the m_____. Are you OK? You're walking kind of strange. Are you l_____?

Andre   I think I've got a bit of a c_____ h_____ in my right leg. It h_____ like the d_____.

Min-Jung   Really? It seems to be getting worse the closer we get to the scales.

Andre   You're h_____.

Min-Jung   All right, here we are. Let's see if all this exercise we've been doing has p_____ o_____.

COMPREHENSION QUESTIONS

1 Did Andre and Min-Jung lift weights while they were at the gym?

2 What did they work out on next?

3 Who felt tuckered out?

4 How long did Min-Jung think they should run on the treadmills?

5 What was Andre's reaction?

6 Has Andre quit smoking completely? If not, how much does he smoke?

7 What did Andre mean when he said, "I've cleaned up my act"?

8 Who was the first person to stop running?

9 How much longer did the other person run for?

10 There are two reasons why Min-Jung is working out. What are they?

11 What will do wonders for Andre's aching muscles?

12 What did Min-Jung want to do before they went to the change rooms?

13 Why did Min-Jung say, "It's time to face the music"?

14 What was Andre's explanation for his limp?

15 Why did Andre say, "You're hilarious"?

DISCUSSION QUESTIONS

DISCUSS THE FOLLOWING QUESTIONS WITH YOUR PARTNER.

PART A: General Discussion Questions

1 Do you think you are in good shape? What aspect of your fitness needs some improvement?

2 What kind of exercise do you prefer to do in the winter? in the summer?

3 Have you ever injured yourself while exercising? How did you hurt yourself?

4 What kinds of exercise do you not like doing?

5 What form of exercise would you like to learn how to do?

PART B: Idiomatic Discussion Questions

1 When was the last time you **worked out**? Have you been working out while you've been here?

2 Have you ever joined a fitness club? Did being a member **pay off**?

3 Tell me about the last time you got **carried away** and did too much exercise. How did you feel the next day?

4 What do you think is the best way to **build up** your endurance?

5 How far can you run before you get **pooped**?

6 What do you **tip the scales at**? (feel free to underestimate)

7 Have you ever had to **clean up your act**? What needed to be changed?

GIVE IT A SHOT

IN THE DIALOGUE, MIN-JUNG SAYS, "TWO TREADMILLS JUST OPENED UP. LET'S GRAB THEM." WHERE WOULD YOU BE IF YOU HEARD THE FOLLOWING SENTENCES?

1 Two treadmills just opened up. Let's grab them. __C__

2 Rack them. I'll break. Two ball, side pocket. ____

3 Paper or plastic? ____

4 It's going. It's going. It's gone! ____

5 Say, "Ahhhh." ____

6 Take a little off the back and sides. ____

7 Would the defendant please rise? ____

8 $100 on 'Seattle Slew' to win / place / show. ____

9 You should proceed to Gate 6 now. ____

10 They're due back by 11:00 pm tomorrow. ____

11 Fill her up. ____

12 Could you pull over at the next corner? ____

13 I'd like to have this pair of pants taken in. ____

14 Paperbacks can be found two aisles over. ____

15 The matinee starts at 3:00. ____

16 I'll have mine over-easy please. ____

17 Last call. ____

18 Please return your seats to the upright position. ____

A Courtroom

B Movie theater

C Fitness club

D Taxi

E Baseball game

F Airport

G Bar

H Video store

I Bookstore/Library

J Pool hall

K Airplane

L Doctor's office

M Restaurant

N Barbershop

O Tailor/Seamstress

P Supermarket

Q Gas station

R Horse track

▪▪CHAPTER ELEVEN▪▪

DRINKING IN A NEIGHBORHOOD BAR

Andre and Hiro are each having a mug of draft beer

Andre Did you pay for the first **round of drinks** while I was on the phone?

Hiro Yeah I did. That beer's yours.

Andre Cheers. I'll be sure and get the next round. Did the good-looking waitress with the brown hair serve us?

Hiro She sure did.

Andre I wish I'd been here. I'm **crazy about** her. I hope she serves us next time.

Hiro Have you noticed that she looks kind of **bummed out** tonight? I wonder why she's **moping around**. She certainly isn't her usual self.

Andre I **heard through the grapevine** that her boyfriend **fooled around on** her. She must have found out about it. That would explain her mood.

Hiro I thought she was seeing the **bouncer**.

Andre She is. That **muscle-bound jerk** is her boyfriend. Can you believe it?

Hiro What does she see in him?

Andre I don't know. Someone as nice as her deserves better than him. He's such a playboy; he's always **cheating on** her.

Hiro He's **a lady's man**? Are you sure? Every time I come in here he **gives me a dirty look**. He always seems to be **pissed off** about something. I can't believe that women find him attractive.

Andre He can really **turn on the charm** when there's a cute girl around. It's **like night and day**.

Hiro	Do you think she'll **stick it out** with him?
Andre	I hope not. I'd love to ask her out on a date, but I'm kind of **leery**. There'd be huge trouble if the bouncer saw me with her.
Hiro	No kidding. I've heard that he's the jealous type. He's also got a well-deserved reputation for having **a short fuse**.
Andre	I certainly wouldn't want to **get into a scrap** with him. He'd beat me senseless. Hey, did I tell you about the last time I was in here?
Hiro	No. What happened?
Andre	My favorite waitress gave me a pitcher of beer **on the house**. I think she might **have a soft spot for** me. I'll have to think of **an opening line** that'll make her laugh.
Hiro	Dream on.
Andre	Oh, shut up! Are you ready for another beer?
Hiro	Sure, I'll have one more. But that's it. I don't want to get too **hammered** tonight. The last time I was in here, I **drank like a fish**. The next morning I had the worst **hangover** ever. I don't want to spend another morning **tossing my cookies**.
Andre	OK. I get the picture. We'll just have **one for the road**. Where's our waitress?
Hiro	I've got some bad news for you buddy. I haven't seen her for quite a while. I think she may have finished her shift.

DEFINITIONS

| *adj.* – adjective | *exclam.* – exclamation | *n.* – noun |
| *adv.* – adverb | *i.* – idiom, phrasal verb | *v.* – verb |

round of drinks (a) *i.* – a number of drinks bought for a group
I'll pay for a round of drinks at the bar if you guys help me tonight.

crazy about something/someone *i.* – love something/someone
She's just crazy about that famous actor. She thinks he's so handsome.

bummed out *i.* – depressed, sad, unhappy
I was bummed out when I didn't get the job that I applied for.

mope around (to) *i.* – move around in a sad manner
He's been moping around ever since his girlfriend broke up with him.

hear through the grapevine (to) *i.* – hear gossip, hear a rumor
I heard through the grapevine that the company might hire some new employees.

fool around on someone (to) *i.* – cheat on someone, have an affair
He has been fooling around on his wife for at least a year.

bouncer *n.* – doorman at a bar/disco
The bouncer at that bar has a temper, so I'd be careful around him.

muscle-bound *adj.* – very muscular
I saw a muscle-bound guy playing touch football at the beach today.

jerk *n.* – terrible man
Sometimes my older brother acts like a real jerk.

cheat on someone (to) *i.* – fool around on someone, have an affair
She cheated on her boyfriend while he was away on vacation in Italy.

lady's man (a) *n.* – lady killer, playboy, stud
I think he's a lady's man because he's with a different woman every weekend.

give someone a dirty look (to) *i.* – scowl/sneer at someone
She gave her ex-boyfriend a dirty look when she saw him at the disco.

pissed off *i.* – angry, mad, teed off, ticked off
I was pissed off at my sister when she borrowed my sweater without asking first

turn on the charm (to) *i.* – become charming
Your friend is quite charismatic. He can really turn on the charm when he wants to.

like night and day *i.* – totally different
She acts differently outside the office. It's like night and day.

stick it out (to) *i.* – endure it
I don't like my job, but I'm going to stick it out because I need the money.

leery *adj.* – apprehensive, wary
I was a little bit leery about learning how to snowboard, but now I love it.

short fuse (a) *i.* – a quick temper, get angry easily
I wouldn't tease him too much if I were you. He has a very short fuse.

get into a scrap (to) *i.* – get into a fight
I almost got into a scrap over the last parking space in the garage.

on the house *i.* – free
My dinner was on the house because the waiter spilled coffee all over me.

have a soft spot for someone (to) *i.* – fond of someone
My father has always had a soft spot for my best friend from high school.

opening line (an) *i.* – a sentence used to start talking with the opposite sex
He started a conversation with the woman by using an opening line.

hammered *adj.* – bombed, drunk, intoxicated, loaded, smashed
He was so hammered that he couldn't drive home last night after the party.

drink like a fish (to) *i.* – drink a lot of alcohol
I can't believe how much alcohol your friend can hold. He drinks like a fish.

hangover *n.* – sickness caused by drinking too much alcohol
I had such a hangover this morning that I didn't get out of bed until noon.

toss one's cookies (to) *i.* – barf, puke, throw up, vomit
He tossed his cookies after eating the undercooked fish for dinner.

one for the road *i.* – one final drink before leaving somewhere
We don't have to leave for another 30 minutes. Let's have one for the road.

EXERCISE 1

MATCH THE WORD/IDIOM WITH THE CORRECT DEFINITION

_M_	1 a lady's man	A	a terrible man
___	2 pissed off	B	a doorman at a bar/disco
___	3 stick it out	C	cheat on someone
___	4 get into a scrap	D	a quick temper
___	5 a jerk	E	apprehensive
___	6 one for the road	F	become charming
___	7 a bouncer	G	very muscular
___	8 give someone a dirty look	H	fond of someone
___	9 fool around on someone	I	move around in a sad manner
___	10 have a soft spot for someone	J	depressed
___	11 toss one's cookies	K	scowl at someone
___	12 leery	L	free
___	13 mope around	M	a playboy
___	14 muscle-bound	N	vomit
___	15 hear through the grapevine	O	angry
___	16 on the house	P	get into a fight
___	17 a short fuse	Q	drunk
___	18 hammered	R	hear gossip
___	19 bummed out	S	one final drink before leaving
___	20 turn on the charm	T	endure it

EXERCISE 2

USE THE WORDS/IDIOMS BELOW TO COMPLETE
EACH OF THE FOLLOWING SENTENCES.

pissed off	a short fuse	on the house
heard through the grapevine	muscle-bound	tossing my cookies
dirty look	an opening line	a soft spot for
stick it out	drank like a fish	cheating on
night and day	leery	bouncer

1   She was horrified to find out that her boyfriend had been _____ her.

2   She _____ that her co-worker will probably get fired at the end of the week.

3   I'm really hungover this morning because I _____ last night.

4   The waiter said that my dinner is _____ because it's my birthday.

5   I have to learn to control my temper. I've got such _____.

6   My brother has been lifting weights for five years. He's really _____.

7   I want to talk to that cute guy sitting at the bar. I'll have to think of _____.

8   The _____ at that bar looks like a terrible guy, but he's actually pretty nice.

9   I was so _____ when somebody vandalized my brand-new sports car.

10 Her personality completely changes when she drinks. It's like _____.

11 The teacher gave her a _____ when he saw her smoking outside the school.

12 I felt like _____ the first time I ate that strange tasting food.

13 The professor lets you arrive late for class. I think he has _____ you.

14 I still feel a little bit _____ about going bungee jumping with you tomorrow.

15 I don't like my job, but I have to _____ until the end of the year.

EXERCISE 3

COMPLETE THE FOLLOWING CROSSWORD PUZZLE
USING WORDS/IDIOMS FROM THE DIALOGUE.

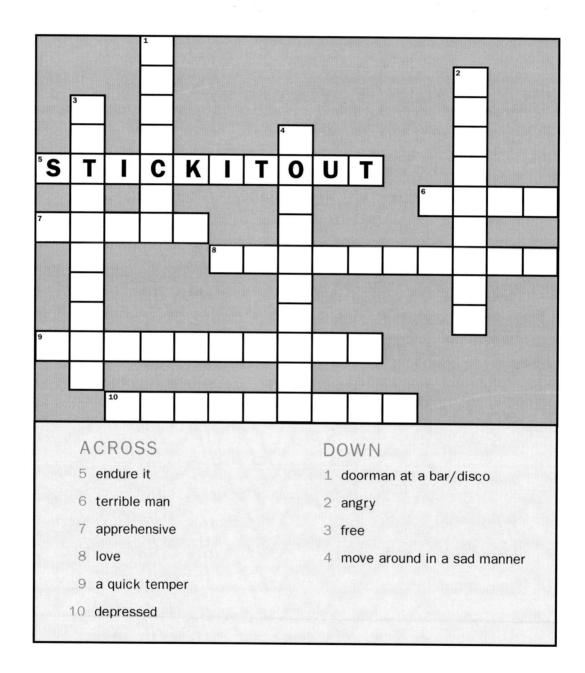

ACROSS

5 endure it

6 terrible man

7 apprehensive

8 love

9 a quick temper

10 depressed

DOWN

1 doorman at a bar/disco

2 angry

3 free

4 move around in a sad manner

EXERCISE 4

1   I **heard through the grapevine** that the manager is going to get fired tomorrow.
 a   The manager told me that the secretary is going to get fired tomorrow.
 b   The secretary informed me that the manager is going to get fired tomorrow.

2   The waiter gave me a dessert **on the house** in order to make up for his mistake.
 a   I got a complimentary dessert in order to make up for the waiter's error.
 b   The waiter made a mistake when he brought me the wrong dessert.

3   I **have a soft spot for** that handsome-looking guy who was in our class last month.
 a   I'm fond of that attractive-looking guy who took class with us last month.
 b   That handsome-looking guy we took class with last month is attracted to me.

4   I **tossed my cookies** because I got food poisoning at the restaurant we went to today.
 a   The food I ate at the restaurant today made me throw up.
 b   I threw some cookies at the waiter because I ate some bad food at the restaurant.

5   I **got into a scrap** last night because some guy insulted my girlfriend at the bar.
 a   Some guy offended my girlfriend at the bar last night, so I got into a fight.
 b   I got into a fight at the bar because some guy was flirting with my girlfriend.

6   My friend **gave me a dirty look** because I didn't let him cheat off me during the test.
 a   My friend scowled at me because I tried to cheat off him during the test.
 b   I didn't let my friend cheat off me during the test, so he sneered at me.

7   He's been **moping around** because he didn't get the promotion he wanted.
 a   He wasn't happy when someone else got the promotion instead of him.
 b   He was happy to continue working at his current position in the company.

8   She got really **pissed off** at him when he started to gossip about her at school.
 a   She was mad because he had made some flattering remarks about her at school.
 b   She was angry because he had started to spread rumors about her at school.

9   He got so **hammered** last night that he doesn't remember how he got home.
 a   He's not sure how he got home last night because he was so intoxicated.
 b   He was so drunk last night that he couldn't find his way home.

10   This course is terribly difficult, but I have to **stick it out** if I want to graduate.
 a   This course is so tough that I'll probably have to take it again.
 b   This course is very hard, but I have to endure it if I want to graduate.

EXERCISE 5

UNSCRAMBLE THE FOLLOWING SENTENCES, ADDING PUNCTUATION WHEN NEEDED. THE BEGINNING AND END OF EACH SENTENCE HAVE ALREADY BEEN DONE FOR YOU. HINT: IT'S HELPFUL TO IDENTIFY THE WORD/IDIOM FROM THE DIALOGUE IN EACH SENTENCE.

1. **I am really** / squash / best / playing / about / my / with / crazy / **friend every Friday.**

   I am really crazy about playing squash with my best friend every Friday_____.

2. **The young man** / around / his / after / huge / girlfriend / fooled / they / a / argument / on / had / **on Saturday night.**

   _____.

3. **My little sister** / ever / has / been / around / since / dog / over / run / her / moping / got / **by a car.**

   _____.

4. **The teenaged boy** / his / he / bad / at / tossed / the / sushi / cookies / some / after / ate / **restaurant this afternoon.**

   _____.

5. **The meal I** / was / the / because / friend / ate / the / knows / my / house / owner / on / **of the diner.**

   _____.

6. **I think the** / soft / for / you / you / have / work / never / because / to / late / spot / a / boss / has/ **at the office.**

   _____.

7. **He gave his** / dirty / saw / with / new / when / look / her / her / boyfriend / he / a / ex-girlfriend / **at the beach.**

   _____.

8. **She was completely** / not / pissed / promotion / off / had / there / worked / she / about / getting / the / because / **for many years.**

   _____.

EXERCISE 6

FIND THE WORDS/IDIOMS LISTED BELOW
IN THE WORD SEARCH GAME.

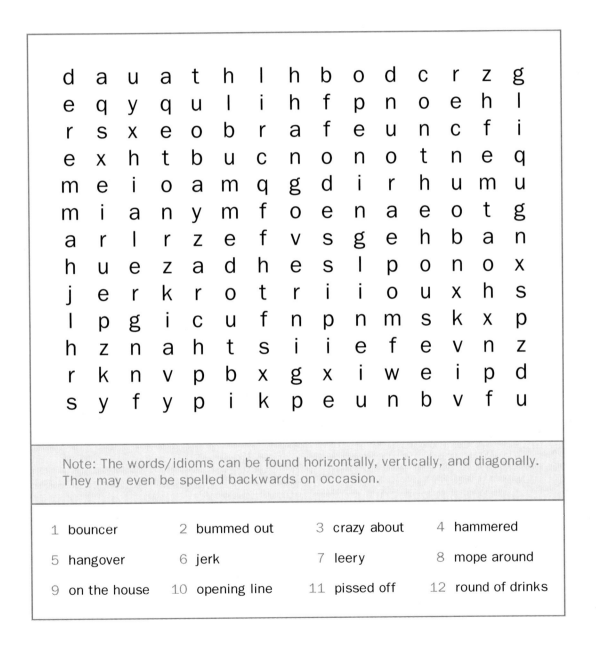

```
d  a  u  a  t  h  l  h  b  o  d  c  r  z  g
e  q  y  q  u  l  i  h  f  p  n  o  e  h  l
r  s  x  e  o  b  r  a  f  e  u  n  c  f  i
e  x  h  t  b  u  c  n  o  n  o  t  n  e  q
m  e  i  o  a  m  q  g  d  i  r  h  u  m  u
m  i  a  n  y  m  f  o  e  n  a  e  o  t  g
a  r  l  r  z  e  f  v  s  g  e  h  b  a  n
h  u  e  z  a  d  h  e  s  l  p  o  n  o  x
j  e  r  k  r  o  t  r  i  i  o  u  x  h  s
l  p  g  i  c  u  f  n  p  n  m  s  k  x  p
h  z  n  a  h  t  s  i  i  e  f  e  v  n  z
r  k  n  v  p  b  x  g  x  i  w  e  i  p  d
s  y  f  y  p  i  k  p  e  u  n  b  v  f  u
```

Note: The words/idioms can be found horizontally, vertically, and diagonally.
They may even be spelled backwards on occasion.

1 bouncer	2 bummed out	3 crazy about	4 hammered
5 hangover	6 jerk	7 leery	8 mope around
9 on the house	10 opening line	11 pissed off	12 round of drinks

Andre and Hiro are each having a mug of draft beer

Andre   Did you pay for the first r_____ of d_____ while I was on the phone?

Hiro   Yeah I did. That beer's yours.

Andre   Cheers. I'll be sure and get the next round. Did the good-looking waitress with the brown hair serve us?

Hiro   She sure did.

Andre   I wish I'd been here. I'm c_____ a_____ her. I hope she serves us next time.

Hiro   Have you noticed that she looks kind of b_____ o_____ tonight? I wonder why she's m_____ a_____. She certainly isn't her usual self.

Andre   I heard t_____ the g_____ that her boyfriend f_____ a_____ on her. She must have found out about it. That would explain her mood.

Hiro   I thought she was seeing the b_____.

Andre   She is. That m_____-bound j_____ is her boyfriend. Can you believe it?

Hiro   What does she see in him?

Andre   I don't know. Someone as nice as her deserves better than him. He's such a playboy; he's always c_____ o_____ her.

Hiro   He's a l_____ m_____? Are you sure? Every time I come in here he gives me a d_____ l_____. He always seems to be p_____ o_____ about something. I can't believe that women find him attractive.

Andre   He can really t_____ on the c_____ when there's a cute girl around. It's like n_____ and d_____.

Hiro	Do you think she'll s_____ it o_____ with him?
Andre	I hope not. I'd love to ask her out on a date, but I'm kind of l_____. There'd be huge trouble if the bouncer saw me with her.
Hiro	No kidding. I've heard that he's the jealous type. He's also got a well-deserved reputation for having a s_____ f_____.
Andre	I certainly wouldn't want to g_____ into a s_____ with him. He'd beat me senseless. Hey, did I tell you about the last time I was in here?
Hiro	No. What happened?
Andre	My favorite waitress gave me a pitcher of beer o_____ the h_____. I think she might h_____ a soft s_____ for me. I'll have to think of an o_____ line that'll make her laugh.
Hiro	Dream on.
Andre	Oh, shut up! Are you ready for another beer?
Hiro	Sure, I'll have one more. But that's it. I don't want to get too h_____ tonight. The last time I was in here, I d_____ like a f_____. The next morning I had the worst h_____ ever. I don't want to spend another morning t_____ my c_____.
Andre	OK. I get the picture. We'll just have o_____ for the r_____. Where's our waitress?
Hiro	I've got some bad news for you buddy. I haven't seen her for quite a while. I think she may have finished her shift.

COMPREHENSION QUESTIONS

TRY TO ANSWER THE FOLLOWING QUESTIONS WITHOUT LOOKING AT THE DIALOGUE. ONCE YOU'VE FINISHED THE QUESTIONS, YOU CAN REFER TO THE DIALOGUE TO CHECK YOUR ANSWERS.

1   What were Andre and Hiro drinking?

2   Who paid for the first round of drinks?

3   Describe the appearance of the waitress that served them.

4   Who's crazy about the waitress?

5   Describe the waitress's mood.

6   What did Andre hear through the grapevine?

7   Why was Hiro surprised that women find the bouncer attractive?

8   What's like night and day?

9   What was Andre leery about doing?

10 Describe the bouncer's personality.

11 What would happen if Andre got into a fight with the bouncer?

12 What did the waitress do for Andre the last time he was in the bar?

13 Who needs to think of an opening line? Why?

14 Why didn't Hiro want to drink very much?

15 Andre probably wasn't going to see the waitress again that night. Why not?

DISCUSSION QUESTIONS

PART A: General Discussion Questions

1 Does your country have a national drink? What is it?

2 What's the drinking age in your country? What is it here?

3 What time do the bars close in your country? How about here?

4 Are you allowed to smoke in the bars in your country? If not, how long has it been prohibited?

5 What's your favorite drink?

PART B: Idiomatic Discussion Questions

1 Where's your favorite place to have a **round of drinks** with your friends?

2 Have you gotten **hammered** recently? Where were you? How much did you drink?

3 Did you have **a hangover** the next morning? What did you take to make yourself feel better?

4 Have you ever seen **a scrap** in a bar? How did it start?

5 Have you ever had a bad experience with **a bouncer** in a bar? If so, describe it.

6 Have you ever received a drink **on the house**? Why did you get it?

7 Describe **a jerk** that you met while in a bar. What did he say/do? How did you react?

GIVE IT A SHOT

IN THE DIALOGUE, ANDRE SAYS THAT HE HAS TO THINK OF AN OPENING LINE THAT WILL MAKE THE WAITRESS LAUGH. READ THE FOLLOWING OPENING LINES OUT LOUD WITH YOUR PARTNER. HOW MANY CAN YOU UNDERSTAND? YOU WILL PROBABLY NEED SOME ASSISTANCE FROM YOUR TEACHER.

1   Man: Excuse me. Were you talking to me?
Woman: No.
Man: Would you please start?

2   Hello. Do you have a name? .... or can I just call you mine?

3   Do you have a map? .... because I keep getting lost in your eyes.

4   Man: Can I have directions?
Woman: To where?
Man: Your heart.

5   Woman: Do you have the time?
Man: It's 11:30.
Woman: No, to write down my phone number.

6   Did the sun come out or did you just smile at me?

7   I'd buy you a drink, but I'd be jealous of the glass.

8   If I could rearrange the alphabet, I'd put U and I together.

9   Is there an airport nearby, or is that just my heart I hear taking off?

10 Woman: Can I borrow a quarter?
Man: What for?
Woman: So I can phone your mom and thank her.

11 Man: Would you like to dance?
Woman: No. Get lost.
Man: I'm sorry you misunderstood me. I said you look fat in those pants.

12 Man: Haven't I seen you someplace before?
Woman: Yeah. That's why I stopped going there.

Warning: If you choose to try some of these out in a bar, do so at your own risk.

■■ CHAPTER TWELVE ■■

CATCHING A MOVIE

CATCHING A MOVIE

Andre and Claudia have just bought some popcorn in the lobby

Andre   Can you believe the prices at the **concession**? Everything here **costs an arm and a leg**.

Claudia   Yeah. It's ridiculous. This bag of popcorn was really expensive. It was such **a rip-off**. Next time we should bring some **munchies** with us.

Andre   Let's wander into the theater before it gets full. I'd like to find some good seats for the show.

They go into the theater and start down the aisle

Claudia   How about this **row**? I think it's about right. Do you mind if I take the seat next to the **aisle**?

Andre   It's all yours. .... Have you **caught any movies** recently?

Claudia   Yeah, I saw this **tearjerker** last weekend. It was a **touching** story about a boy and his dog. I have to admit I **had a lump in my throat** by the end of the movie. It was a bit of a struggle to **hold back the tears**. You should have seen the guy next to me; I thought he was going to start **bawling**. The story really **got to** him.

Andre   Who knows? Maybe it reminded him of the dog he had when he was growing up. Anyway, it doesn't sound like my kind of movie.

Claudia   How about the thriller that's playing at the Cineplex? Have you seen it?

Andre   Yeah. I saw it on Tuesday night. That movie will **scare you to death**. There are so many **twists and turns** that you're not sure what's going to happen next. It really keeps you **on the edge of your seat**. I won't give away the ending, but it **caught me off guard**.

Claudia	I've heard it's great. The special effects are supposed to **blow you away**. The movie critics have given it **two thumbs up**. It seems like everybody's talking about it.
Andre	Well, it's an amazing film. I'm sure it'll be **nominated** for some Academy Awards.
Claudia	Would you want to see it again?
Andre	I don't know. Why?
Claudia	I'd like to see it, but I'm not sure my homestay roommate would go with me. She's not **into** those kinds of movies. She's a bit of a **wimp** when it comes to anything scary. She even **freaks out** sometimes when she has to stay at home by herself.
Andre	Why don't you ask Min-Jung to go with you? She's a **movie buff**; I'm sure she'd love to see it.
Claudia	There's an idea. I'll **give her a ring** tomorrow and see if she wants to go. Do you know her phone number? I think I may have lost it.
Andre	Yeah, I do. I'll give it to you after the show.
	The lights in the theater start to dim
Claudia	Oh. The **coming attractions** are starting. Pass me the popcorn.

DEFINITIONS

adj. – adjective	**exclam.** – exclamation	**n.** – noun
adv. – adverb	**i.** – idiom, phrasal verb	**v.** – verb

concession *n.* – snack bar, refreshment stand
The price of a chocolate bar is always very high at the concession.

cost an arm and a leg (to) *i.* – very expensive
The designer coat she bought in that trendy store cost an arm and a leg.

rip-off (a) *i.* – overcharged, overpriced
The jacket that he bought at the mall yesterday was such a rip-off.

munchies *n.* – snack food
I brought some munchies to eat while we watch the football game on TV.

row *n.* – a line of seats
We had front row seats for the big rock concert at the coliseum.

aisle *n.* – passageway between seating areas
I had to sit next to the aisle because all the window seats were taken.

catch a movie (to) *i.* – see a movie
Would you like to catch a movie with me on Thursday night?

tearjerker *n.* – very sad movie
I cried a little bit when I watched that tearjerker on TV last night.

touching *adj.* – heartbreaking, moving, stirring
He told me a touching story about his early childhood.

have a lump in one's throat (to) *i.* – become emotional
I had a lump in my throat by the end of that sad movie.

hold back the tears (to) *i.* – control/stop one's tears
My mother couldn't hold back the tears as she drove me to the airport.

bawl (to) *v.* – cry very loudly
The young boy started bawling when his mother wouldn't buy him a toy.

get to someone (to) *i.* – make someone sad or emotional
Her story really got to me. I had a tear in my eye after I heard it.

scare someone to death (to) _i._ – scare someone very much
I'm sure that horror movie will scare you to death.

twists and turns _n._ – changes in the plot
There were so many twists and turns that it was difficult to understand the movie.

on the edge of one's seat _i._ – filled with suspense
I was on the edge of my seat as the actress walked down a dark alley.

catch someone off guard (to) _i._ – catch someone unprepared
The ending to that horror movie caught me off guard.

blow someone away (to) _i._ – amaze/astonish/astound someone
The laser show at the rock concert really blew me away.

two thumbs up _i._ – excellent, highly recommended
That movie we saw at the theater was very funny. It gets two thumbs up.

nominate (to) _v._ – select for a possible award/position
That actor's performance should be nominated for an Academy Award.

into something _i._ – enjoy something
I love rollerblading around town in my free time. I'm really into it.

wimp _n._ – chicken, coward, sissy, wuss
He is such a wimp that he cries every time I tease him.

freak out (to) _i._ – extremely emotional, upset
I freaked out when I got lost in the mountains for a few hours.

movie buff _n._ – movie fan
My friend is a movie buff. She knows everything about the movie industry.

give someone a ring _i._ – phone someone
Could you please give me a ring as soon as you get to the office?

coming attractions _n._ – movies to be released soon
I love watching the coming attractions before the movie begins.

EXERCISE 1

MATCH THE WORD/IDIOM WITH
THE CORRECT DEFINITION

M	1 cost an arm and a leg		A	movie fan
___	2 two thumbs up		B	coward
___	3 catch a movie		C	filled with suspense
___	4 touching		D	selected for
___	5 hold back the tears		E	highly recommended
___	6 row		F	snack food
___	7 on the edge of one's seat		G	control one's tears
___	8 blow someone away		H	phone someone
___	9 nominated for		I	very sad movie
___	10 wimp		J	changes in the plot
___	11 movie buff		K	amaze someone
___	12 coming attractions		L	moving, stirring
___	13 concession		M	very expensive
___	14 munchies		N	cry very loudly
___	15 tearjerker		O	scare someone very much
___	16 bawl		P	catch someone unprepared
___	17 scare someone to death		Q	see a movie
___	18 twists and turns		R	snack bar
___	19 catch someone off guard		S	a line of seats
___	20 give someone a ring		T	movies to be released soon

EXERCISE 2

USE THE WORDS/IDIOMS BELOW TO COMPLETE
EACH OF THE FOLLOWING SENTENCES.

get caught off guard	to bawl	munchies
twists and turns	gave me a ring	caught a movie
cost an arm and a leg	the concession	buff
touching	tearjerker	scared to death
wimp	rip-off	row

1 We need to go to the store and buy some _____ for the party tonight.

2 The young girl quietly sobbed as she watched a _____ at the theater.

3 I was _____ when my car broke down on a deserted highway late at night.

4 The snowboard equipment I bought this year was very expensive. It _____.

5 I didn't buy any food at _____ because the line-up was a mile long.

6 The boy started _____ when he realized that he had lost his favorite toy.

7 I was surprised when an old friend from high school _____ last night.

8 I know everything about The Battle of Gettysburg. I'm a Civil War _____.

9 My brother is petrified of snakes. He's such a _____ whenever he sees one.

10 Now I realize that I paid way too much for this jacket. It was such a _____.

11 We had to pay the scalper lots of money for front _____ seats to the concert.

12 That novel is very interesting because it has lots of _____.

13 The teacher told us a _____ story about a poor family struggling to survive.

14 She _____ at the theater on Tuesday night with her friends from school.

15 My father is always prepared for any emergency. He hates to _____.

EXERCISE 3

WHAT WORD/IDIOM FROM THE DIALOGUE MATCHES THE FOLLOWING DEFINITIONS? WHEN THE EXERCISE HAS BEEN COMPLETED, THE IDIOM FOR 'VERY EXPENSIVE' WILL BE SPELLED VERTICALLY.

1	snack food	m u n (c) h i e s
2	line of seats	_(_)_
3	snack bar	_ _ _ _ _ (_) _ _ _ _
4	highly recommended	_ _ _ (_) _ _ _ _ _ _ _
5	passageway between seating areas	_ _ (_) _ _
6	see a movie	_ _ _ _ _ (_) _ _ _ _ _
7	selected for	_ _ _ (_) _ _ _ _ _ _ _
8	sad movie	_ _ (_) _ _ _ _ _ _ _
9	scare her very much	_ _ _ (_) _ _ _ _ _ _ _ _ _ _
10	coward	_ _ (_) _
11	overcharged	(_) _ _ _ - _ _ _
12	changes in the plot	_ _ _ _ _ _ _ (_) _ _ _ _ _ _
13	control one's tears	_ _ (_) _ _ _ _ _ _ _ _ _ _ _ _
14	movies to be released soon	_ _ _ _ _ _ _ _ _ (_) _ _ _ _ _ _
15	cry very loudly	_ _ (_)
16	movie fan	_ _ _ (_) _ _ _ _
17	phone him	(_) _ _ _ _ _ _ _ _ _ _

Unscramble the following words/idioms from the dialogue.

18	cctha ihm fof uradg	_ _ _ _ _ _ _ _ _ _ _ _ _ _ _ _
19	wlob ouy yaaw	_ _ _ _ _ _ _ _ _ _ _
20	veig reh a ginr	_ _ _ _ _ _ _ _ _ _ _ _
21	dolh cakb het raets	_ _ _ _ _ _ _ _ _ _ _ _ _ _ _ _
22	otw mubtsh pu	_ _ _ _ _ _ _ _ _ _ _

EXERCISE 4

1 I became emotional as I watched a TV program on homeless children.

   I had a lump in my throat as I watched a TV program on homeless children_____.

2 Driving down that steep hill in the snowstorm scared me very much.

   _____.

3 I'm worried about you walking home this late. Phone me once you get to your place.

   _____.

4 She was filled with suspense as she watched the leading actor walk into the dark house.

   _____.

5 He was amazed when he saw the Eiffel Tower during his first trip to France.

   _____.

6 My friends caught me unprepared when they threw me a surprise birthday party.

   _____.

7 We should remember to buy some snack food for the long drive home.

   _____.

8 That state-of-the-art big screen TV I bought yesterday was very expensive.

   _____.

9 She's going to buy a hotdog at the refreshment stand before the hockey game starts.

   _____.

10 That movie is very confusing because there are too many changes in the plot.

   _____.

1. **My brother and** / which / argued / one / of / over / us / the / get / aisle / I / seat / would / **on the bus.**

   My brother and I argued over which one of us would get the aisle seat on the bus.

2. **They invited us** / movie / to / dinner / them / a / after / catch / we / finish / with / **at the restaurant.**

   _____.

3. **The children were** / abandoned / when / old / death / they / walked / the / into / to / scared / **house at night.**

   _____.

4. **The president of** / guard / company / the / workers / off / caught / when / the / he / **showed up unannounced.**

   _____.

5. **My youngest son** / for / at / his / minutes / he / least / bawled / after / fell / off / 30 / **bike this morning.**

   _____.

6. **My older sister** / edge / of / on / her / was / the / movie / because / was / the / seat / so / **filled with suspense.**

   _____.

7. **I was really** / friends / a / away / blown / voyage / my / bon / threw / party / me / for / when / **on the weekend.**

   _____.

8. **I could not** / back / when / hold / the / saw / the / tears / report / about / the / news / victims / of / I / **the terrorist bombing.**

   _____.

EXERCISE 6

FIND THE WORDS/IDIOMS LISTED BELOW IN THE WORD SEARCH GAME.

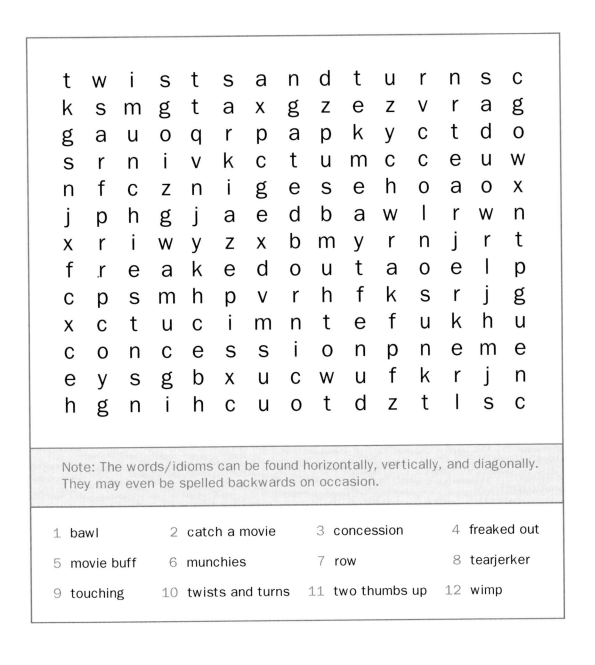

```
t  w  i  s  t  s  a  n  d  t  u  r  n  s  c
k  s  m  g  t  a  x  g  z  e  z  v  r  a  g
g  a  u  o  q  r  p  a  p  k  y  c  t  d  o
s  r  n  i  v  k  c  t  u  m  c  c  e  u  w
n  f  c  z  n  i  g  e  s  e  h  o  a  o  x
j  p  h  g  j  a  e  d  b  a  w  l  r  w  n
x  r  i  w  y  z  x  b  m  y  r  n  j  r  t
f  r  e  a  k  e  d  o  u  t  a  o  e  l  p
c  p  s  m  h  p  v  r  h  f  k  s  r  j  g
x  c  t  u  c  i  m  n  t  e  f  u  k  h  u
c  o  n  c  e  s  s  i  o  n  p  n  e  m  e
e  y  s  g  b  x  u  c  w  u  f  k  r  j  n
h  g  n  i  h  c  u  o  t  d  z  t  l  s  c
```

Note: The words/idioms can be found horizontally, vertically, and diagonally. They may even be spelled backwards on occasion.

1 bawl	2 catch a movie	3 concession	4 freaked out
5 movie buff	6 munchies	7 row	8 tearjerker
9 touching	10 twists and turns	11 two thumbs up	12 wimp

EXERCISE 7

FILL IN THE WORDS/IDIOMS THAT ARE MISSING FROM THE DIALOGUE.

Andre and Claudia have just bought some popcorn in the lobby

Andre   Can you believe the prices at the c_____? Everything here c_____ an arm and a l_____.

Claudia   Yeah. It's ridiculous. This bag of popcorn was really expensive. It was such a r_____-off. Next time we should bring some m_____ with us.

Andrc   Let's wander into the theater before it gets full. I'd like to find some good seats for the show.

They go into the theater and start down the aisle

Claudia   How about this r_____? I think it's about right. Do you mind if I take the seat next to the a_____?

Andre   It's all yours. .... Have you c_____ any m_____ recently?

Claudia   Yeah, I saw this t_____ last weekend. It was a t_____ story about a boy and his dog. I have to admit I had a l_____ in my t_____ by the end of the movie. It was a bit of a struggle to h_____ back the t_____. You should have seen the guy next to me; I thought he was going to start b_____. The story really g_____ to him.

Andre   Who knows? Maybe it reminded him of the dog he had when he was growing up. Anyway, it doesn't sound like my kind of movie.

Claudia   How about the thriller that's playing at the Cineplex? Have you seen it?

Andre   Yeah. I saw it on Tuesday night. That movie will s_____ you to d_____. There are so many t_____ and t_____ that you're not sure what's going to happen next. It really keeps you on the e_____ of your s_____. I won't give away the ending, but it c_____ me off g_____.

Claudia   I've heard it's great. The special effects are supposed to b_____ you away. The movie critics have given it t_____ t_____ up. It seems like everybody's talking about it.

Andre   Well, it's an amazing film. I'm sure it'll be n_____ for some Academy Awards.

Claudia   Would you want to see it again?

Andre   I don't know. Why?

Claudia   I'd like to see it, but I'm not sure my homestay roommate would go with me. She's not i_____ those kinds of movies. She's a bit of a w_____ when it comes to anything scary. She even f_____ o_____ sometimes when she has to stay at home by herself.

Andre   Why don't you ask Min-Jung to go with you? She's a m_____ b_____; I'm sure she'd love to see it.

Claudia   There's an idea. I'll g_____ her a r_____ tomorrow and see if she wants to go. Do you know her phone number? I think I may have lost it.

Andre   Yeah, I do. I'll give it to you after the show.

The lights in the theater start to dim

Claudia   Oh. The c_____ a_____ are starting. Pass me the popcorn.

COMPREHENSION QUESTIONS

TRY TO ANSWER THE FOLLOWING QUESTIONS WITHOUT LOOKING AT THE DIALOGUE. ONCE YOU'VE FINISHED THE QUESTIONS, YOU CAN REFER TO THE DIALOGUE TO CHECK YOUR ANSWERS.

1   What did Andre and Claudia buy at the concession?

2   What costs an arm and a leg?

3   What are Andre and Claudia going to do the next time they come to the theater?

4   Who picked the seats at the theater?

5   What seat did Claudia want?

6   Describe the last movie Claudia saw.

7   What did Claudia say about the man who sat next to her at the last movie she saw?

8   What was Andre's explanation for that man's reaction to the movie?

9   Describe the movie Andre saw at the Cineplex on Tuesday night.

10   What did Andre say about the ending of the movie he saw?

11   What did the critics think of the movie Andre saw?

12   Why won't Claudia's homestay roommate go to the thriller with her?

13   Who's a movie buff?

14   How will Claudia get in contact with Min-Jung?

15   Why did Andre and Claudia stop talking?

DISCUSSION QUESTIONS

PART A: General Discussion Questions

1 What are three of your favorite movies? Why do you like them so much?

2 What actor/actress do you really enjoy watching?

3 How much does a movie ticket cost in your country? How much is it here?

4 Can you buy tickets that reserve you a specific seat in the theater in your country? Can you do that here?

5 What was the first English language movie you saw in your country? Were subtitles used in the movie? These days, can you understand most movies without reading the subtitles?

PART B: Idiomatic Discussion Questions

1 What's your favorite type of movie? For example: **tearjerker**, action, romance, comedy, mystery, documentary, science fiction, thriller, etc.

2 Tell me about a movie that kept you **on the edge of your seat**.

3 What kind of **munchies** do you like to eat when you're watching a movie?

4 What movie did you see as a child that **scared you to death**? Explain.

5 Do you know the four movies that were **nominated for** best picture last year? Which movie won the Oscar?

6 What **costs an arm and a leg** here but is much cheaper in your country? And vice versa.

7 Have you gotten **ripped-off** while you've been here or on vacation somewhere else? Explain.

GIVE IT A SHOT

ARE YOU A MOVIE BUFF? CAN YOU MATCH THE FOLLOWING LINES OF DIALOGUE WITH THE MOVIE IT CAME FROM?

K	1 "Here's Johnny."	A	Titanic
___	2 "Show me the money."	B	The Terminator
___	3 "I'm the king of the world."	C	A Few Good Men
___	4 "I'll have what she's having."	D	E.T.
___	5 "I'm not bad, I'm just drawn that way."	E	Forrest Gump
___	6 "You can't handle the truth."	F	The Sixth Sense
___	7 "I'm your number one fan."	G	Jerry Maguire
___	8 "Life's a box of chocolates."	H	Wall Street
___	9 "I'll be back."	I	The Empire Strikes Back
___	10 "Frankly, my dear, I don't give a damn."	J	When Harry Met Sally
___	11 "I see dead people."	K	The Shining
___	12 "E.T. phone home."	L	Misery
___	13 "Luke, I am your father."	M	Casablanca
___	14 "Greed .... is good."	N	Who Framed Roger Rabbit
___	15 "Here's looking at you, kid."	O	Gone With The Wind

If you scored between:

11–15   You're a definite movie buff.
6–10   Your movie knowledge is pretty impressive.
1–5   You should get out of the house more often.

••CHAPTER THIRTEEN••

DRIVING TO A CABIN FOR THE WEEKEND

Jose stops to pick up Andre on the way to the cabin

Jose   Hi. **Hop in**. What's the matter? You look terrible. Somebody definitely **got up on the wrong side of the bed** this morning.

Andre   I'm **wiped out**. The people who live across the hall from me were up all night **ranting and raving**. They seem to have a huge argument about once every two weeks. I didn't **get a wink of sleep** last night. I'll be all right if I **snooze** on the drive up to the cabin. Where'd you get this 4x4 from? You didn't rent it, did you?

Jose   No way. My uncle lent it to me for the weekend while he's out of town on business.

Andre   He doesn't mind if you borrow it?

Jose   As long as I fill up the gas tank and return the jeep in one piece, he doesn't seem to mind at all.

Andre   He sounds like a nice guy. It must be **handy** having some relatives that live here while you're studying English.

Jose   That's for sure. My uncle **showed me the ropes** when I first arrived and he **gives me a hand** whenever I need it.

Andre   Look at the **bumper sticker** on that car in front of us. It's kind of funny.

The bumper sticker reads: "Eat right, Exercise, Die Anyway"

Jose   We may just die if this **goof** behind me doesn't stop **tailgating** us.

Andre   Don't you hate drivers like that? He's the type of guy who will always **cut you off** or **butt in** at the front of a line-up. People like him really **make my blood boil**.

Jose	Easy does it! Why don't you try to find the new CD I bought? I think it's **tucked under** your seat.
Andre	Here it is. Do you want to listen to it?
Jose	Yeah. You'll have to **fiddle with** the volume control on the CD player, though. It's sort of **touchy**.
Andre	There we go. How's that sound?
Jose	Perfect.
Andre	How long a drive is it to the cabin?
Jose	It's about a two-hour drive. The cabin is next to a beautiful lake, but it's **in the sticks**. We'll have to go off-road for about 30 minutes. I'm sure you'll love the place once we get there. The cabin's **rustic**, but very **cozy**. It has a huge fireplace that we always sit in front of at night. It's a great place to **unwind**. .... Is there something wrong? Why do you keep **fidgeting** around?
Andre	My back is **driving me nuts**! It's incredibly sore. I must have pulled a muscle when I was playing racquetball yesterday.
Jose	Maybe you should do some stretching before you play. It might help. Why don't you curl up and **get some shut-eye**? I'll wake you up when we get there.
Andre	Sounds like an offer I can't refuse. Talk to you in a couple of hours.

DEFINITIONS

adj. – adjective	*exclam.* – exclamation	*n.* – noun
adv. – adverb	*i.* – idiom, phrasal verb	*v.* – verb

hop in (to) *i.* – get in a vehicle
Let's hop in the car and drive over to your house.

get up on the wrong side of the bed (to) *i.* – wake up in a bad mood
He looks terrible this morning. I think he got up on the wrong side of the bed.

wiped out *i.* – exhausted, pooped, tired, tuckered out, worn out
She was wiped out after hiking through the woods for 5 hours.

rant and rave (to) *v.* – scream and shout
They had a huge argument. They were ranting and raving for most of the night.

get a wink of sleep (to) *i.* – a short period of sleep
He had insomnia last night, so he didn't get a wink of sleep.

snooze (to) *v.* – nap, sleep
My dog loves to snooze on the big sofa in the living room.

handy *adj.* – convenient
It's really handy having a computer in my dormitory room.

show someone the ropes (to) *i.* – tell or show someone how something works
My older sister showed me the ropes when I was a freshman at university.

give someone a hand (to) *i.* – help someone
Could you give me a hand with the housework today?

bumper sticker *n.* – a slogan or joke on a sticker that is displayed on a car
I laughed out loud when I read the bumper sticker on the car in front of us.

goof *n.* – geek, loser, nerd
She doesn't like your brother because he is such a goof.

tailgate (to) *v.* – follow another car too closely
We're going to get into an accident if you keep tailgating that car.

cut someone off (to) *i.* – cross someone's path
We almost got into an accident when that huge truck cut us off.

butt in (to) *i.* – cut in, join a line-up at the front or in the middle
I really hate drivers who try to butt in at the front of a line-up.

make one's blood boil (to) *i.* – make someone very angry
His appalling behavior at our wedding made my blood boil.

tuck under/into something (to) *i.* – place under/into something
My father tucked $40 into my pocket just before I left for the dance.

fiddle with something (to) *i.* – finely adjust something, manipulate something
I've been fiddling with the DVD player, but I can't seem to get it to work.

touchy *adj.* – sensitive
I wouldn't talk to him about that. It's a very touchy subject.

in the sticks *i.* – in the countryside
He grew up in the sticks, but went to university in a big city.

rustic *adj.* – rural
The cabin that we stayed at last weekend had a rustic charm.

cozy *adj.* – warm and comfortable
We felt cozy sitting in front of the roaring fire late at night.

unwind (to) *v.* – relax
Playing tennis with my friend on the weekend helps me to unwind.

fidget (to) *v.* – move around, restless
The little girl couldn't sit still during the trip. She kept fidgeting around in her seat.

drive someone nuts (to) *i.* – make someone crazy
The constant noise from the construction site is driving me nuts.

get some shut-eye (to) *i.* – get some sleep
I feel really tired today. I think I need to get some shut-eye this afternoon.

EXERCISE 1

_G_	1 handy		A	in the countryside
___	2 wiped out		B	finely adjust something
___	3 in the sticks		C	make someone very angry
___	4 cut someone off		D	sensitive
___	5 goof		E	a sticker that is displayed on a car
___	6 make one's blood boil		F	get some sleep
___	7 fidget around		G	convenient
___	8 unwind		H	help someone
___	9 get some shut-eye		I	scream and shout
___	10 drive someone nuts		J	cut in
___	11 bumper sticker		K	get in a vehicle
___	12 rant and rave		L	place under something
___	13 get up on the wrong side of the bed		M	geek
___	14 butt in		N	relax
___	15 tuck under something		O	follow another car too closely
___	16 fiddle with something		P	wake up in a bad mood
___	17 hop in		Q	exhausted
___	18 touchy		R	move around, restless
___	19 tailgate		S	make someone crazy
___	20 give someone a hand		T	cross someone's path

EXERCISE 2

USE THE WORDS/IDIOMS BELOW TO COMPLETE EACH OF THE FOLLOWING SENTENCES.

makes my blood boil	unwind	fiddling with
give me a hand	some shut-eye	fidgets
showed me the ropes	butt in	ranting and raving
the sticks	bumper sticker	handy
the wrong side of the bed	goof	hop in

1   I can't believe the nerve of that driver. He just _____ at the front of the line.

2   His rude and abusive behavior at every business meeting _____.

3   I've been _____ the VCR for a while, but I still can't get it to work.

4   I'm exhausted after working the graveyard shift. I need to get _____.

5   The boss was _____ because a salesman had made a very costly mistake.

6   My parents don't live in the city. They have a small farm in _____.

7   My little sister always _____ around when we go for a long drive in the car.

8   This weekend I really need to _____ after a stressful week at the office.

9   I don't like the pants you're wearing. They make you look like a _____.

10 You're grumpy this morning. I think you got up on _____.

11 Did you see the funny _____ on that car that just passed us in the fast lane?

12 My boss was helpful when I started working for the company. He _____.

13 Why don't we _____ my car and drive over to your place right now?

14 Could you _____ moving the sofa out of the truck and into the house?

15 Wow! Your apartment is so close to the school. That sure is _____.

EXERCISE 3

WHAT WORD/IDIOM FROM THE DIALOGUE MATCHES THE FOLLOWING DEFINITIONS? WHEN THE EXERCISE HAS BEEN COMPLETED, THE IDIOM FOR 'MAKE HIM VERY ANGRY' WILL BE SPELLED VERTICALLY.

1   get some sleep   g e t   s o(m)e   s h u t - e y e
2   scream and shout   _ _ _ _   (_)_ _   _ _ _ _
3   in the countryside   _ _   _ _ _   _ _ _ _(_)_
4   move around, restless   _ _ _ _(_)_

5   convenient   (_)_ _ _ _
6   relax   _ _ _(_)_ _
7   rural   _ _(_)_ _ _

8   cut in   (_)_ _ _   _ _
9   a short period of sleep   _ _ _   _   _ _ _ _   _ _   _(_)_ _ _
10 sensitive   _(_)_ _ _ _
11 get in a vehicle   _(_)_   _ _
12 exhausted   _ _ _ _(_)   _ _ _

13 sticker   (_)_ _ _ _   _ _ _ _ _ _
14 warm and comfortable   _(_)_ _
15 help him   _(_)_ _   _ _ _   _   _ _ _ _
16 follow another car too closely   _ _ (_)_ _ _ _

Unscramble the following words/idioms from the dialogue.

17 vierd hmi tusn   _ _ _ _   _ _ _   _ _ _ _
18 whso imh eht sroep   _ _ _ _   _ _ _   _ _ _   _ _ _ _ _
19 tcu ouy fof   _ _ _   _ _ _   _ _ _
20 ktcude ruedn   _ _ _ _ _ _   _ _ _ _
21 idldfe tihw   _ _ _ _ _ _   _ _ _ _

EXERCISE 4

CHOOSE THE ANSWER THAT MATCHES
THE FOLLOWING STATEMENTS.

1 I need to **get some shut-eye** before I go to work at the factory tonight.
   a I have to get some sleep before I start working the night shift.
   b I think I'm going to snooze while I'm at the factory tonight.

2 I didn't get very much sleep last night, so I **woke up on the wrong side of the bed**.
   a I didn't get enough sleep last night, so I was irritable this morning.
   b I didn't get very much sleep last night, so I slept in this morning.

3 His appalling behavior at the annual meeting this afternoon **made my blood boil**.
   a His terrible behavior at the annual meeting this afternoon made me furious.
   b His gracious behavior at the annual meeting today made me very angry.

4 My little sister always **fidgets** around in the car when we go for a long drive.
   a My little sister talks a lot whenever we go for a long drive in the car.
   b Whenever we go for a long drive in the car, my little sister can't sit still.

5 His car wouldn't start after he spent an hour **fiddling with** the carburetor.
   a His car wouldn't start even though he had worked on the carburetor for an hour.
   b His car finally started after he had worked on the carburetor for an hour.

6 My neighbor offered to **give me a hand** when I was shoveling my driveway.
   a My neighbor offered to assist me while I was removing the snow from my driveway.
   b My neighbor offered to help me when I was sweeping the leaves from my driveway.

7 I couldn't get any sleep because my neighbors were **ranting and raving** all night long.
   a My neighbors prevented me from sleeping because their stereo was too loud.
   b I couldn't sleep last night because my neighbors were screaming and shouting.

8 I was **wiped out** after cross-country skiing through the forest for over 3 hours.
   a I was fatigued after cross-country skiing in the woods for more than 3 hours.
   b I fell down after cross-country skiing through the forest for more than 3 hours

9 Your little brother's mischievous behavior at the birthday party really **drove me nuts**.
   a Your younger brother's naughty behavior at the party irritated me.
   b Your little brother's courteous behavior at the party bothered me.

10 The boss **showed me the ropes** when I first started working for the company.
    a The boss ignored me when I was a new employee at the company.
    b I got a lot of help from the boss when I first started working at the company.

EXERCISE 5

UNSCRAMBLE THE FOLLOWING SENTENCES, ADDING PUNCTUATION WHEN NEEDED. THE BEGINNING AND END OF EACH SENTENCE HAVE ALREADY BEEN DONE FOR YOU. HINT: IT'S HELPFUL TO IDENTIFY THE WORD/IDIOM FROM THE DIALOGUE IN EACH SENTENCE.

1 **I felt so** / bed / in / morning / that / I / cozy / want / to / get / didn't / up / and / this / **go to work.**

I felt so cozy in bed this morning that I didn't want to get up and go to work   .

2 **My boyfriend was** / mood / a / in / wrong / he / up / the / got / because / side / on / bad / **of the bed.**

_____.

3 **My daughter always** / when / me / wanted / to / her / bed / into / night / at / tuck / **she was young.**

_____.

4 **I didn't sleep** / going / well / very / last / so / I'm / to / night / snooze / the / on / **sofa this afternoon.**

_____.

5 **The young boy** / around / kept / the / because / he / table / at / fidgeting / dinner / **was really bored.**

_____.

6 **The driver of** / other / was / when / inadvertently / him / cut / I / car / the / off / furious / **on the freeway.**

_____.

7 **The woman in** / grocery / blood / when / told / daughter / the / she / my / my / boil / store / made / **to shut up.**

_____.

8 **I didn't get** / a / hall / sleep / last / because / people / the / across / of / wink / night / were / the / **having a party.**

_____.

EXERCISE 6

REWRITE THE FOLLOWING SENTENCES USING A WORD/IDIOM FROM THE DIALOGUE.

1 Do you have time to help me with the yard work this afternoon?

<u>Do you have time to give me a hand with the yard work this afternoon</u>_____?

2 That guy made me very angry when he punched my younger brother in the face.

_____.

3 I think the book you're looking for was placed under the sofa in the living room.

_____.

4 I love to relax on the patio in my backyard after a tough day at work.

_____.

5 My co-worker showed me how the office operates when I was a new employee.

_____.

6 I got into my brand-new car and drove out to the beach on Sunday afternoon.

_____.

7 We got lost in the countryside when we were on vacation last summer.

_____.

8 She was exhausted because she had spent over 10 hours working at the office.

_____.

9 The drunken man was screaming and shouting as he staggered down the street.

_____.

10 I really don't like aggressive drivers who follow my car too closely.

_____.

EXERCISE 7

FILL IN THE WORDS/IDIOMS THAT ARE MISSING FROM THE DIALOGUE.

Jose stops to pick up Andre on the way to the cabin

Jose Hi. H_____ in. What's the matter? You look terrible. Somebody definitely got up on the w_____ side of the b_____ this morning.

Andre I'm w_____ o_____. The people who live across the hall from me were up all night r_____ and r_____ . They seem to have a huge argument about once every two weeks. I didn't get a w_____ of s_____ last night. I'll bc all right if I s_____ on the drive up to the cabin. Where'd you get this 4x4 from? You didn't rent it, did you?

Jose No way. My uncle lent it to me for the weekend while he's out of town on business.

Andre He doesn't mind if you borrow it?

Jose As long as I fill up the gas tank and return the jeep in one piece, he doesn't seem to mind at all.

Andre He sounds like a nice guy. It must be h_____ having some relatives that live here while you're studying English.

Jose That's for sure. My uncle s_____ me the r_____ when I first arrived and he g_____ me a h_____ whenever I need it.

Andre Look at the b_____ s_____ on that car in front of us. It's kind of funny.

The bumper sticker reads: "Eat right, Exercise, Die Anyway"

Jose We may just die if this g_____ behind me doesn't stop t_____ us.

Andre Don't you hate drivers like that? He's the type of guy who will always c_____ you off or b_____ in at the front of a line-up. People like him really make my b_____ b_____ .

Jose	Easy does it! Why don't you try to find the new CD I bought? I think it's t_____ u_____ your seat.
Andre	Here it is. Do you want to listen to it?
Jose	Yeah. You'll have to f_____ w_____ the volume control on the CD player, though. It's sort of t_____.
Andre	There we go. How's that sound?
Jose	Perfect.
Andre	How long a drive is it to the cabin?
Jose	It's about a two-hour drive. The cabin is next to a beautiful lake, but it's in the s_____. We'll have to go off-road for about 30 minutes. I'm sure you'll love the place once we get there. The cabin's r_____, but very c_____. It has a huge fireplace that we always sit in front of at night. It's a great place to u_____. .... Is there something wrong? Why do you keep f_____ around?
Andre	My back is d_____ me n_____! It's incredibly sore. I must have pulled a muscle when I was playing racquetball yesterday.
Jose	Maybe you should do some stretching before you play. It might help. Why don't you curl up and get some s_____-e_____? I'll wake you up when we get there.
Andre	Sounds like an offer I can't refuse. Talk to you in a couple of hours.

COMPREHENSION QUESTIONS

TRY TO ANSWER THE FOLLOWING QUESTIONS WITHOUT LOOKING AT THE DIALOGUE. ONCE YOU'VE FINISHED THE QUESTIONS, YOU CAN REFER TO THE DIALOGUE TO CHECK YOUR ANSWERS.

1 How did Andre look when Jose stopped to pick him up?

2 Why did Andre look that way?

3 Andre will be all right if he does what?

4 What kind of vehicle was Jose driving? Did he rent it?

5 Who helped Jose when he first arrived? How did he help him?

6 What did the bumper sticker on the car in front of them say?

7 Why was Jose concerned about the driver behind them?

8 What did Andre say about that type of driver?

9 What was tucked under Andre's seat?

10 What was the matter with the CD player?

11 How long a drive is it to the cabin?

12 Describe the cabin they're going to.

13 What do they usually do at the cabin in the evening?

14 Why was Andre fidgeting around in the vehicle?

15 When will Jose wake Andre up?

DISCUSSION QUESTIONS

PART A: General Discussion Questions

1 Do you have a driver's license? How old were you when you got it?

2 Who taught you how to drive? Do you have to attend a driving school in order to get a license in your country?

3 How often do you drive in your country? How about here?

4 What's your ideal car?

5 If you could have the use of a convertible sports car for two days, where would you go?

PART B: Idiomatic Discussion Questions

1 What **drives you nuts** about driving in your country? How about here?

2 Tell me about a time that another driver **made your blood boil**. What did he/she do?

3 Are **bumper stickers** popular in your country? Can you translate any of them into English?

4 Would you prefer to spend the weekend at a **cozy** cabin **in the sticks** or at a luxurious hotel downtown? Explain your choice.

5 What are your favorite ways to **unwind**? Give three examples.

6 Who **showed you the ropes** when you first arrived here?

7 Have you **gotten up on the wrong side of the bed** recently? Why did you feel so bad?

GIVE IT A SHOT

ANDRE AND JOSE SEE A FUNNY BUMPER STICKER ON A CAR WHILE DRIVING TO THE CABIN. READ THE FOLLOWING BUMPER STICKERS OUT LOUD WITH A PARTNER. HOW MANY CAN YOU UNDERSTAND? YOU WILL PROBABLY NEED SOME ASSISTANCE FROM YOUR TEACHER.

1. Hang up and drive.

2. No radio – Already stolen.

3. Keep honking – I'm reloading.

4. Horn broken – Watch for finger.

5. Honk if you like peace and quiet.

6. If you don't like my driving, stay off the sidewalk.

7. You never really learn to swear until you learn to drive.

8. Have a nice day .... somewhere else.

9. The more people I meet, the more I like my dog.

10. I can handle pain until it hurts.

11. Don't steal. The government hates the competition.

12. A clear conscience is usually the sign of a bad memory.

13. Hard work pays off in the future. Laziness pays off now.

14. Money isn't everything, but sure keeps the kids in touch.

15. I don't find it hard to meet expenses. They're everywhere.

16. Borrow money from pessimists – they don't expect it back.

17. Few women admit their age; fewer men act it.

18. You're only young once, but you can stay immature forever.

••CHAPTER FOURTEEN••

FINISHING CLASSES

FINISHING CLASSES

Andre is chatting with Hans in the hallway at school

Andre   I can't believe I'm finally finished.

Hans   Congratulations. How did your last day at school go?

Andre   It was pretty easy. I hardly **cracked a book** today. **As a matter of fact**, we spent most of the last class just **shooting the breeze**.

Hans   What did you guys talk about?

Andre   A lot of students were talking about going home. It seems like I'm not the only one who has **mixed emotions** about leaving.

Hans   What do you mean?

Andre   Well, one moment I'm excited about getting out of here, and then the next I'm **down in the dumps** because I can't stay longer.

Hans   I'll probably be **in the same boat** when it comes time for me to leave. I still can't believe that you'll be gone in just over a month. Are you sure that you can't **stick around** until I go home at the end of March?

Andre   Sorry, there's no way I can stay that long. My parents are expecting me back in December. There'd be **hell to pay** if I didn't make it home by then. Can you believe how quickly this year **went by**? It feels like I just got here a few months ago.

Hans   I know what you mean. **Time flies**. Before I know it, you'll be gone.

Andre   We've still got some time left. We're not **parting ways** just yet. Don't get **choked up** about it already.

Hans   Very funny. I'll try to **hold back the tears**.

Andre	Have you been able to find anybody to **take my place** at the apartment?
Hans	Not yet. It's not that easy to find a roommate that I'm **compatible** with. **Like it or lump it**, I'm going to have to find somebody else.
Andre	I guess you'll just have to keep looking.
Hans	I suppose so. By the way, do you think your English has improved while you've been here?
Andre	Yeah, **by leaps and bounds**. I don't mean to **boast**, but I scored 93 on the last internet TOEFL test I took.
Hans	**Holy smoke!** That's incredible! Why didn't you say anything about your result before?
Andre	I didn't want to **brag** about it. I know that you still have to take the test.
Hans	Don't remind me. You must have **worked your butt off** to get a score like that.
Andre	**You can say that again.** I spent hours and hours at the library **poring over** all the practice exams and grammar exercises. It was worth the effort given the result I got. I'm so glad that I didn't **goof off** like I did when I first arrived here.
Hans	What are you going to do in your **spare time** now that you're finished with school?
Andre	I don't know. I wouldn't mind **hitting the slopes** a few times before I go. Other than that, I'll probably just **take it easy**.
Hans	That sounds like a good plan.

adj. – adjective	*exclam.* – exclamation	*n.* – noun
adv. – adverb	*i.* – idiom, phrasal verb	*v.* – verb

crack a book (to) *i.* – open a book
I didn't crack a book last night because I'd already prepared for the test.

as a matter of fact *i.* – actually
I'm really tired right now. As a matter of fact, I'm going home to bed.

shoot the breeze (to) *i.* – chat, gab, talk
I spent the last hour shooting the breeze with my friend at the coffee shop.

mixed emotions *i.* – both positive and negative feelings
She has mixed emotions about getting back together with her ex-boyfriend.

down in the dumps *i.* – blue, bummed out, depressed, sad
He's been down in the dumps since his dog went missing.

in the same boat *i.* – in the same situation
We're in the same boat because neither of us has a date for Saturday night.

stick around (to) *i.* – stay
I'm going to stick around at school after class today.

hell to pay *i.* – great punishment as a result of one's actions
There was hell to pay when I forgot to pick up my mother at the shopping mall.

go by (to) *i.* – pass
Time has certainly gone by quickly this year.

time flies *i.* – time passes quickly
Time flies when you're having fun.

part ways (to) *i.* – separate from someone
I'm going to miss you when we part ways at the end of the month.

choked up *i.* – emotional, upset
She was choked up when she got fired from her job for no reason.

hold back the tears (to) *i.* – control/stop one's tears
The little girl couldn't hold back the tears when she scraped her knee.

take one's place (to) *i.* – replace someone
I can't go to the concert with them, so my friend is going to take my place.

compatible **adj.** – like-minded, well-suited
I think they make a very nice couple. They're very compatible.

like it or lump it (to) **i.** – something must be accepted, like it or not
Like it or lump it, you have to help me paint the house today.

by leaps and bounds **i.** – a lot, very much
My English has improved by leaps and bounds since I started to study hard.

boast (to) **v.** – brag, speak in a proud manner
That guy always boasts about how successful his company is.

holy smoke **eclam.** – holy cow, wow
Holy smoke! I just saw a movie star get into a limousine outside the hotel.

brag (to) **v.** – boast, speak in a proud manner
She started to brag after she got a high score on the test.

work one's butt off (to) **i.** – work very hard
I've been working my butt off at university for the last three months.

you can say that again **i.** – I agree with you
Steve: Did you see her? She was gorgeous!
Jim: You can say that again.

pore over something (to) **i.** – study very hard
I pored over my notes this morning in preparation for the final exam.

goof off (to) **i.** – waste time
The teacher made him stay after class because he goofed off during the lesson.

spare time **n.** – free time
She really enjoys reading mystery novels in her spare time.

hit the slopes (to) **i.** – go skiing/snowboarding
I'm planning to hit the slopes with my friends on the weekend.

take it easy (to) **i.** – relax, kick back
I'll probably just take it easy at home with my family tonight.

EXERCISE 1

MATCH THE WORD/IDIOM WITH THE CORRECT DEFINITION

D	1 as a matter of fact	A	I agree with you
___	2 mixed emotions	B	in the same situation
___	3 take one's place	C	chat
___	4 spare time	D	actually
___	5 time flies	E	go skiing/snowboarding
___	6 part ways	F	like-minded
___	7 boast	G	waste time
___	8 work one's butt off	H	separate from someone
___	9 pore over something	I	open a book
___	10 hit the slopes	J	a lot
___	11 crack a book	K	replace someone
___	12 down in the dumps	L	speak in a proud manner
___	13 in the same boat	M	positive and negative feelings
___	14 stick around	N	study very hard
___	15 compatible	O	time passes quickly
___	16 hold back the tears	P	stay
___	17 by leaps and bounds	Q	depressed
___	18 goof off	R	control one's tears
___	19 you can say that again	S	work very hard
___	20 shoot the breeze	T	free timc

USE THE WORDS/IDIOMS BELOW TO COMPLETE EACH OF THE FOLLOWING SENTENCES.

part ways with	goofed off	mixed emotions
work his butt off	spare time	holy smoke
hold back the tears	hell to pay	brags
poring over	a matter of fact	compatible with
took my place	hit the slopes	in the same boat

1　I can't stand the way he _____ about how much money he makes.

2　He'll have to _____ if he hopes to graduate at the top of his class.

3　My little sister couldn't _____ as she watched a touching movie on TV.

4　We're _____ because we both have to work overtime tonight.

5　I'm sad about you moving away. I really don't want to _____ you.

6　I have _____ about changing jobs at the end of this year.

7　That student failed out of university because he always _____ in class.

8　He has been _____ the practice exams at the library for the last three hours.

9　I want to _____ tomorrow because I'd like to try out my new snowboard.

10　I'm really hungry. As _____, I'm going to have something to eat right now.

11　I really enjoy playing games on my computer in my _____.

12　There was _____ when I broke one of my mother's favorite antique chairs.

13　I bought a new printer today. Unfortunately, it's not _____ my computer.

14　I couldn't go to the summer camp so my brother _____.

15　_____! That car just smashed into the telephone pole across the street.

EXERCISE 3

WHAT WORD/IDIOM FROM THE DIALOGUE MATCHES THE FOLLOWING
DEFINITIONS? WHEN THE EXERCISE HAS BEEN COMPLETED, THE IDIOM
FOR 'I AGREE WITH YOU' WILL BE SPELLED VERTICALLY.

1   relax   t a k e it e a s(y)
2   brag   _(_)_ _ _
3   a lot   _ _   _ _ _ _ _   _ _ _   _ _(_)_ _ _

4   emotional   (_)_ _ _ _ _   _ _
5   free time   _ _(_)_ _   _ _ _ _
6   stay   _ _ _ _ _   _ _ _ _(_)_

7   chat   (_)_ _ _ _   _ _ _   _ _ _ _ _ _
8   separate   _ _ _ _   _(_)_ _
9   pass   _ _   _(_)

10 control one's tears   _ _ _ _   _ _ _ _   (_)_ _   _ _ _ _
11 holy cow   (_)_ _ _   _ _ _ _ _
12 actually   _ _   _   _(_)_ _ _   _ _   _ _ _ _
13 like-minded   _ _ _ _ _(_)_ _ _

14 open a book   _ _ _ _ _   (_)   _ _ _ _
15 waste time   (_)_ _ _   _ _ _
16 in the same situation   _ _   _ _ _   _(_)_ _   _ _ _ _
17 go skiing   _(_)_   _ _ _   _ _ _ _ _
18 depressed   _ _ _ _   _(_)   _ _ _   _ _ _ _ _

Unscramble the following words/idioms from the dialogue.

19 lelh ot ypa   _ _ _ _   _ _   _ _ _
20 xdemi nmtioose   _ _ _ _ _   _ _ _ _ _ _ _ _
21 etmi lsief   _ _ _ _   _ _ _ _ _
22 otohs het rebzee   _ _ _ _ _   _ _ _   _ _ _ _ _ _

EXERCISE 4

1 She has been **down in the dumps** because her father passed away last week.
   a She has been despondent because her father died recently.
   b She has been cheery ever since her father passed away.

2 He said that he's going to take up painting in his **spare time** this year.
   a He said that he's going to start painting again in his free time this year.
   b He said that he wants to learn how to paint in his free time this year.

3 I **hit the slopes** with my friends at a local ski resort on Friday afternoon.
   a I had a serious crash while skiing at a local ski resort on Friday afternoon.
   b I went skiing with my friends at a local ski resort on Friday afternoon.

4 She spent the afternoon **shooting the breeze** with her boyfriend in the park.
   a It was too windy to spend the afternoon in the park with her boyfriend.
   b She was in the park chatting with her boyfriend all afternoon.

5 I could barely **hold back the tears** while I was watching that movie on TV.
   a I almost started to cry while I watched that touching movie on TV.
   b I quietly sobbed while watching that emotional movie on TV.

6 She wants to **stick around** longer to see if her friends finally show up at the party.
   a She wants to get going because she doesn't think her friends are going to show up.
   b She'd like to stay here longer because she wants to see if her friends show up.

7 There was **hell to pay** when I tossed a baseball through the living room window.
   a My parents reprimanded me severely when I broke the living room window.
   b My parents praised me after I tossed a baseball through the living room window.

8 He had to **work his butt off** in order to get into that prestigious university.
   a He had to work very hard in order to get into that dreadful university.
   b He had to study very hard in order to be accepted by that prominent university.

9 That man spends too much time **boasting** about how brilliant his two sons are.
   a That man brags about his sons all the time because he is very proud them.
   b That man is very modest about how brilliant his two sons are.

10 He's going to get fired because he **goofs off** at the office on a daily basis.
   a He won't have a job much longer because he wastes too much time at work.
   b He'll probably lose his job because he arrives late for work everyday.

EXERCISE 5

UNSCRAMBLE THE FOLLOWING SENTENCES, ADDING PUNCTUATION WHEN NEEDED. THE BEGINNING AND END OF EACH SENTENCE HAVE ALREADY BEEN DONE FOR YOU. HINT: IT'S HELPFUL TO IDENTIFY THE WORD/IDIOM FROM THE DIALOGUE IN EACH SENTENCE.

1 **I always shoot** / friends / breeze / hall / the / my / with / in / the / before / **the class begins.**

   <u>I always shoot the breeze with my friends in the hall before the class begins</u> .

2 **I was very** / when / girlfriend / I / at / the / and / part / had / my / sad / to / ways / **airport last week.**

   _____ .

3 **Everyone on the** / was / in / dumps / we / lost / after / the / down / team / **the championship game.**

   _____ .

4 **My ability to** / improved / leaps / after / bounds / and / snowboard / I / by / **took several lessons.**

   _____ .

5 **I hate it** / a / when / snobby / football / boyfriend / your / about / boasts / great / what / **player he is.**

   _____ .

6 **There will be** / train / hell / to / if / forget / meet / dad / the / pay / you /at / to / your / **station this afternoon.**

   _____ .

7 **I'll have to** / my / in / work / biology / order / pass / to / butt / the / off / **course I'm taking.**

   _____ .

8 **That employee got** / he / fired / always / was / because / goofing / when / should / off / he / **have been working.**

   _____ .

EXERCISE 6

FIND THE WORDS/IDIOMS LISTED BELOW
IN THE WORD SEARCH GAME.

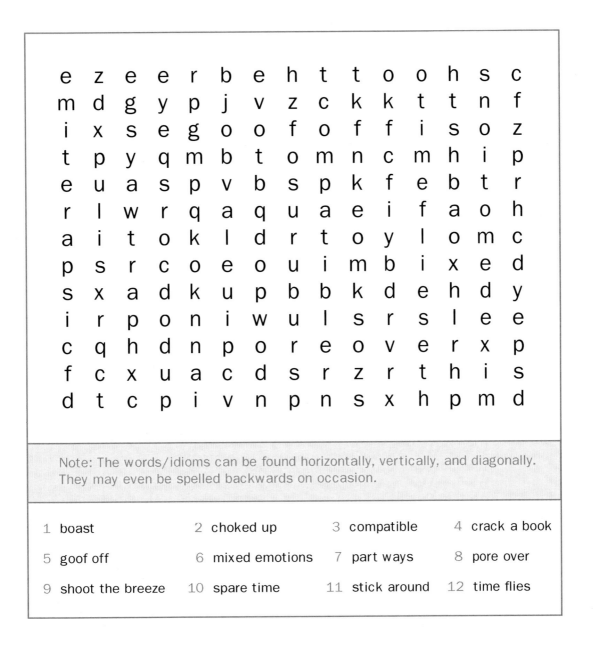

```
e  z  e  e  r  b  e  h  t  t  o  o  h  s  c
m  d  g  y  p  j  v  z  c  k  k  t  t  n  f
i  x  s  e  g  o  o  f  o  f  f  i  s  o  z
t  p  y  q  m  b  t  o  m  n  c  m  h  i  p
e  u  a  s  p  v  b  s  p  k  f  e  b  t  r
r  l  w  r  q  a  q  u  a  e  i  f  a  o  h
a  i  t  o  k  l  d  r  t  o  y  l  o  m  c
p  s  r  c  o  e  o  u  i  m  b  i  x  e  d
s  x  a  d  k  u  p  b  b  k  d  e  h  d  y
i  r  p  o  n  i  w  u  l  s  r  s  l  e  e
c  q  h  d  n  p  o  r  e  o  v  e  r  x  p
f  c  x  u  a  c  d  s  r  z  r  t  h  i  s
d  t  c  p  i  v  n  p  n  s  x  h  p  m  d
```

Note: The words/idioms can be found horizontally, vertically, and diagonally.
They may even be spelled backwards on occasion.

1 boast	2 choked up	3 compatible	4 crack a book
5 goof off	6 mixed emotions	7 part ways	8 pore over
9 shoot the breeze	10 spare time	11 stick around	12 time flies

Andre is chatting with Hans in the hallway at school

Andre   I can't believe I'm finally finished.

Hans   Congratulations. How did your last day at school go?

Andre   It was pretty easy. I hardly c_____ a b_____ today. As a m_____ of f_____, we spent most of the last class just s_____ the b_____.

Hans   What did you guys talk about?

Andre   A lot of students were talking about going home. It seems like I'm not the only one who has m_____ e_____ about leaving.

Hans   What do you mean?

Andre   Well, one moment I'm excited about getting out of here, and then the next I'm d_____ in the d_____ because I can't stay longer.

Hans   I'll probably be in the s_____ b_____ when it comes time for me to leave. I still can't believe that you'll be gone in just over a month. Are you sure that you can't s_____ a_____ until I go home at the end of March?

Andre   Sorry, there's no way I can stay that long. My parents are expecting me back in December. There'd be h_____ to p_____ if I didn't make it home by then. Can you believe how quickly this year w_____ b_____? It feels like I just got here a few months ago.

Hans   I know what you mean. T_____ f_____. Before I know it, you'll be gone.

Andre   We've still got some time left. We're not p_____ w_____ just yet. Don't get c_____ u_____ about it already.

Hans   Very funny. I'll try to hold b_____ the t_____.

Andre   Have you been able to find anybody to t_____ my p_____ at the apartment?

Hans   Not yet. It's not that easy to find a roommate that I'm c_____ with. L_____ it or l_____ it, I'm going to have to find somebody else.

Andre   I guess you'll just have to keep looking.

Hans   I suppose so. By the way, do you think your English has improved while you've been here?

Andre   Yeah, by l_____ and b_____. I don't mean to b_____, but I scored 93 on the last internet TOEFL test I took.

Hans   H_____ s_____! That's incredible! Why didn't you say anything about your result before?

Andre   I didn't want to b_____ about it. I know that you still have to take the test.

Hans   Don't remind me. You must have w_____ your b_____ off to get a score like that.

Andre   You c_____ say that a_____. I spent hours and hours at the library p_____ o_____ all the practice exams and grammar exercises. It was worth the effort given the result I got. I'm so glad that I didn't g_____ o_____ like I did when I first arrived here.

Hans   What are you going to do in your s_____ t_____ now that you're finished with school?

Andre   I don't know. I wouldn't mind h_____ the s_____ a few times before I go. Other than that, I'll probably just t_____ it e_____.

Hans   That sounds like a good plan.

COMPREHENSION QUESTIONS

TRY TO ANSWER THE FOLLOWING QUESTIONS WITHOUT LOOKING AT THE DIALOGUE. ONCE YOU'VE FINISHED THE QUESTIONS, YOU CAN REFER TO THE DIALOGUE TO CHECK YOUR ANSWERS.

1   Where was Andre talking to Hans?

2   Did Andre study hard at school on his last day?

3   What did the students talk about in Andre's last class?

4   Why did Andre have mixed emotions?

5   What did Hans mean when he said, "I'll probably be in the same boat"?

6   When does Andre have to return to his country?

7   Why can't Andre stay until the end of March?

8   Do you think Hans was getting choked up? Why? Why not?

9   Why hasn't Hans found someone to take Andre's place at the apartment?

10 Has Andre's English improved over the last year? By how much has it improved?

11 What was Andre's score on the internet TOEFL test? Do you think that's a high score?

12 Why didn't Andre tell Hans about his test score before?

13 Where did Andre prepare for the TOEFL test? How much time did he spend there?

14 Did Andre study hard when he first arrived in the country?

15 What does Andre plan to do in his spare time?

DISCUSSION QUESTIONS

DISCUSS THE FOLLOWING QUESTIONS WITH YOUR PARTNER.

PART A: General Discussion Questions

1 When do you finish your studies at this school?

2 Do you feel like you've had enough time here to improve your English?

3 How many months do you think you'd have to stay here in order to see a dramatic improvement in your English?

4 Have you taken the TOEFL exam? Were you satisfied with your score? If you haven't taken the test, how do you think you'd do on it?

5 How do you think you'll feel when you finally finish your studies here?

PART B: Idiomatic Discussion Questions

1 Have you been **goofing off** or studying hard recently? Why?

2 What do you do in your **spare time** here? How about in your country?

3 Describe a period of time in your life when you had to **work your butt off**.

4 There would be **hell to pay** if my parents knew that I .... when I was ....

5 Did you have **mixed emotions** when you left your country to come here? Why? Why not?

6 Which student at the school will you miss the most when it comes time to **part ways?**

7 Have you been **down in the dumps** at any point while you've been here? Why?

IN THE DIALOGUE, ANDRE SAYS THAT HE FEELS 'DOWN IN THE DUMPS' ABOUT GOING HOME. HOW MANY OF THE FOLLOWING WORDS/EXPRESSIONS FOR SADNESS AND HAPPINESS ARE YOU FAMILIAR WITH? YOU MAY NEED SOME ASSISTANCE FROM YOUR TEACHER.

Sad:

blue
bummed out
dejected
depressed
despondent
down (in the dumps)
gloomy
miserable
unhappy

Happy:

cheerful
ecstatic
elated
in high spirits
in seventh heaven
on cloud nine
pleased
thrilled
tickled pink

Choose the correct answer to complete the following sentences.

1 He was (on cloud nine/gloomy) when he won the election for governor of the state.

2 She was (dejected/tickled pink) when her parents gave her a new car on her birthday.

3 He was (in seventh heaven/miserable) after he found out his dog had been run over.

4 She was (in high spirits/despondent) as they began their hike into the beautiful forest.

5 The student was (elated/down in the dumps) when he failed the entrance exam again.

6 You look kind of (gloomy/cheerful) today. What's wrong with you?

7 She was (despondent/thrilled) to be considered one of the best writers in the country.

8 They were (bummed out/ecstatic) because they couldn't buy tickets for the concert.

9 I always feel (cheerful/blue) when it rains for days on end.

10 I'm (depressed/in seventh heaven) every time my girlfriend tells me she loves me.

▪▪ CHAPTER FIFTEEN ▪▪

SNOWBOARDING AT A WINTER RESORT

Min-Jung is waiting for Andre in the line-up for the chairlift

Min-Jung What kept you?

Andre Sorry, I **took a spill** half way down the run. It took me a little while to recover from it.

Min-Jung How'd it happen? You're such a **hotdog**. Were you **showing off** again?

Andre Not a chance. Some crazy skier **cut me off**. He didn't even realize that he made me lose control to avoid **smacking into** him.

Min-Jung **Heads up**. We're next for the chairlift. Here we go.

They get on the chairlift and head up the hill

Andre What run will you try next?

Min-Jung I think I'll **take a stab** at the 'Widow Maker'.

Andre Are you certain you're **up to** it? That's a tough run. You might be **getting in over your head**.

Min-Jung Don't **psych me out** now. Every once in a while I have to take on a new challenge. I'm **going for** it. Have you seen Jose on the slopes today?

Andre Yeah I have. I was surprised to see him because he was **under the weather** on Thursday. I think it's his first time snowboarding. I'll say this; he sure is fearless.

Min-Jung No kidding. I saw him **wipe out** a couple of times. The guy's going to be **black-and-blue**. I bet he's really **cranky** tomorrow. He'll be **moaning** and **groaning** about how his body's killing him.

Andre	You're probably right. Hey, did you have a chance to go to that second-hand snowboard sale you were telling me about?
Min-Jung	I did, but I got there too late. There wasn't very much to choose from by the time I arrived. It's too bad because I could use a new board. This one is **on its last legs**.
Andre	It does look pretty beat up. Is your front binding OK? Something looks **out of whack**.
Min-Jung	I almost broke it last season. I'll have to **make do** until I can afford to buy a new board.
Andre	You'll be lucky if it lasts the day **from the looks of it**. Have you decided what time you're going to leave?
Min-Jung	I'm going to **take off** pretty soon. I promised to meet up with Claudia for dinner tonight. Oh, it's time to get off the chairlift. Are you all set?
Andre	**Hold your horses**. I have to put my gloves on. Which way is it to the 'Widow Maker'?
Min-Jung	**Hang a left** after we get off the chairlift. Why? Are you going to **tag along**?
Andre	Sure. I'll try to **keep up with** you.
Min-Jung	Great! Now I don't have to **kick the bucket** alone.

take a spill (to) *i.* – take a fall
A woman just took a spill on the icy sidewalk in front of that store.

hotdog *n.* – a showoff
Look at the way that guy skates around the rink. He's such a hotdog.

show off (to) *i.* – display one's ability in too proud a manner
My baby brother always shows off whenever company visits our house.

cut someone off (to) *i.* – cross someone's path
I almost fell down when that careless snowboarder cut me off.

smack into someone/something (to) *i.* – crash into someone/something
He smacked into a tree when he lost control of his truck on the corner.

heads up *exclam.* – be alert
Heads up! There's a car coming this way.

take a stab at something (to) *i.* – try something
She's going to take a stab at rock climbing this weekend.

up to doing something *i.* – able to do something, ready to do something
I don't think I'll ever be up to running a marathon.

get in over one's head (to) *i.* – attempt something too difficult
I got in over my head when I took that fourth year chemistry course.

psych someone out (to) *i.* – make someone lose confidence
The tennis player tried to psych out his opponent before the match began.

go for it (to) *i.* – do it, try it
I don't care if it's the most difficult ski run on the mountain. I'm going for it.

under the weather *i.* – ill, sick
My roommate has been under the weather for the past few days.

wipe out (to) *i.* – fall
She wiped out when she tried to turn her bike on the gravel road.

black-and-blue *adj.* – covered in bruises
His face was black-and-blue after he got into a fight at school.

cranky *adj.* – grouchy, grumpy, irritable
He's cranky this morning because he didn't get any sleep last night.

moan (to) *v.* – express pain, groan
She was moaning because she pulled a muscle in her back.

groan (to) *v.* – express pain, moan
The rugby player groaned when three opponents tackled him at the same time.

on its last legs *i.* – almost broken, ready to collapse or fail
Your motorcycle is in terrible condition. I think it's on its last legs.

out of whack *i.* – out of alignment
What's wrong with the front tire on your bike? Something looks out of whack.

make do (to) *i.* – do one's best with something that is sub-standard.
I don't have the proper hammer. I'll just have to make do with this one for now.

from the looks of something *i.* – from the appearance of something
Does this computer still work? It's ready to be replaced from the looks of it.

take off (to) *i.* – get going, hit the road, leave
I think I'm going to take off after we finish eating lunch at the restaurant.

hold your horses (to) *i.* – wait
I'm not ready to leave just yet. Hold your horses.

hang a left/right (to) *i.* – take a left/right
You should go down the street and then hang a left at the bank on the corner.

tag along with someone (to) *i.* – follow someone
Do you mind if I tag along with you and your friends this afternoon?

keep up with someone (to) *i.* – progress at the same speed as someone else
She is a much better runner than I am. I don't think I can keep up with her.

kick the bucket (to) *i.* – die, pass away
I hope I don't kick the bucket when I go skydiving next weekend.

EXERCISE 1

MATCH THE WORD/IDIOM WITH THE CORRECT DEFINITION

_K_	1 hotdog	A	out of alignment
___	2 kick the bucket	B	attempt something too difficult
___	3 black-and-blue	C	wait
___	4 cranky	D	almost broken
___	5 cut someone off	E	take a left
___	6 tag along with someone	F	be alert
___	7 smack into someone	G	sick
___	8 hold your horses	H	covered in bruises
___	9 hang a left	I	leave
___	10 under the weather	J	fall
___	11 wipe out	K	a showoff
___	12 moan	L	from the appearance of it
___	13 take off	M	follow someone
___	14 go for it	N	groan
___	15 heads up	O	make someone lose confidence
___	16 on its last legs	P	crash into someone
___	17 out of whack	Q	cross someone's path
___	18 psych someone out	R	do it
___	19 get in over one's head	S	die
___	20 from the looks of it	T	irritable

EXERCISE 2

USE THE WORDS/IDIOMS BELOW TO COMPLETE
EACH OF THE FOLLOWING SENTENCES.

hold your horses	up to	tagged along
a spill	black-and-blue	in over my head
keeping up with	hotdog	under the weather
make do	kick the bucket	cut me off
took a stab at	psych out	smacked into

1 My sister has been sneezing and coughing all day. She certainly is _____.

2 I'm having a difficult time _____ the other students in my physics class.

3 I got _____ when I took that graduate course in computer programming.

4 The boxer tried to _____ his opponent at the press conference
before the fight.

5 I _____ windsurfing when I was on vacation at the lake last summer.

6 _____! I'll be ready to leave in a few minutes.

7 My sister's legs were _____ after the field hockey game finished.

8 Are you _____ going for a long run with us this morning?

9 I _____ another snowboarder when I lost control on the steep part
of the run.

10 This isn't the right tool for the job, but I suppose I'll have to _____ with it.

11 He just loves it when people watch him ski down the hill. He's such a _____.

12 I _____ with him when he went to the amusement park last night.

13 Can you believe that driver? He doesn't even realize that he _____.

14 She thought she was going to _____ when she went skydiving last summer.

15 This morning I took _____ when I stumbled over a rock on the sidewalk.

EXERCISE 3

COMPLETE THE FOLLOWING CROSSWORD PUZZLE
USING WORDS/IDIOMS FROM THE DIALOGUE.

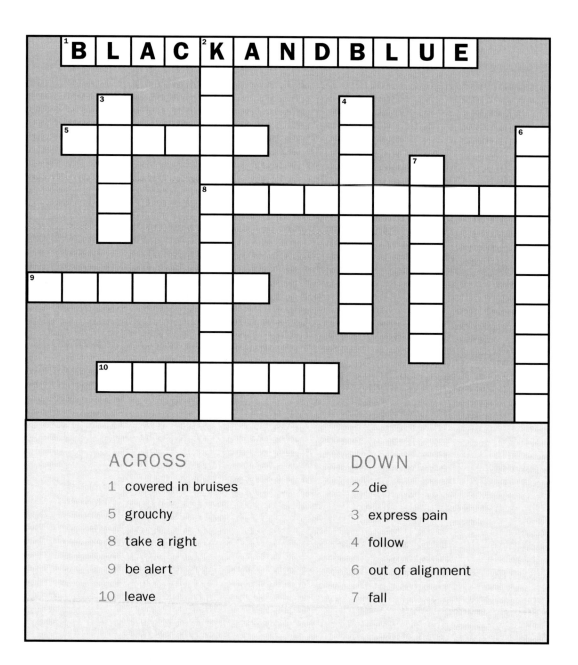

ACROSS

1 covered in bruises

5 grouchy

8 take a right

9 be alert

10 leave

DOWN

2 die

3 express pain

4 follow

6 out of alignment

7 fall

EXERCISE 4

1 He hasn't come to work this week because he's been sick.

   He hasn't come to work this week because he's been under the weather_____.

2 My legs were always covered in bruises when I was a young boy.

   _____.

3 I attempted something too difficult when I enrolled in a fourth year biology class.

   _____.

4 I thought I was going to die when my brakes failed on that steep hill.

   _____.

5 I'm getting dressed as fast as I can. Just wait!

   _____.

6 My friends want to leave now because they want to avoid the rush hour traffic.

   _____.

7 He hit a telephone pole when he lost control of his car on that sharp corner.

   _____.

8 You should go down the alley and then take a left at the next corner.

   _____.

9 She was irritable because her sister kept interrupting her while she was studying.

   _____.

10 My friend always tries to make me lose confidence before we play squash.

   _____.

EXERCISE 5

UNSCRAMBLE THE FOLLOWING SENTENCES, ADDING PUNCTUATION WHEN NEEDED. THE BEGINNING AND END OF EACH SENTENCE HAVE ALREADY BEEN DONE FOR YOU. HINT: IT'S HELPFUL TO IDENTIFY THE WORD/IDIOM FROM THE DIALOGUE IN EACH SENTENCE.

1 **They need to** / away / right / in / take / to / it / make / to / off / the / order / **meeting on time.**

They need to take off right away in order to make it to the meeting on time.

2 **You're going to** / bucket / you / kick / smoking / keep / if / the / on / and / **drinking like that.**

3 **He told me** / along / street / hang / left / the / to / a / and / then / go / at / **the grocery store.**

4 **Our friend is** / she'll / so / the / exam / probably / the / under / miss / midterm / weather / **on Tuesday afternoon.**

5 **I don't think** / up / that / going / a / hike / the / 10-mile / through / for / to / I'm / **wilderness with you.**

6 **Would you mind** / I / along / you / you / the / go / when / if / tagged / with / to / **computer store today?**

7 **I really got** / my / when / took / university / head / over / five / worked / courses / in / and / I / **part-time at night.**

8 **I'm going to** / stab / while / on / with / Hawaii / in / my / a / surfing / at / I'm / take / vacation / **family this summer.**

1	make him lose confidence	p s y c h h i m o(u)t
2	almost broken	_(_) _ _ _ _ _ _ _ _ _ _ _
3	a showoff	_ _ _(_)_ _
4	leave	_ _ _(_) _ _ _
5	wait	_ _ _ _ _ _ _(_) _ _ _ _ _
6	follow	(_)_ _ _ _ _ _ _
7	die	_ _ _ _ _(_)_ _ _ _ _ _ _
8	take a left	_ _ _ _ _ _(_)_ _
9	out of alignment	_ _ _ _ _ (_)_ _ _ _
10	fall	_ _ _(_) _ _ _
11	moan	_ _ _(_)_
12	do it	_ _ _ _ _ _(_)
13	be alert	(_)_ _ _ _ _ _
14	cover in bruises	_ _ _ _ _ - _ _ _ - _ _ _(_)
15	irritable	_(_)_ _ _

16	eepk pu tihw	_ _ _ _ _ _ _ _ _ _
17	aonm	_ _ _ _
18	ldoh oyru sseorh	_ _ _ _ _ _ _ _ _ _ _ _ _
19	keta a tbsa ta	_ _ _ _ _ _ _ _ _ _ _
20	teg ni vero erh edah	_ _ _ _ _ _ _ _ _ _ _ _ _ _ _ _

EXERCISE 7

FILL IN THE WORDS/IDIOMS THAT ARE
MISSING FROM THE DIALOGUE.

Min-Jung is waiting for Andre in the line-up for the chairlift

Min-Jung   What kept you?

Andre   Sorry, I t_____ a s_____ half way down the run. It took me a little while to recover from it.

Min-Jung   How'd it happen? You're such a h_____. Were you s_____ off again?

Andre   Not a chance. Some crazy skier c_____ me o_____. He didn't even realize that he made me lose control to avoid s_____ i_____ him.

Min-Jung   H_____ u_____. We're next for the chairlift. Here we go.

They get on the chairlift and head up the hill

Andre   What run will you try next?

Min-Jung   I think I'll t_____ a s_____ at the 'Widow Maker'.

Andre   Are you certain you're u_____ t_____ it? That's a tough run. You might be getting in o_____ your h_____.

Min-Jung   Don't p_____ me o_____ now. Every once in a while I have to take on a new challenge. I'm g_____ f_____ it. Have you seen Jose on the slopes today?

Andre   Yeah I have. I was surprised to see him because he was u_____ the w_____ on Thursday. I think it's his first time snowboarding. I'll say this; he sure is fearless.

Min-Jung   No kidding. I saw him w_____ o_____ a couple of times. The guy's going to be b_____-and-b_____. I bet he's really c_____ tomorrow. He'll be m_____ and g_____ about how his body's killing him.

Andre	You're probably right. Hey, did you have a chance to go to that second-hand snowboard sale you were telling me about?
Min-Jung	I did, but I got there too late. There wasn't very much to choose from by the time I arrived. It's too bad because I could use a new board. This one is o_____ its last l_____.
Andre	It does look pretty beat up. Is your front binding OK? Something looks o_____ of w_____.
Min-Jung	I almost broke it last season. I'll have to m_____ d_____ until I can afford to buy a new board.
Andre	You'll be lucky if it lasts the day f_____ the l_____ of it. Have you decided what time you're going to leave?
Min-Jung	I'm going to t_____ o_____ pretty soon. I promised to meet up with Claudia for dinner tonight. Oh, it's time to get off the chairlift. Are you all set?
Andre	H_____ your h_____. I have to put my gloves on. Which way is it to the 'Widow Maker'?
Min-Jung	H_____ a l_____ after we get off the chairlift. Why? Are you going to t_____ a_____?
Andre	Sure. I'll try to k_____ u_____ with you.
Min-Jung	Great! Now I don't have to k_____ the b_____ alone.

COMPREHENSION QUESTIONS

TRY TO ANSWER THE FOLLOWING QUESTIONS WITHOUT LOOKING AT THE DIALOGUE. ONCE YOU'VE FINISHED THE QUESTIONS, YOU CAN REFER TO THE DIALOGUE TO CHECK YOUR ANSWERS.

1   Where was Min-Jung waiting for Andre?

2   What happened to Andre on the last run?

3   What run will Min-Jung take a stab at next?

4   Why did Andre say, "You might be getting in over your head"?

5   Has Andre seen Jose on the slopes today? Why was he surprised to see him?

6   Was Jose an experienced snowboarder?

7   Was Jose an aggressive or timid snowboarder?

8   Why will Jose be moaning and groaning tomorrow?

9   Why couldn't Min-Jung buy a board at the used snowboard sale she went to?

10 Describe the condition of the board Min-Jung was using.

11 What was wrong with her front binding?

12 Why will Min-Jung leave soon?

13 Which way is it to the 'Widow Maker' after getting off the chairlift?

14 Will Min-Jung go down the 'Widow Maker' by herself?

15 Why did Min-Jung say, "Now I don't have to kick the bucket alone"?

DISCUSSION QUESTIONS

DISCUSS THE FOLLOWING QUESTIONS WITH YOUR PARTNER.

PART A: General Discussion Questions

1 Have you ever been to a ski resort? Tell me about it.

2 Can you ski and/or snowboard? Which do you prefer to do?

3 Is skiing or snowboarding more popular in your country?

4 How much money do you think you'd have to spend to buy all the equipment needed to ski/snowboard?

5 What other kinds of winter sports have you participated in?

PART B: Idiomatic Discussion Questions

1 What have you always wanted to **take a stab at**, but never got around to doing?

2 If you could **tag along** with someone famous for one day, what celebrity would you pick?

3 Have you ever **gotten in over your head**? Give an example from school, work or sports.

4 Did you ever **show off** as a child? What were you so proud of?

5 Have you been **under the weather** while living here? What were your symptoms? How long did it take to get over your cold? What kind of medication did you take?

6 What makes you **cranky**? Give three examples.

7 Tell me about the last time you **wiped out**. Did you hurt yourself? Did anyone see you do it?

GIVE IT A SHOT

SNOWBOARDERS OFTEN USE SLANG FROM THE LIST BELOW.
HOW MUCH OF THE FOLLOWING SLANG HAVE YOU HEARD
WHILE SNOWBOARDING?

Chatter the noise made from a vibrating board at high speed
Corduroy the finely grooved ridges left on a run after it's been groomed
Goofy a boarder who rides with his right foot forward
Lame bad, poor
Fat/Phat exceptional, great
Poseur a person with the best equipment who pretends to snowboard very well
Regular a boarder who rides with his left foot forward
Rolling down the windows rotating your arms wildly when off balance
Session a period of time spent snowboarding
Sick exceptional, great
Stick Snowboard
Stoked excited, psyched up

Use the slang from the list above to complete the following sentences.

1   When I was renting a board, they asked me if I was regular or _____.

2   My old board was so _____ that I had to buy a new one.

3   That guy with all the nice equipment can't snowboard. He's such a _____.

4   It's sunny today and there's lots of fresh powder. I'm so _____.

5   I lost control when I was making a turn because my board started to _____.

6   The design of your new Burton snowboard is great. It's so p_____.

7   The conditions were perfect today. We had a great _____.

8   When did you get those new Oakley goggles? I like them. They're s_____.

9   I had to buy a new _____ because my old board was falling apart.

10   I learned how to snowboard with my left foot forward. I'm _____.

11   Let's take this run because it has lots of _____.

12   You looked so funny just before you wiped out. You were really r_____.

■■ CHAPTER SIXTEEN ■■

RETURNING HOME

RETURNING HOME

Andre is talking to Jose in front of the school

Jose   Are you more or less ready for tomorrow?

Andre   Well, I suppose so. I've bought most of the souvenirs I need and I finished packing last night. Man, have I ever got **a ton** of stuff to take back with me. I **dread lugging** it all the way home.

Jose   Are you **heading** straight back to Switzerland or are you going to travel around a bit before you return?

Andre   I'm going to Florida for ten days before I fly home.

Jose   It'll be nice to escape the cold weather for a while. Do you have some friends or family there?

Andre   Actually not. I'll be **living out of my suitcase** while I'm **knocking around** the Sunshine State.

Jose   Are you **looking forward to** getting back to Geneva?

Andre   I'm a little bit worried about it. I think at first I'll **feel out of place**. After being away for so long, it's kind of like **going back to square one**. I'm a little jealous of the classmates that I went to school with because most of them have already found jobs. It'll probably take me a while to **get the ball rolling**.

Jose   Just **bide your time**. I'm sure if you're patient, a job that's in your field will **turn up** eventually. What about that new computer company that you said was hiring a lot of workers?

Andre   I may have **missed the boat** on that. They stop interviewing this week. I doubt if they'll still be hiring by the time I get home. It's too bad really; I was hoping to **get in on the ground floor**.

Jose   Will your parents help you out until you **get back on your feet**?

Andre   They'll **foot the bill** if I go to graduate school in the States, but other than that
        I'll have to **pay my own way**. To tell the truth, I'm really stressed out about the
        whole situation.

Jose   Don't let it **weigh on your mind** right now. You should enjoy your trip to Florida.
        You can worry about the future once you get back to Switzerland.

Andre   I suppose you're right. I shouldn't let it **get me down**.

Jose   When you finally get home do you think you'll get back together with your **old
        flame**? From what you said before, it sounded like you two were pretty serious
        at one time.

Andre   We were at one point, but then we just kind of drifted apart. I have a feeling that
        she'll **give me the cold shoulder** the next time we **cross paths**.

Jose   I guess only time will tell.

Andre   Did I mention that Hans is throwing me a **bon voyage party** at the
        apartment tonight?

Jose   No you didn't. What time does it **get underway**?

Andre   At 7:30 **sharp**. Will you be able to **swing by**?

Jose   Sure. I **wouldn't miss it for the world**.

ton (a) *n.* – a bunch, a load, a lot, a pile, a stack
I can't go out with you tonight because I have to do a ton of homework.

dread doing something (to) *v.* – fear doing something in the future
I always dreaded going to the dentist when I was a child.

lug something (to) *v.* – carry something heavy
He had to lug two heavy suitcases from one side of the airport to the other.

head somewhere (to) *v.* – go somewhere
It's getting late. I think I'm going to head home now.

live of out of one's suitcase (to) *i.* – stay in different places briefly, never unpacking
She lived out of her suitcase while she was traveling around Europe.

knock around somewhere (to) *i.* – travel around somewhere
He wants to spend about two weeks knocking around southern California.

look forward to doing something (to) *i.* – excited about doing something in the future
She's looking forward to seeing you at the baseball game on Saturday.

feel out of place (to) *i.* – feel uncomfortable somewhere
I didn't have a good time at the party because I felt out of place.

go back to square one (to) *i.* – return to the beginning, start over
He had to go back to square one after he lost his job at the assembly plant.

get the ball rolling (to) *i.* – get the process going
I'm certain my business plan will be a success if I can just get the ball rolling.

bide one's time (to) *i.* – wait patiently
Just bide your time. I'm sure you'll find a job after you graduate from business school.

turn up (to) *i.* – show up
Only a few students turned up for the lecture this afternoon.

miss the boat (to) *i.* – miss an opportunity or chance
She really missed the boat when she didn't go for an interview at that company.

get in on the ground floor (to) *i.* – get involved with something at the start
If you want to make money on that stock, you should get in on the ground floor.

get back on one's feet (to) *i.* – become independent again
It took him a while to get back on his feet after the car accident.

foot the bill (to) *i.* – pay the bill
My parents will foot the bill if I decide to go to college next year.

pay one's own way (to) *i.* – pay for something yourself
I'm going to pay my own way when I go to university next year.

weigh on one's mind (to) *i.* – worry someone
Tomorrow's final exam is weighing on my mind.

get someone down (to) *i.* – depress someone
That movie had a depressing ending. It really got me down.

old flame *i.* – ex-lover
I saw my old flame when I went to the mall on Sunday afternoon.

give someone the cold shoulder (to) *i.* – ignore someone
She was angry at her boyfriend, so she gave him the cold shoulder.

cross paths (to) *i.* – meet by chance, run into someone
I don't think we'll ever cross paths again.

bon voyage party *n.* – farewell party
My friends are throwing me a bon voyage party at the apartment tonight.

get underway (to) *i.* – get started
Do you know what time the rock concert gets underway?

sharp *adv.* – exactly, on the dot
I'll meet you in front of the movie theater at 7:00 sharp.

swing by somewhere (to) *i.* – stop by somewhere, visit somewhere
She's going to swing by the apartment after she gets off work.

wouldn't miss something for the world *i.* – would never miss something
I wouldn't miss your graduation ceremony for the world.

EXERCISE 1

MATCH THE WORD/IDIOM WITH THE CORRECT DEFINITION

M	1 dread doing something	A	miss an opportunity
___	2 bide one's time	B	depress someone
___	3 miss the boat	C	feel uncomfortable somewhere
___	4 old flame	D	would never miss something
___	5 give someone the cold shoulder	E	wait patiently
___	6 swing by somewhere	F	farewell party
___	7 get someone down	G	a lot of something
___	8 sharp	H	pay the bill
___	9 wouldn't miss it for the world	I	meet by chance
___	10 feel out of place	J	ignore someone
___	11 turn up	K	start over
___	12 cross paths	L	travel around somewhere
___	13 weigh on one's mind	M	fear doing something
___	14 foot the bill	N	show up
___	15 bon voyage party	O	stop by somewhere
___	16 knock around somewhere	P	carry something heavy
___	17 look forward to doing something	Q	worry someone
___	18 a ton of something	R	exactly
___	19 lug something	S	excited about doing something
___	20 go back to square one	T	ex-lover

EXERCISE 2

USE THE WORDS/IDIOMS BELOW TO COMPLETE
EACH OF THE FOLLOWING SENTENCES.

back to square one	felt out of place	lug
living out of my suitcase	the ground floor	get the ball rolling
ton of	swung by	underway
the cold shoulder	sharp	bon voyage party
looking forward to	old flame	head

1 I'll be _____ while I'm traveling around the southern part of Italy.

2 It will take a while for me to _____ after I return to my hometown.

3 They went _____ after their house was destroyed in the hurricane.

4 She made a lot of money on that stock because she got in on _____.

5 What time does the surprise party for your best friend get _____?

6 I have to do a _____ work at the office before I go home today.

7 My suitcase is very heavy. Could you please help me _____ it out to the car?

8 I was uncomfortable at my new job because nobody spoke to me. I _____.

9 She was surprised when her family threw a _____ for her last night.

10 My girlfriend was so angry at me that she gave me _____ at lunchtime.

11 She was really surprised when her _____ suddenly called one day last week.

12 I'm _____ having dinner with that attractive woman from work.

13 Don't be late. I'll meet you in front of the subway station at 6:00 _____.

14 I think we should _____ over to my brother's house before it gets too late.

15 I _____ his place on my way to the stadium earlier this afternoon.

EXERCISE 3

WHAT WORD/IDIOM FROM THE DIALOGUE MATCHES THE FOLLOWING DEFINITIONS? WHEN THE EXERCISE HAS BEEN COMPLETED, THE IDIOM FOR 'GET THE PROCESS GOING' WILL BE SPELLED VERTICALLY.

1	stop by	s w i n(g) b y
2	depress her	_ _ _ _(_)_ _ _ _ _
3	meet by chance	_ _ _ _ _ _ _(_)_ _
4	feel uncomfortable	_ _ _ _ _ _(_) _ _ _ _ _ _ _
5	go	(_)_ _ _
6	farewell party	_ _ _ _ _ _ _(_) _ _ _ _ _
7	pay the bill	_ _ _ _ _ _ _ (_)_ _ _
8	exactly	_ _(_)_ _
9	excited about the future	(_)_ _ _ _ _ _ _ _ _ _ _
10	ignore him	_ _ _ _ _ _ _ _ _ _ _ _(_)_ _ _ _ _ _ _ _ _
11	show up	_ _(_)_ _ _
12	start over	_ _ _ _ _ _ _(_) _ _ _ _ _ _ _ _ _
13	carry something heavy	(_)_ _
14	ex-lover	_ _ _ _(_)_ _ _
15	miss an opportunity	_(_)_ _ _ _ _ _ _ _ _
16	travel around	_ _ _ _ _ _ _ _(_)_
17	get started	(_)_ _ _ _ _ _ _ _ _ _

Unscramble the following words/idioms from the dialogue.

18	rddea	_ _ _ _ _
19	teg imh wdon	_ _ _ _ _ _ _ _ _ _
20	yap ym now ayw	_ _ _ _ _ _ _ _ _ _ _
21	ewihg no ish nmid	_ _ _ _ _ _ _ _ _ _ _ _ _
22	elvi uto fo shi uisacset	_ _ _ _ _ _ _ _ _ _ _ _ _ _ _ _ _ _ _

EXERCISE 4

REWRITE THE FOLLOWING SENTENCES USING A WORD/IDIOM FROM THE DIALOGUE.

1 She's going to travel around Europe after she graduates from university.

   <u>She's going to knock around Europe after she graduates from university</u> .

2 I felt uncomfortable when I first started working for that high-tech company.

   _____ .

3 The city tour starts at 9 o'clock in the morning in front of the hotel.

   _____ .

4 I'm sure that if you wait patiently, another job opportunity will come along.

   _____ .

5 I had to carry four heavy bags of groceries all the way home from the market.

   _____ .

6 My ex-lover slapped me in the face when she saw me at the movies with another girl.

   _____ .

7 She said that she'd visit the office right after the meeting finishes.

   _____ .

8 I missed a great opportunity when I chose not to invest money in that company.

   _____ .

9 The bad weather we've had recently is really depressing me.

   _____ .

10 Even though we both live in the same town, we rarely meet each other by chance.

   _____ .

EXERCISE 5

UNSCRAMBLE THE FOLLOWING SENTENCES, ADDING PUNCTUATION WHEN NEEDED. THE
BEGINNING AND END OF EACH SENTENCE HAVE ALREADY BEEN DONE FOR YOU. HINT:
IT'S HELPFUL TO IDENTIFY THE WORD/IDIOM FROM THE DIALOGUE IN EACH SENTENCE.

1 **My parents will** / the / bill / I / university / in / to / foot / go / when / **California next year.**

   My parents will foot the bill when I go to university in California next year   .

2 **I went home** / felt / because / of / at / early / I / so / place / out / **that posh restaurant.**

   _____.

3 **My family is** / looking / to / really / you / come / when / meeting / forward / they / **to New York.**

   _____.

4 **My co-worker gave** / cold / when / ran / him / me / the / on / into / shoulder / I / **the street today.**

   _____.

5 **I spent three** / knocking / Asia / weeks / I / my / before / around / final / started / **year of university.**

   _____.

6 **He had to** / back / square / after / dropped / college / go / one / to / of / out / he / in /
   his first year.

   _____.

7 **My friend helped** / my / across / parking / and / me / suitcases / lug / the / lot / **into the airport.**

   _____.

8 **I have not** / him / crossed / though / both / and / in / work / paths / live / we / even / with /
   the same city.

   _____.

EXERCISE 6

FIND THE WORDS/IDIOMS LISTED BELOW
IN THE WORD SEARCH GAME.

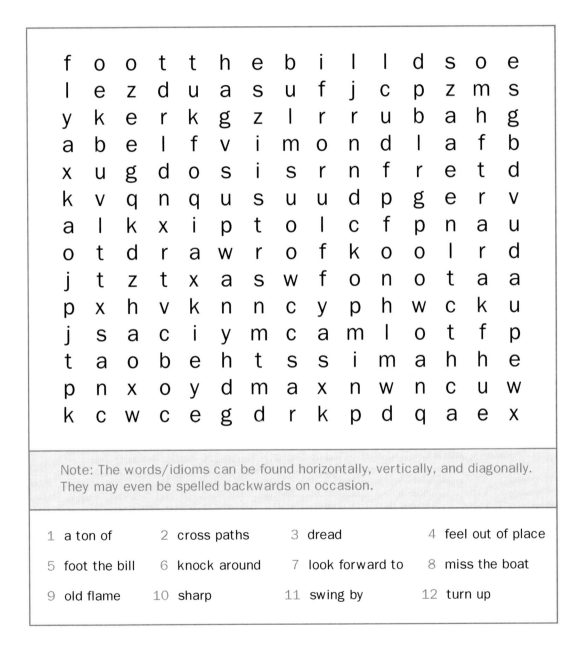

```
f  o  o  t  t  h  e  b  i  l  l  d  s  o  e
l  e  z  d  u  a  s  u  f  j  c  p  z  m  s
y  k  e  r  k  g  z  l  r  r  u  b  a  h  g
a  b  e  l  f  v  i  m  o  n  d  l  a  f  b
x  u  g  d  o  s  i  s  r  n  f  r  e  t  d
k  v  q  n  q  u  s  u  u  d  p  g  e  r  v
a  l  k  x  i  p  t  o  l  c  f  p  n  a  u
o  t  d  r  a  w  r  o  f  k  o  o  l  r  d
j  t  z  t  x  a  s  w  f  o  n  o  t  a  a
p  x  h  v  k  n  n  c  y  p  h  w  c  k  u
j  s  a  c  i  y  m  c  a  m  l  o  t  f  p
t  a  o  b  e  h  t  s  s  i  m  a  h  h  e
p  n  x  o  y  d  m  a  x  n  w  n  c  u  w
k  c  w  c  e  g  d  r  k  p  d  q  a  e  x
```

Note: The words/idioms can be found horizontally, vertically, and diagonally.
They may even be spelled backwards on occasion.

1 a ton of	2 cross paths	3 dread	4 feel out of place
5 foot the bill	6 knock around	7 look forward to	8 miss the boat
9 old flame	10 sharp	11 swing by	12 turn up

EXERCISE 7

Andre is talking to Jose in front of the school

Jose   Are you more or less ready for tomorrow?

Andre   Well, I suppose so. I've bought most of the souvenirs I need and I finished packing last night. Man, have I ever got a t_____ of stuff to take back with me. I d_____ I_____ it all the way home.

Jose   Are you h_____ straight back to Switzerland or are you going to travel around a bit before you return?

Andre   I'm going to Florida for ten days before I fly home.

Jose   It'll be nice to escape the cold weather for a while. Do you have some friends or family there?

Andre   Actually not. I'll be I_____ out of my s_____ while I'm k_____ around the Sunshine State.

Jose   Are you I_____ f_____ to getting back to Geneva?

Andre   I'm a little bit worried about it. I think at first I'll feel o_____ of p_____. After being away for so long, it's kind of like going b_____ to s_____ one. I'm a little jealous of the classmates that I went to school with because most of them have already found jobs. It'll probably take me a while to get the b_____ r_____.

Jose   Just b_____ your t_____. I'm sure if you're patient, a job that's in your field will t_____ u_____ eventually. What about that new computer company that you said was hiring a lot of workers?

Andre   I may have m_____ the b_____ on that. They stop interviewing this week. I doubt if they'll still be hiring by the time I get home. It's too bad really; I was hoping to get in on the g_____ f_____.

Jose	Will your parents help you out until you get back o_____ your f_____?
Andre	They'll f_____ the b_____ if I go to graduate school in the States, but other than that I'll have to p_____ my own w_____. To tell the truth, I'm really stressed out about the whole situation.
Jose	Don't let it w_____ on your m_____ right now. You should enjoy your trip to Florida. You can worry about the future once you get back to Switzerland.
Andre	I suppose you're right. I shouldn't let it g_____ me d_____.
Jose	When you finally get home do you think you'll get back together with your o_____ f_____? From what you said before, it sounded like you two were pretty serious at one time.
Andre	We were at one point, but then we just kind of drifted apart. I have a feeling that she'll give me the c_____ s_____ the next time we c_____ p_____.
Jose	I guess only time will tell.
Andre	Did I mention that Hans is throwing me a b_____ v_____ party at the apartment tonight?
Jose	No you didn't. What time does it get u_____?
Andre	At 7:30 s_____. Will you be able to s_____ b_____?
Jose	Sure. I wouldn't m_____ it for the w_____.

COMPREHENSION QUESTIONS

TRY TO ANSWER THE FOLLOWING QUESTIONS WITHOUT LOOKING AT THE DIALOGUE. ONCE YOU'VE FINISHED THE QUESTIONS, YOU CAN REFER TO THE DIALOGUE TO CHECK YOUR ANSWERS.

1. Where was Andre talking to Jose?

2. What did Andre finish doing last night?

3. What does Andre dread doing?

4. Does Andre know anyone in the Sunshine State?

5. How does Andre think he'll feel once he returns to Switzerland?

6. Who was Andre jealous of? Why?

7. What kind of company was Andre interested in working for?

8. Why has he probably missed the boat on that opportunity?

9. Will Andre's parents help him out when he returns home?

10. What did Andre mean when he said, "I shouldn't let it get me down"?

11. Do you think Andre will get back together with his old flame?

12. What does Andre think will happen the next time he runs into his ex-girlfriend?

13. What's happening tonight?

14. What time does it get underway?

15. Will Jose be able to swing by?

DISCUSSION QUESTIONS

DISCUSS THE FOLLOWING QUESTIONS WITH YOUR PARTNER.

PART A: General Discussion Questions

1 Will you go directly back to your country after you finish school? If not, what will you do?

2 Do you plan on having a farewell party before you return to your country?

3 What will you miss about studying English here?

4 How do you think you'll feel once you get back to your hometown?

5 What is the first thing you want to do once you return home?

PART B: Idiomatic Discussion Questions

1 Did you **feel out of place** when you first arrived here? How long did it take until you felt at home?

2 What do you **dread** doing once you return to your country? What do you **look forward to** doing?

3 When you return home will you **go back to square one**? pick up right where you left off?

4 Have you **missed the boat** on anything while you've been away from your country?

5 Do you have an **old flame** in your hometown? What do you think will happen if you run into him/her?

6 Who was the last person to **give you the cold shoulder**? Why did they do it?

7 If you could spend a summer **knocking around** any country in the world, where would you go? Why?

GIVE IT A SHOT

IN THE DIALOGUE, ANDRE SAYS THAT HE'S GOING TO TRAVEL AROUND THE SUNSHINE STATE BEFORE HE RETURNS HOME. ARE YOU FAMILIAR WITH ANY OTHER STATE NICKNAMES? TRY TO MATCH UP THE FOLLOWING STATES WITH THE CORRECT NICKNAME.

PART A

_D_	1 Alaska	A	Golden State
___	2 Arizona	B	Peach State
___	3 California	C	Aloha State
___	4 Florida	D	Land of the Midnight Sun
___	5 Georgia	E	Sunshine State
___	6 Hawaii	F	Wolverine State
___	7 Kentucky	G	Grand Canyon State
___	8 Michigan	H	Bluegrass State

PART B

_B_	1 Nebraska	A	Evergreen State
___	2 Nevada	B	Cornhusker State
___	3 New Mexico	C	Empire State
___	4 New York	D	Land of Enchantment
___	5 Washington	E	Mount Rushmore State
___	6 Oregon	F	Lone Star State
___	7 South Dakota	G	Beaver State
___	8 Texas	H	Silver State

▪▪ RELATED WEBSITES ▪▪

RELATED WEBSITES

CHAPTER 1   ARRIVING IN THE COUNTRY

Airport Information:
http://www.worldairportguide.com/airport/
http://www.traveljam.com/tools.htm
http://www.airlineandairportlinks.com/

Currency Converters:
http://www.xe.com/ucc/
http://www.oanda.com/convert/classic

World Clock - Time Zones:
http://www.timeanddate.com/worldclock/

Local Weather Forecasts:
http://weather.wn.com/

International Telephone Directory:
http://www.anywho.com/

CHAPTER 2   WANDERING AROUND THE CITY

City Guides (International):
http://www.wordtravels.com/Cities/

City Guides (USA):
http://www.onlinecityguide.com/

City Guides (Canada):
http://www.canada.com/cityguides/index.html

Restaurant Guides (USA):
http://www.dine.com/
http://www.dinesite.com/

Restaurant Guides (Canada):
http://www.restaurant.ca/

CHAPTER 3   SITTING IN THE STUDENT LOUNGE

n/a

CHAPTER 4   ATTENDING A TOEFL CLASS

TOEFL Information:
http://www.toefl.org/
http://www.toeflden.com/
http://www.stuff.co.uk/toefl.htm

Colleges/Universities (USA):
http://www.campustours.com/

Colleges/Universities (Canada):
http://www.univsource.com/canadaregion.htm

CHAPTER 5   EATING DINNER WITH A ROOMMATE

Easy Recipes For Students:
http://www.yumyum.com/student/

Gourmet Recipes:
http://www.recipesource.com/
http://www.cooksrecipes.com/
http://www.epicurious.com/
http://www.marthastewart.com/

Vegetarian Recipes:
http://www.vrg.org/recipes/
http://vegweb.com/

CHAPTER 6   SHOPPING FOR CLOTHES IN A MALL

Outlet Malls:
http://www.outletsonline.com/
http://www.outletbound.com/
http://www.mallseeker.com/
http://www.outlet-stores.us/

CHAPTER 7   PICKING UP A FRIEND AT THE AIRPORT

Airline Toll-Free Numbers:
http://www.tollfreeairline.com/

World Clock - Time Zones:
http://www.timeanddate.com/worldclock/

Airport Information:
http://www.worldairportguide.com/airport/
http://www.traveljam.com/tools.htm
http://www.airlineandairportlinks.com/

CHAPTER 8   SUNTANNING ON THE BEACH

Best Beaches (USA):
http://www.petrix.com/beaches
http://www.americasbestonline.net/beaches.htm

Skin Cancer Prevention:
http://www.skincancerfacts.org.uk/

RELATED WEBSITES

CHAPTER 9   WAITING FOR A FIREWORKS SHOW

Fireworks Event Calendar:
http://www.fireworksguide.com/

Fireworks Safety:
http://www.fireworksafety.com/

How Fireworks Work:
http://www.howstuffworks.com/fireworks.htm

The History of Fireworks:
http://www.pyrouniverse.com/history.htm

CHAPTER 10   WORKING OUT AT A FITNESS CLUB

YMCA/YWCA (USA):
http://www.ymca.net/
http://www.ywca.org/

YMCA/YWCA (Canada):
http://www.ymca.ca/
http://www.ywcacanada.ca/

CHAPTER 11   DRINKING IN A NEIGHBORHOOD BAR

Neighborhood Bars (North America):
http://www.pubcrawler.com/
http://www.realbeer.com/destinations/

Neighborhood Bars (USA):
http://www.allaboutbeer.com/brewpubs/

Neighborhood Bars (Canada):
http://www.realbeer.com/canada/

Support Group:
http://www.aa.org/

CHAPTER 12   CATCHING A MOVIE

General Movie Information:
http://www.imdb.com/
http://www.hollywood.com/
http://movies.com/

Movie Times and Locations:
http://www.moviefone.com/
http://www.fandango.com/

Academy Awards:
http://www.oscars.org/index.html

Sundance Film Festival:
http://www.sundance.org/

Independent And Art House Theaters:
http://www.indiefilmpage.com/theaters.html

IMAX Show Times and Locations:
http://www.imax.com/

CHAPTER 13   DRIVING TO A CABIN FOR THE WEEKEND

National Highway Traffic Safety Administration:
http://www.nhtsa.dot.gov/

Driving Maps (North America):
http://www.mapquest.com/
http://www.maps.expedia.com/

National Parks (USA):
http://www.nps.gov/
http://www.us-national-parks.net/

National Parks (Canada):
http://www.canadianparks.com/
http://www.parkscanada.gc.ca/index_e.asp

Youth Hostels:
http://www.hihostels.com/

Bed and Breakfast Inns:
http://www.iloveinns.com/

Hotels:
http://www.hotels.com/
http://www.all-hotels.com/
http://hotelguide.net/
http://www.orbitz.com/
http://www.historichotels.org/

CHAPTER 14   FINISHING CLASSES

Find another ESL School:
http://www.eslbase.com/schools/
http://www.esl-guide.com/
http://www.studyusa.com/
http://www.esldirectory.com/

RELATED WEBSITES

THE FOLLOWING WEBSITES HAVE INFORMATION RELATED TO THE TOPICS COVERED IN EACH OF THE CHAPTERS.
NOTE: THE AUTHOR IS NOT RESPONSIBLE FOR THE CONTENT FOUND ON THE WEBSITES LISTED BELOW.

CHAPTER 15   SNOWBOARDING AT A WINTER RESORT

General Ski/Snowboard Information:
http://www.skinet.com/
http://www.snowboarding.com/

Find A Ski Resort:
http://www.ski-guide.com/

Resort Weather And Snow Conditions:
http://www.snocountry.com/main.php

Skis/Snowboards/Boots/Bindings/Clothing/Accessories:
http://www.skisite.com/manuf.cfm

International Ski Federation:
http://www.fis-ski.com/

CHAPTER 16   RETURNING HOME

Book A Flight:
http://www.orbitz.com/
http://travel.excite.com/
http://www.travelocity.com/
http://www.cheaptickets.com/

Airline Toll-Free Numbers:
http://www.tollfreeairline.com/

Airline Safety Records:
http://www.airsafe.com/
http://www.airline-safety-records.com/
http://aviation-safety.net/

World Clock - Time Zones:
http://www.timeanddate.com/worldclock/

Airport Information:
http://www.worldairportguide.com/airport/
http://www.traveljam.com/tools.htm
http://www.airlineandairportlinks.com/

Local Weather Forecasts:
http://weather.wn.com/

Currency Converters:
http://www.xe.com/ucc/
http://www.oanda.com/convert/classic

International Telephone Directory:
http://www.anywho.com/

■■ ANSWER KEY ■■

ANSWER KEY

EXERCISE 1 (Pg. 6)

1	H	6	Q	11	M	16	I
2	E	7	K	12	R	17	D
3	N	8	O	13	G	18	J
4	T	9	B	14	C	19	F
5	A	10	S	15	L	20	P

EXERCISE 2 (Pg. 7)

1	gulped down	6	pinned up against	11	Fill me in
2	stretch my legs	7	pester	12	bombed
3	burst into tears	8	running off at the mouth	13	B.O.
4	dive	9	brat	14	get over
5	jetlag	10	came across	15	safe and sound

EXERCISE 3 (Pg. 8)

ACROSS:

2 come across
4 fill me in
7 at home
9 spoiled
10 jetlag
13 dive

DOWN:

1 safe and sound
3 settle down
5 in no time
6 pester
8 blabber
11 gulp down
12 get over

EXERCISE 4 (Pg. 9)

1	B	5	B	8	B
2	B	6	A	9	B
3	A	7	B	10	A
4	A				

EXERCISE 5 (Pg. 10)

1 **The passenger is** looking forward to stretching his legs when the bus **ride is over.**
2 **She asked him** to be quiet because he had been running off at the **mouth for hours.**
3 **The boy was** pinned up against the window because there were six children in the backseat **of the car.**
4 **My father told** me to settle down when I made too much noise during his **favorite TV program.**
5 **We arrived at** the airport safe and sound even though the plane **had engine trouble.**
6 **The young girl** burst into tears when she saw her brother break her favorite toy **into many pieces.**
7 **He could not** get over the fact that his sister had won a gold medal **at the Olympics.**
8 **The teacher was** appalled to hear the foul language the students were using **in the classroom.**

EXERCISE 6 (Pg. 11)

```
s  z  u  g  n  b  a  r  x  l  f  t  x  h  f
t  c  n  e  h  b  h  e  o  h  a  o  b  v  h
r  t  d  t  a  r  b  a  a  i  v  k  z  u  i
e  d  b  o  p  t  h  p  x  r  e  b  c  x  h
t  u  k  v  p  t  h  r  e  d  p  l  i  d  y
c  o  m  e  a  c  r  o  s  s  g  m  c  s  z
h  a  c  r  l  k  g  e  m  j  t  d  p  g  g
m  q  s  v  l  n  r  v  t  e  a  e  c  z  p
y  x  p  r  i  b  e  i  x  t  v  y  r  s  r
l  s  c  n  w  o  d  p  l  u  g  v  r  z
e  h  f  k  g  k  d  o  o  a  r  d  i  d  l
g  k  u  p  g  h  m  g  z  g  x  z  v  u  n
s  o  d  c  r  x  v  z  p  e  f  k  s  x  r
```

GIVE IT A SHOT (Pg. 16)

Part A

1 G	4 C	7 A
2 D	5 H	8 F
3 I	6 E	9 B

Part B

1 B	4 C	7 A
2 D	5 G	8 F
3 I	6 H	9 E

CHAPTER 2   WANDERING AROUND THE CITY

EXERCISE 1 (Pg. 22)

1 S	6 N	11 A	16 C
2 D	7 R	12 M	17 L
3 K	8 P	13 H	18 I
4 J	9 B	14 Q	19 O
5 T	10 E	15 F	20 G

ANSWER KEY

EXERCISE 2 (Pg. 23)

1 take in the sights
2 check out
3 ran out of
4 a drag
5 like the back of his hand
6 shopping spree
7 a change of pace
8 wrong side of the tracks
9 to wander
10 a bundle
11 a knot in my stomach
12 kick myself
13 kitty-corner
14 Take it from me
15 wiped out

EXERCISE 3 (Pg. 24)

1 a knot in my stomach
2 take in the sights
3 check out
4 wipe out
5 a drag
6 a shopping spree
7 run up a bill
8 cover a lot of ground
9 stroll
10 kitty-corner
11 a bundle
12 take a break
13 run out of
14 as far as I know
15 play it safe
16 a change of pace
17 wander
18 down-and-out
19 a bundle of nerves
20 off the beaten path
21 in check
22 know like the back of my hand
23 kick myself
24 knows his way around
25 take it from me
26 cover a lot of ground

EXERCISE 4 (Pg. 25)

1 **As far as I know**, the park is four blocks down the street and on the right.
2 I'd like to **take in the sights** as soon as we finish breakfast this morning.
3 I had **a knot in my stomach** when I saw my ex-girlfriend on the street.
4 The tidal wave completely **wiped out** the small fishing village 20 miles down the coast.
5 **Check out** that handsome guy standing in front of the vending machine.
6 I spent **a bundle** on that state-of-the-art computer I bought yesterday.
7 The store you're looking for is **kitty-corner** to the gas station in the next block.
8 They might get into trouble if they end up **on the wrong side of the tracks**.
9 That subject is such **a drag** that I'm considering changing classes.
10 We can't make pancakes this morning because we've **run out of milk**.

EXERCISE 5 (Pg. 26)

1 **I think it's** too late to walk home from here, so let's play it safe and **take a taxi**.
2 **I'm going to** take in the sights while my wife goes scuba diving in the ocean **with her friend**.
3 **She had a** knot in her stomach when she had to give a speech in front **of 200 people**.
4 **I don't really** know my way around this city yet because I've only been here **for two days**.
5 **The muscular sprinter** was a bundle of nerves before the 100-meter final at **the track meet**.
6 **She exceeded her** credit card limit when she went on a three-day shopping spree **in New York**.
7 **The elderly couple** strolled through the colorful flower garden on a **sunny Friday afternoon**.
8 **The group of** boys got nervous when they ended up on the wrong side of the tracks **late at night**.

EXERCISE 6 (Pg. 27)

```
c  x  r  u  n  o  u  t  o  f  y  m  o  y  p
h  n  i  b  q  j  u  a  z  x  z  s  o  k  k
a  g  h  q  j  o  n  k  q  p  f  n  p  c  w
n  n  j  z  e  b  v  e  l  d  n  u  b  e  u
g  h  s  p  o  i  c  a  x  q  d  q  w  h  c
e  h  i  n  l  c  y  b  b  e  f  x  l  c  t
o  w  a  u  k  i  h  r  y  w  v  l  i  n  e
f  g  u  j  t  f  l  e  s  y  m  k  c  i  k
p  z  t  s  d  l  k  a  c  q  z  i  g  b  b
a  f  a  i  o  u  h  k  w  k  f  k  j  r  t
c  f  c  r  e  d  n  a  w  w  o  a  c  f  p
e  t  t  n  n  q  g  o  p  t  u  t  u  c
y  s  x  a  s  m  b  v  d  l  i  b  t  k  d
```

GIVE IT A SHOT (Pg. 32)

1 strolled
2 sneaked
3 staggered
4 limped
5 strutted
6 marched
7 stumbled
8 toddled
9 swaggered
10 stomped

CHAPTER 3   SITTING IN THE STUDENT LOUNGE

EXERCISE 1 (Pg. 38)

1	K	6	H	11	N	16	D
2	P	7	S	12	Q	17	G
3	O	8	C	13	F	18	M
4	R	9	E	14	A	19	I
5	B	10	T	15	J	20	L

EXERCISE 2 (Pg. 39)

1	cream of the crop	6	crushed	11	his days are numbered
2	slacked off	7	young at heart	12	run
3	slated for	8	run a few errands	13	hook up with
4	two's company, three's a crowd	9	cram	14	sleep on it
5	made a fuss	10	up to	15	lose any sleep over it

EXERCISE 3 (Pg. 40)

ACROSS:

4 knuckle down
6 up to
9 cream of the crop
10 cram

DOWN:

1 run of the mill
2 slated for
3 young at heart
5 hook up with
7 slack off
8 crushed

EXERCISE 4 (Pg. 41)

1	A	5	A	9	B
2	B	6	B	10	B
3	A	7	A		
4	B	8	A		

EXERCISE 5 (Pg. 42)

1 **His days are** numbered because he's been late for work **too many times.**
2 **I have to** run a few errands this afternoon, so I probably won't be **back until 5:00.**
3 **The young man** made a fuss when the store wouldn't let him **return the computer.**
4 **My father is** still young at heart even though he just celebrated **his 70th birthday.**
5 **I'll be sure** to keep my fingers crossed when you go for an interview with **that new company.**
6 **We're going to** hook up with our friends at the café that's across the **street from here.**
7 **I'm going to** have to knuckle down soon, or I could fail the math **course I'm taking.**
8 **My younger sister** is stressed out because she has been spending too much **time at work.**

EXERCISE 6 (Pg. 43)

1	run of the mill	9	young at heart	17	lose sleep over
2	hitch	10	make a fuss over	18	keep her fingers crossed
3	a pile of	11	up to	19	run of the mill
4	cram	12	crushed	20	run some errands
5	stressed out	13	getting on	21	hook up with
6	knuckle down	14	slack off	22	make a fuss over
7	slated for	15	run		
8	his days are numbered	16	hook up with		

EXERCISE 1 (Pg. 54)

1	D	6	T	11	O	16	L
2	H	7	E	12	S	17	C
3	R	8	K	13	F	18	N
4	A	9	P	14	Q	19	J
5	M	10	B	15	G	20	I

EXERCISE 2 (Pg. 55)

1 has it in for
2 on the tip on my tongue
3 go over
4 weight off my shoulders
5 coming down with
6 made a dent in
7 hung up on
8 chews her out
9 mull it over
10 mind like a steel trap
11 badmouth
12 at the end of his rope
13 vivid
14 hits the books
15 new flame

EXERCISE 3 (Pg. 56)

ACROSS:

2 coming along
5 have it in for
6 cover for
7 new flame
8 surf the net

DOWN:

1 hit the books
2 catch hell
3 run into
4 come up with

EXERCISE 4 (Pg. 57)

1 I was **at the end of my rope** after spending the whole day trying to fix my car.
2 She's going to **go over** her notes at the library before she takes the final exam.
3 I needed some more time to **mull over** the purchase of that brand-new sports car.
4 It was **a weight off his shoulders** when he finally found a job that was in his field.
5 The cop **told off/chewed out/came down hard on** the driver because he had sped through a school zone.
6 He said that he met his **new flame** on a blind date last weekend.
7 That guy always gets high marks at school because he **has a mind/memory like a steel trap**.
8 She was **hung up on** that question because she hadn't listened to the teacher's instructions.
9 I've only **made a dent in** the work I have to do for tomorrow's class.
10 I don't like the way her boyfriend is always **badmouthing** our friends.

EXERCISE 5 (Pg. 58)

1 **It was a** huge weight off my shoulders when I found out that **I wasn't pregnant.**
2 **I have had** it in for him ever since he lied about using my car **without my knowledge.**
3 **I don't like** your new boyfriend because he's always badmouthing my **friends and me.**
4 **I have been** mulling over this decision for a while, but I'm still not sure **what to do.**
5 **The young woman** was hung up on her ex-boyfriend even though he had cheated on **her many times.**
6 **I spent over** three hours surfing the net trying to find more information **for my presentation.**
7 **I'm going to** have to hit the books because I haven't been studying **nearly enough recently.**
8 **The teenaged boy** really caught hell when his father saw him smoking in the park **with his friends.**

EXERCISE 6 (Pg. 59)

```
g  u  h  b  u  c  a  t  c  h  h  e  l  l  i
d  r  t  d  q  t  d  e  m  i  s  v  f  p  r
d  o  i  a  q  u  z  h  t  h  u  l  i  u  o
q  f  w  z  m  o  d  t  s  u  r  q  g  q  k
b  r  p  x  h  w  h  u  s  n  f  z  l  h  h
s  e  u  e  s  e  k  o  m  g  t  h  q  w  e
n  v  e  m  b  h  t  m  u  u  h  e  z  v  o
z  o  m  o  b  c  l  d  l  p  e  f  f  d  a
x  c  o  m  i  n  g  a  l  o  n  g  e  s  p
h  k  c  v  k  t  g  b  o  n  e  f  n  c  x
s  h  k  h  o  s  g  j  v  g  t  a  x  p  h
z  h  e  m  a  l  f  w  e  n  m  k  v  p  s
q  k  v  l  x  u  h  b  r  u  n  i  n  t  o
```

GIVE IT A SHOT (Pg. 64)

1 hit the roof	5 made a fuss	9 teed off
2 furious	6 went ballistic	10 miffed
3 annoyed	7 made a scene	
4 flew off the handle	8 livid	

CHAPTER 5   EATING DINNER WITH A ROOMMATE

EXERCISE 1 (Pg. 70)

1 F	5 L	9 G	13 K	17 D
2 N	6 T	10 R	14 P	18 I
3 A	7 C	11 E	15 Q	19 O
4 S	8 M	12 H	16 J	20 B

EXERCISE 2 (Pg. 71)

1 gives me the creeps
2 chow down
3 on the fritz
4 popped by
5 in the long run
6 jack-of-all-trades
7 thaw out
8 the teacher's good side
9 let her down
10 in mint condtion
11 turned beet red
12 made it from scratch
13 drop in on
14 in the buff
15 let him off the hook

EXERCISE 3 (Pg. 72)

ACROSS:

1 on the fritz
3 come to
5 ripped off
8 in mint condition
10 dough

DOWN:

2 in the long run
3 chow down
4 turn beet red
6 fix lunch
7 in the buff
9 thaw out

EXERCISE 4 (Pg. 73)

1 I'm going to **drop in on** my friend on my way home from the swimming pool.
2 The washing machine has been **on the fritz** ever since you tried to wash those blankets.
3 I just want you to relax. I'm going to **fix dinner** for you tonight.
4 My mother's desserts are always delicious because she **makes them from scratch**.
5 I don't like shopping in that area because the merchants usually **rip me off**.
6 My friends will probably **pop by** the bank before they come here.
7 You're going to have to start **working out** if you want to lose some weight.
8 He **turned beet red** when I told him that his zipper was wide open.
9 She said that I **let her down** when I forgot to water the plants while she was away.
10 I was awfully surprised when I saw that woman suntanning **in the buff** on the beach.

EXERCISE 5 (Pg. 74)

1 **I'd like to** drop in on my friend because I haven't seen her in a **very long time**.
2 **You'll have a** lot more money in the long run if you save a little **bit each month**.
3 **The computer is** on the fritz again, so we'll have to take it to the **repair shop tomorrow**.
4 **I told him** that he was lucky when the professor let him off the hook **for missing class**.
5 **The beautiful antique** table was in mint condition, so I decided to **buy it yesterday**.
6 **My stupid boyfriend** let me down when he didn't show up for our date **on Friday night**.
7 **The big dog** in that yard gives me the creeps because he always **snarls at me**.
8 **I really got** ripped off when I bought this pair of sunglasses at **the mall today**.

EXERCISE 6 (Pg. 75)

1 on me
2 thaw
3 a jack-of-all-trades
4 in the buff
5 in mint condition
6 turn beet red
7 on the fritz
8 drop in on
9 in the long run
10 let him down
11 doesn't look half bad
12 come to
13 rip me off
14 decadent
15 work out
16 the can
17 dough
18 let him off the hook
19 chow down
20 stay on his good side
21 slipped her mind
22 in the buff

GIVE IT A SHOT (Pg. 80)

1 sipping
2 devoured
3 nibbled on
4 downed
5 knocked back
6 nibble on
7 sipped it
8 have
9 wolfed down
10 drank
11 sipped
12 gobbled down

CHAPTER 6   SHOPPING FOR CLOTHES IN A MALL

EXERCISE 1 (Pg. 86)

1 M
2 F
3 P
4 A
5 J
6 T
7 E
8 R
9 G
10 K
11 Q
12 D
13 O
14 I
15 H
16 B
17 S
18 L
19 C
20 N

EXERCISE 2 (Pg. 87)

1 jam-packed
2 take in
3 first thing in the morning
4 long gone
5 cash
6 mark down
7 shot his mouth off at
8 had her name on it
9 shell out
10 full of herself
11 hit the spot
12 a last resort
13 dressed to the nines
14 clashes
15 Get a load of

EXERCISE 3 (Pg. 88)

ACROSS:

1 marked down
4 break the bank
7 hit
8 steep
9 take in
11 rack
12 shell out

DOWN:

2 dressed to kill
3 snapped up
5 hit the spot
6 cash
10 clash

EXERCISE 4 (Pg. 89)

1 B	3 A	5 B	7 B	9 B
2 B	4 A	6 A	8 A	10 B

EXERCISE 5 (Pg. 90)

1 **I'm going to** keep my job for the time being, even though I **don't like it**.
2 **The young women** were dressed to kill when they went to the hottest club in **town last night**.
3 **We'll have to** leave first thing in the morning if you want to get **there by lunchtime**.
4 **He said that** a cold glass of juice would really hit the spot after doing **all that exercise**.
5 **After he won** the competition, he was so full of himself that people started **to dislike him**.
6 **I hope he** doesn't shoot his mouth off during the annual meeting at the **head office today**.
7 **You really shouldn't** sell yourself short, because you have the education and experience to **do that job**.
8 **How much would** you be willing to shell out for a brand-new apartment **in that area**?

EXERCISE 6 (Pg. 91)

```
y  o  n  i  q  e  n  o  g  g  n  o  l  k  s
u  f  o  d  a  o  l  a  t  e  g  l  m  d  e
t  w  b  g  l  f  y  p  l  u  i  r  a  c  k
n  g  k  n  a  b  e  h  t  k  a  e  r  b  s
z  l  e  t  s  p  t  i  o  h  v  b  k  x  h
e  w  v  g  t  u  i  t  u  o  l  l  e  h  s
x  i  o  i  r  d  d  t  z  l  o  w  d  b  a
y  n  n  t  e  e  d  h  i  l  i  j  d  z  l
s  c  i  t  s  p  e  e  t  s  y  z  o  c  c
x  w  z  s  o  p  l  s  o  c  a  f  w  e  u
n  x  e  y  r  a  n  p  r  n  a  y  n  d  i
f  r  m  n  t  n  k  o  a  k  m  x  i  x  l
d  x  g  q  w  s  o  t  d  i  q  u  i  b  b
```

CHAPTER 7   PICKING UP A FRIEND AT THE AIRPORT

EXERCISE 1 (Pg. 102)

1 F	5 J	9 L	13 E	17 D
2 H	6 A	10 N	14 S	18 P
3 M	7 T	11 R	15 G	19 K
4 Q	8 B	12 O	16 I	20 C

EXERCISE 2 (Pg. 103)

1 a stone's throw away
2 went cold turkey
3 grumpy
4 get over
5 time to spare

6 cravings for
7 pack on the pounds
8 grab a bite
9 gridlock
10 to take five

11 spare-tire
12 Holy cow
13 half-and-half
14 lucked out
15 head

EXERCISE 3 (Pg. 104)

1 go cold turkey
2 a stone's throw away
3 that does it
4 luck out
5 make great time
6 the john
7 get over
8 spare-tire

9 holy cow
10 grab a bite to eat
11 kill time
12 head
13 go ballistic
14 you bet
15 butt
16 time to spare

17 take five
18 grumpy
19 craving
20 pack on the pounds
21 gridlock
22 make great time
23 pack on the pounds
24 go ballistic

EXERCISE 4 (Pg. 105)

1 Could we **grab a bite to eat** at the diner before we go to the concert?
2 After smoking for more than 10 years, he **went cold turkey**.
3 We've been working for more than 4 hours. What do you say we **take five**?
4 My father **went ballistic/hit the roof** when my younger brother was arrested for vandalism.
5 He's got a **spare-tire** because he overeats and never exercises.
6 I was up all night studying. I definitely need a **pick-me-up** this morning.
7 The ambulance couldn't get to the accident scene because of the **gridlock**.
8 Do you happen to know where **the john** is?
9 He was really **grumpy** this morning because he drank too much last night.
10 I'll be sure and **head** over to his house right after the basketball game finishes.

EXERCISE 5 (Pg. 106)

1 **He really started** to pack on the pounds after he turned **forty years old**.
2 **These days, there's** always gridlock in the city between 4 **and 6 o'clock**.
3 **I'd like to** grab a bite to eat at that new restaurant that just opened **on the corner**.
4 **He was terribly** grumpy this morning because his newborn baby kept him **up all night**.
5 **She really hit** the roof when her husband completely forgot about their **tenth wedding anniversary**.
6 **The student couldn't** get over the fact that she hadn't been accepted into **Harvard Law School**.
7 **We're lucky because** the store you want to visit is only a stone's throw **away from here**.
8 **I saw a** lot of bald men with spare-tires when I went to my **high-school reunion**.

EXERCISE 6 (Pg. 107)

```
t  g  e  t  o  v  e  r  v  m  g  k  x  q  q
i  q  q  v  z  u  m  n  z  o  b  c  g  s  t
z  e  v  k  u  i  i  y  b  x  v  q  p  a  d
t  h  v  s  c  g  t  a  t  b  u  a  r  a  y
i  i  c  i  c  o  l  d  t  u  r  k  e  y  p
b  r  f  q  f  l  l  a  a  e  n  h  l  k  m
h  y  k  p  i  e  i  d  t  i  z  s  w  f  u
o  b  q  s  e  q  k  i  i  l  c  z  v  u  r
l  j  t  i  m  i  r  a  c  r  a  v  i  n  g
y  i  b  y  u  e  f  n  t  f  g  u  g  p  j
c  h  u  b  b  y  u  r  c  f  q  y  c  u  k
o  m  r  x  d  n  d  m  c  j  t  d  s  u  d
w  l  i  u  l  x  q  e  k  w  k  e  f  z  p
```

EXERCISE 1 (Pg. 118)

1	J	5	H	9	R	13	S	17	G
2	F	6	C	10	E	14	A	18	O
3	L	7	T	11	P	15	D	19	B
4	N	8	I	12	Q	16	M	20	K

EXERCISE 2 (Pg. 119)

1 bundle up
2 came across
3 bending my ear
4 like crazy
5 get away with
6 one-track mind
7 bugs
8 got some sun
9 suits you to a T
10 knock it off
11 take a dip
12 pour
13 hot
14 can't handle
15 muggy

EXERCISE 3 (Pg. 120)

ACROSS:

1 like crazy
3 hot
5 bundle up
7 cloud over
9 a load of
10 kick back
11 pour

DOWN:

2 come across
3 hang out
4 bugs
6 heat wave
8 doze off

ANSWER KEY

EXERCISE 4 (Pg. 121)

1 A	3 A	5 B	7 A	9 B
2 B	4 B	6 B	8 B	10 A

EXERCISE 5 (Pg. 122)

1 **I think the** ski jacket you bought for yourself really suits you **to a T**.
2 **I told him** that we are going to hang out at the café until he **joins us there**.
3 **I can't go** to the movies with you because I have a load of homework **to do tonight**.
4 **She has been** fishing for compliments ever since she got her hair cut at **that trendy salon**.
5 **He said that** it's supposed to cloud over this afternoon and then **start raining tonight**.
6 **The teacher always** lets him get away with skipping class **every Friday afternoon**.
7 **While I was** wandering through the mall with my friend, I came across **a beautiful blouse**.
8 **I've been studying** like crazy because I have to write two final exams the **day after tomorrow**.

EXERCISE 6 (Pg. 123)

1 doze off	9 a load of	17 heat wave
2 like crazy	10 a one-track mind	18 bugs
3 skimpy	11 take a dip	19 get some sun
4 handle	12 by all means	20 bend his ear
5 knock it off	13 kick back	21 muggy
6 hot	14 get some sun	22 skimpy
7 pour	15 bundle up	23 a one-track mind
8 cloud over	16 hang out	

CHAPTER 9 WAITING FOR A FIREWORKS SHOW

EXERCISE 1 (Pg. 134)

1 E	5 L	9 P	13 G	17 F
2 J	6 R	10 N	14 C	18 K
3 S	7 M	11 A	15 T	19 B
4 I	8 D	12 Q	16 H	20 O

EXERCISE 2 (Pg. 135)

1 flirted with	6 get up the guts	11 mobbed
2 a crush	7 get in touch with	12 the silent treatment
3 chickened out	8 on the lookout for	13 hit it off
4 on the verge	9 kicks off	14 bored stiff
5 Everybody and his brother	10 grab a bite	15 out of this world

EXERCISE 3 (Pg. 136)

ACROSS:

2 catch
6 sit tight
7 kicks off
8 breathtaking
10 hit it off

DOWN:

1 bored stiff
3 chicken out
4 grab a bite
5 run a fever
9 show up

EXERCISE 4 (Pg. 137)

1 My boyfriend was over an hour late for our date. That's **par for the course**.
2 The stores are always **mobbed** during the Christmas shopping season.
3 My older sister **made a killing** selling real estate in San Francisco last year.
4 He said that his friends are supposed to **show up** in about 15 minutes.
5 She has always **had the hots for/had a crush on** that handsome guy who lives across the street.
6 Don't worry. I'll **get in touch with** you first thing tomorrow.
7 She was going to ask him to dance, but then she **chickened out.**
8 The summer craft fair **kicks off** at 9 o'clock tomorrow morning.
9 **Everybody and his brother** went to see the new exhibition at the art gallery this weekend.
10 His wife **gave him the silent treatment** for three days after he forgot their wedding anniversary.

EXERCISE 5 (Pg. 138)

1 **I may have** finally gotten up the guts to ask her out on a **date this weekend.**
2 **I've been waiting** for my best friend to get in touch with me for **over two hours**.
3 **The meal we** ate was out of this world because it was prepared by a **famous European chef.**
4 **Would you like** to grab a bite to eat with me at that little restaurant **down the street**?
5 **The professor was** not very pleased when she showed up late for the final **exam this morning.**
6 **The young woman** couldn't get the bartender off her mind because he was so **charming and handsome.**
7 **The nursing student** hit it off with the interesting doctor she met at the medical **conference in Chicago.**
8 **The shopping mall** was mobbed with fans as the famous actress strolled from **store to store.**

ANSWER KEY

EXERCISE 6 (Pg. 139)

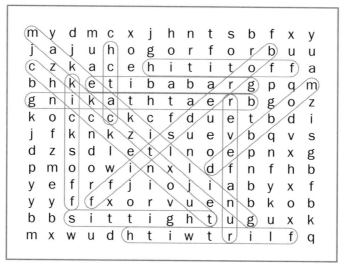

EXERCISE 1 (Pg. 150)

1 C	5 N	9 T	13 G	17 M
2 K	6 I	10 F	14 R	18 E
3 Q	7 O	11 A	15 J	19 P
4 H	8 D	12 S	16 L	20 B

EXERCISE 2 (Pg. 151)

1 limped	6 out of breath	11 hilarious
2 tipped the scales	7 call it a day	12 pay off
3 do me some good	8 clean up my act	13 stomach
4 build up	9 light as a feather	14 open up
5 kick the habit	10 working out	15 hit

EXERCISE 3 (Pg. 152)

ACROSS:

3 kick the habit
9 face the music
10 pooped
11 build up
12 open up

DOWN:

1 stomach
2 limp
4 charley horse
5 hit
6 out of shape
7 hilarious
8 work out

EXERCISE 4 (Pg. 153)

1 The soccer coach told the player that he'd have to **clean up his act**.
2 The comedian I saw at the nightclub last night was **hilarious**.
3 She was **out of breath** after running from one side of the campus to the other.
4 Two seats on the bus just **opened up**. Why don't we take them?
5 I ate tons of food over the Christmas vacation. I'm afraid to see **what I tip the scales at**.
6 I can't **stomach** the way he criticizes everyone he works with at the office.
7 I think we've done enough for one day. What do you say we **call it a day**?
8 We **hit** the shopping mall after we finished studying at the library.
9 He's been **limping** ever since he twisted his ankle
10 I don't think you've put on any weight at all. You're still **light as a feather**.

EXERCISE 5 (Pg. 154)

1 **He was so** out of shape that he could only run for a few **minutes before stopping**.
2 **That muscular guy** always works out at the gym at 8:30 **every Sunday morning**.
3 **The boys were** tuckered out because they had spent the day hiking **through the woods**.
4 **I think it** would do us some good to get out of the sun and **into the shade**.
5 **They decided to** call it a day after they had worked on the project for **over five hours**.
6 **My uncle decided** it was time to clean up his act after suffering a **serious heart attack**.
7 **Her arms and** legs were very sore because she got carried away at the fitness **club last night**.
8 **She said that** her back was killing her, so she won't be able to go dancing **with us tonight**.

EXERCISE 6 (Pg. 155)

1 carried away
2 out of shape
3 build up
4 call it a day
5 killing me
6 face the music
7 hurt like the devil
8 tip the scales at
9 a second wind
10 stomach
11 pay off
12 charley horse
13 by the way
14 work out
15 kick the habit
16 pooped
17 hilarious
18 tuckered out
19 out of breath
20 do us some good
21 clean up my act
22 hilarious

GIVE IT A SHOT (Pg. 160)

1 C
2 J
3 P
4 E
5 L
6 N
7 A
8 R
9 F
10 H
11 Q
12 D
13 O
14 I
15 B
16 M
17 G
18 K

ANSWER KEY

EXERCISE 1 (Pg. 166)

1	M	5	A	9	C	13	I	17	D
2	O	6	S	10	H	14	G	18	Q
3	T	7	B	11	N	15	R	19	J
4	P	8	K	12	E	16	L	20	F

EXERCISE 2 (Pg. 167)

1 cheating on
2 heard through the grapevine
3 drank like a fish
4 on the house
5 a short fuse
6 muscle-bound
7 an opening line
8 bouncer
9 pissed off
10 night and day
11 dirty look
12 tossing my cookies
13 a soft spot for
14 leery
15 stick it out

EXERCISE 3 (Pg. 168)

ACROSS:

5 stick it out
6 jerk
7 leery
8 crazy about
9 a short fuse
10 bummed out

DOWN:

1 bouncer
2 pissed off
3 on the house
4 mope around

EXERCISE 4 (Pg. 169)

1	B	6	B
2	A	7	A
3	A	8	B
4	A	9	A
5	A	10	B

EXERCISE 5 (Pg. 170)

1 **I am really** crazy about playing squash with my best **friend every Friday.**
2 **The young man** fooled around on his girlfriend after they had a huge argument **on Saturday night.**
3 **My little sister** has been moping around ever since her dog got run over **by a car.**
4 **The teenaged boy** tossed his cookies after he ate some bad sushi at the **restaurant this afternoon.**
5 **The meal I** ate was on the house because my friend knows the owner **of the diner.**
6 **I think the** boss has a soft spot for you because you never have to work late **at the office.**
7 **He gave his** ex-girlfriend a dirty look when he saw her with her new boyfriend **at the beach.**
8 **She was completely** pissed off about not getting the promotion because she had worked there **for many years.**

EXERCISE 6 (Pg. 171)

```
d  a  u  a  t  h  l  h  b  o  d  c  r  z  g
e  q  y  q  u  l  i  h  f  p  n  o  e  h  l
r  s  x  e  o  l  r  a  f  e  u  c  f  e  i
e  x  h  t  b  b  c  n  o  n  o  n  e  m  q
m  e  i  o  a  u  q  g  d  i  r  t  m  u  u
m  i  a  n  y  m  f  o  e  n  a  h  t  g  g
a  r  l  r  z  e  f  v  s  g  e  b  a  n  n
h  u  e  z  a  d  h  e  s  l  p  o  n  o  x
j  e  r  k  r  o  t  r  i  i  o  u  o  x  s
l  p  g  i  c  u  f  n  n  n  m  s  x  h  p
h  z  n  a  h  t  s  i  i  e  f  e  v  n  z
r  k  n  v  p  b  x  g  x  i  w  e  i  p  d
s  y  f  y  p  i  k  p  e  u  n  b  v  f  u
```

CHAPTER 12   CATCHING A MOVIE

EXERCISE 1 (Pg. 182)

1 M	5 G	9 D	13 R	17 O
2 E	6 S	10 B	14 F	18 J
3 Q	7 C	11 A	15 I	19 P
4 L	8 K	12 T	16 N	20 H

EXERCISE 2 (Pg. 183)

1 munchies
2 tearjerker
3 scared to death
4 cost an arm and a leg
5 the concession
6 to bawl
7 gave me a ring
8 buff
9 wimp
10 rip-off
11 row
12 twists and turns
13 touching
14 caught a movie
15 get caught off guard

EXERCISE 3 (Pg. 184)

1 munchies
2 row
3 concession
4 two thumbs up
5 aisle
6 catch a movie
7 nominated for
8 tearjerker
9 scare her to death
10 wimp
11 a rip-off
12 twists and turns
13 hold back the tears
14 coming attractions
15 bawl
16 movie buff
17 give him a ring
18 catch him off guard
19 blow you away
20 give her a ring
21 hold back the tears
22 two thumbs up

EXERCISE 4 (Pg. 185)

1 I **had a lump in my throat** as I watched a TV program on homeless children.
2 Driving down that steep hill in the snowstorm **scared me to death**.
3 I'm worried about you walking home this late. **Give me a ring** once you get to your place.
4 She was **on the edge of her seat** as she watched the leading actor walk into the dark house.
5 He was **blown away** when he saw the Eiffel Tower during his first trip to France.
6 My friends **caught me off guard** when they threw me a surprise birthday party.
7 We should remember to buy some **munchies** for the long drive home.
8 That state-of-the-art big screen TV I bought yesterday **cost an arm and a leg**.
9 She's going to buy a hotdog at the **concession** before the hockey game starts.
10 That movie is very confusing because there are too many **twists and turns**.

EXERCISE 5 (Pg. 186)

1 **My brother and** I argued over which one of us would get the aisle seat **on the bus**.
2 **They invited us** to catch a movie with them after we finish dinner **at the restaurant**.
3 **The children were** scared to death when they walked in the old abandoned **house at night**.
4 **The president of** the company caught the workers off guard when he **showed up unannounced**.
5 **My youngest son** bawled for at least 30 minutes after he fell off his **bike this morning**.
6 **My older sister** was on the edge of her seat because the movie was so **filled with suspense**.
7 **I was really** blown away when my friends threw a bon voyage party for me **on the weekend**.
8 **I could not** hold back the tears when I saw the news report about the victims of **the terrorist bombing**.

EXERCISE 6 (Pg. 187)

```
t w i s t s a n d t u r n s c
k s m g t a x g z e z v r a g
g a u o q r p a p k y c t d o
s r n i v k c t u m c c e u w
n f c z n i g e s e h o a o x
j p h g j a e d b a w l r w n
x r i w y z x b m y r n j r t
f r e a k e d o u t a o e l p
c p s m h p v r h f k s r j g
x c t u c i m n t e f u k h u
c o n c e s s i o n p n e m e
e y s g b x u c w u f k r j n
h g n i h c u o t d z t l s c
```

GIVE IT A SHOT (Pg. 192)

1 K	4 J	7 L	10 O	13 I
2 G	5 N	8 E	11 F	14 H
3 A	6 C	9 B	12 D	15 M

CHAPTER 13 DRIVING TO A CABIN FOR THE WEEKEND

EXERCISE 1 (Pg. 198)

1 G	5 M	9 F	13 P	17 K
2 Q	6 C	10 S	14 J	18 D
3 A	7 R	11 E	15 L	19 O
4 T	8 N	12 I	16 B	20 H

EXERCISE 2 (Pg. 199)

1 butt in
2 makes my blood boil
3 fiddling with
4 some shut-eye
5 ranting and raving
6 the sticks
7 fidgets
8 unwind
9 goof
10 the wrong side of the bed
11 bumper sticker
12 showed me the ropes
13 hop in
14 give me a hand
15 handy

EXERCISE 3 (Pg. 200)

1 get some shut-eye
2 rant and rave
3 in the sticks
4 fidget
5 handy
6 unwind
7 rustic
8 butt in
9 get a wink of sleep
10 touchy
11 hop in
12 wiped out
13 bumper sticker
14 cozy
15 give him a hand
16 tailgate
17 drive him nuts
18 show him the ropes
19 cut you off
20 tucked under
21 fiddle with

EXERCISE 4 (Pg. 201)

1 A	3 A	5 A	7 B	9 A
2 A	4 B	6 A	8 A	10 B

EXERCISE 5 (Pg. 202)

1 **I felt so** cozy in bed this morning that I didn't want to get up and **go to work.**
2 **My boyfriend was** in a bad mood because he got up on the wrong side **of the bed.**
3 **My daughter always** wanted me to tuck her into bed at night when **she was young.**
4 **I didn't sleep** very well last night, so I'm going to snooze on the **sofa this afternoon.**
5 **The young boy** kept fidgeting around at the dinner table because he **was really bored.**
6 **The driver of** the other car was furious when I inadvertently cut him off **on the freeway.**
7 **The woman in** the grocery store made my blood boil when she told my daughter **to shut up.**
8 **I didn't get** a wink of sleep last night because the people across the hall were **having a party.**

ANSWER KEY

EXERCISE 6 (Pg. 203)

1 Do you have time to **give me a hand** with the yard work this afternoon?
2 That guy **made my blood boil** when he punched my younger brother in the face.
3 I think the book you're looking for was **tucked** under the sofa in the living room.
4 I love to **unwind** on the patio in my backyard after a tough day a work.
5 My co-worker **showed me the ropes** when I was a new employee.
6 **I hopped into** my brand-new car and drove out to the beach on Sunday afternoon.
7 We got lost **in the sticks** when we were on vacation last summer.
8 She was **wiped out** because she had spent over 10 hours working at the office.
9 The drunken man was **ranting and raving** as he staggered down the street.
10 I really don't like aggressive drivers who **tailgate** me.

CHAPTER 14   FINISHING CLASSES

EXERCISE 1 (Pg. 214)

1 D	5 O	9 N	13 B	17 J
2 M	6 H	10 E	14 P	18 G
3 K	7 L	11 I	15 F	19 A
4 T	8 S	12 Q	16 R	20 C

EXERCISE 2 (Pg. 215)

1 brags	6 mixed emotions	11 spare time
2 work his butt off	7 goofed off	12 hell to pay
3 hold back the tears	8 poring over	13 compatible with
4 in the same boat	9 hit the slopes	14 took my place
5 part ways with	10 a matter of fact	15 Holy smoke

EXERCISE 3 (Pg. 216)

1 take it easy	9 go by	17 hit the slopes
2 boast	10 hold back the tears	18 down in the dumps
3 by leaps and bounds	11 holy smoke	19 hell to pay
4 choked up	12 as a matter of fact	20 mixed emotions
5 spare time	13 compatible	21 time flies
6 stick around	14 crack a book	22 shoot the breeze
7 shoot the breeze	15 goof off	
8 part ways	16 in the same boat	

EXERCISE 4 (Pg. 217)

1 A	3 B	5 A	7 A	9 A
2 B	4 B	6 B	8 B	10 A

EXERCISE 5 (Pg. 218)

1 **I always shoot** the breeze with my friends in the hall before **the class begins.**
2 **I was very** sad when my girlfriend and I had to part ways at the **airport last week.**
3 **Everyone on the** team was down in the dumps after we lost **the championship game.**
4 **My ability to** snowboard improved by leaps and bounds after I **took several lessons.**
5 **I hate it** when your snobby boyfriend boasts about what a great football **player he is.**
6 **There will be** hell to pay if you forget to meet your dad at the train **station this afternoon.**
7 **I'll have to** work my butt off in order to pass the biology **course I'm taking.**
8 **That employee got** fired because he was always goofing off when he should **have been working.**

EXERCISE 6 (Pg. 219)

GIVE IT A SHOT (Pg. 224)

1 on cloud nine
2 tickled pink
3 miserable
4 in high spirits
5 down in the dumps
6 gloomy
7 thrilled
8 bummed out
9 blue
10 in seventh heaven

CHAPTER 15   SNOWBOARDING AT A WINTER RESORT

EXERCISE 1 (Pg. 230)

1 K	5 Q	9 E	13 I	17 A
2 S	6 M	10 G	14 R	18 O
3 H	7 P	11 J	15 F	19 B
4 T	8 C	12 N	16 D	20 L

EXERCISE 2 (Pg. 231)

1 under the weather
2 keeping up with
3 in over my head
4 psych out
5 took a stab at

6 Hold your horses
7 black-and-blue
8 up to
9 smacked into
10 make do

11 hotdog
12 tagged along
13 cut me off
14 kick the bucket
15 a spill

EXERCISE 3 (Pg. 232)

ACROSS:

1 black and blue
5 cranky
8 hang a right
9 heads up
10 take off

DOWN:

2 kick the bucket
3 groan
4 tag along
6 out of whack
7 wipe out

EXERCISE 4 (Pg. 233)

1 He hasn't come to work this week because he's been **under the weather**.
2 My legs were always **black-and-blue** when I was a young boy.
3 I **got in over my head** when I enrolled in a fourth year biology course.
4 I thought I was going to **kick the bucket** when my brakes failed on that steep hill.
5 I'm getting dressed as fast as I can. Just **hold your horses**!
6 My friends want to **take off** now because they want to avoid the rush hour traffic.
7 He **smacked into** a telephone pole when he lost control of his car on that sharp corner.
8 You should go down the alley and then **hang a left** at the next corner.
9 She was **cranky** because her sister kept interrupting her while she was studying.
10 My friend always tries to **psych me out** before we play squash.

EXERCISE 5 (Pg. 234)

1 **They need to** take off right away in order to make it to the **meeting on time**.
2 **You're going to** kick the bucket if you keep on smoking and **drinking like that**.
3 **He told me** to go along the street and then hang a left at **the grocery store**.
4 **Our friend is** under the weather so she'll probably miss the midterm exam **on Tuesday afternoon**.
5 **I don't think** that I'm up to going for a 10-mile hike through the **wilderness with you**.
6 **Would you mind** if I tagged along with you when you go to the **computer store today**?
7 **I really got** in over my head when I took five university courses and worked **part-time at night**.
8 **I'm going to** take a stab at surfing while I'm on vacation in Hawaii with my **family this summer**.

EXERCISE 6 (Pg. 235)

1 psych him out
2 on its last legs
3 hotdog
4 take off
5 hold your horses

6 tag along
7 kick the bucket
8 hang a left
9 out of whack
10 wipe out

11 groan
12 go for it
13 heads up
14 black-and-blue
15 cranky

16 keep up with
17 moan
18 hold your horses
19 take a stab at
20 get in over her head

GIVE IT A SHOT (Pg. 240)

1 goofy
2 lame
3 poseur
4 stoked

5 chatter
6 phat
7 session
8 sick

9 stick
10 regular
11 corduroy
12 rolling down the windows

CHAPTER 16   RETURNING HOME

EXERCISE 1 (Pg. 246)

1 M	5 J	9 D	13 Q	17 S
2 E	6 O	10 C	14 H	18 G
3 A	7 B	11 N	15 F	19 P
4 T	8 R	12 I	16 L	20 K

EXERCISE 2 (Pg. 247)

1 living out of my suitcase
2 get the ball rolling
3 back to square one
4 the ground floor
5 underway

6 ton of
7 lug
8 felt out of place
9 bon voyage party
10 the cold shoulder

11 old flame
12 looking forward to
13 sharp
14 head
15 swung by

EXERCISE 3 (Pg. 248)

1 swing by
2 get her down
3 cross paths
4 feel out of place
5 head
6 bon voyage party
7 foot the bill
8 sharp

9 look forward to
10 give him the cold shoulder
11 turn up
12 go back to square one
13 lug
14 old flame
15 miss the boat
16 knock around

17 get underway
18 dread
19 get him down
20 pay my own way
21 weigh on his mind
22 live out of his suitcase

EXERCISE 4 (Pg. 249)

1 She's going to **knock around** Europe after she graduates from university.
2 I **felt out of place** when I first started working for that high-tech company.
3 The city tour **gets underway** at 9 o'clock in the morning in front of the hotel.
4 I'm sure that if you **bide your time**, another job opportunity will come along.
5 I had to **lug** four heavy bags of groceries all the way home from the market.
6 My **old flame** slapped me in the face when she saw me at the movies with another girl.
7 She said that she'd **swing by** the office right after the meeting finishes.
8 I **missed the boat** when I chose not to invest money in that company.
9 The bad weather we've had recently is really **getting me down**.
10 Even though we both live in the same town, we rarely **cross paths**.

EXERCISE 5 (Pg. 250)

1 **My parents will** foot the bill when I go to university in **California next year.**
2 **I went home** early because I felt so out of place at **that posh restaurant.**
3 **My family is** really looking forward to meeting you when they come **to New York.**
4 **My co-worker gave** me the cold shoulder when I ran into him on **the street today.**
5 **I spent three** weeks knocking around Asia before I started my final **year of university.**
6 **He had to** go back to square one after he dropped out of college in **his first year.**
7 **My friend helped** me lug my suitcases across the parking lot and **into the airport.**
8 **I have not** crossed paths with him even though we both live and work in **the same city.**

EXERCISE 6 (Pg. 251)

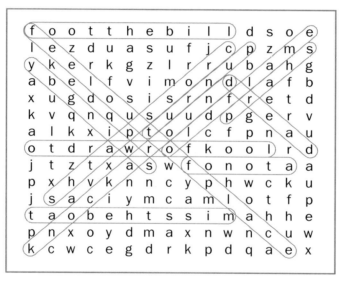

GIVE IT A SHOT (Pg. 256)

Part A

1	D	5	B
2	G	6	C
3	A	7	H
4	E	8	F

Part B

1	B	5	A
2	H	6	G
3	D	7	E
4	C	8	F

■■ GLOSSARY ■■

GLOSSARY

GLOSSARY

have a lump in one's throat (to)	become emotional	178,180
have a soft spot for someone (to)	fond of someone	163,165
have it in for someone (to)	get even with someone, seek revenge	50,53
have one's name on it (to)	perfectly suited to someone	83,84
have the hots for someone (to)	be very attracted to someone	131,133
head somewhere (to)	go somewhere	99,101,242,244
heads up	be alert	226,228
hear through the grapevine (to)	hear gossip, hear a rumor	162,164
heat wave	many days of hot weather	114,116
hell to pay	great punishment as a result of one's actions	210,212
high-cut	a swimsuit that shows a lot of leg	115,117
hilarious	very funny	147,149
hit it off (to)	become good friends with someone quickly	131,133
hit somewhere (to)	visit somewhere	82,84,147,149
hit the books (to)	study	50,52
hit the roof (to)	furious, livid, very angry	99,101
hit the slopes (to)	go skiing/snowboarding	211,213
hit the spot (to)	satisfying	83,85
hitch	problem	35,37
hold back the tears (to)	control/stop one's tears	178,180,210,212
hold your horses (to)	wait	227,229
holy cow	holy smoke, wow	99,101
holy smoke	holy cow, wow	211,213
hook up with someone (to)	meet someone	35,37
hop in (to)	get in a vehicle	194,196
hot	sexy, gorgeous	115,117
hotdog	a showoff	226,228
humongous	enormous, gigantic, huge, immense	2,4
hung up on something/someone	stuck on something/someone, unable to continue	50,52
hurt like the devil (to)	hurt very much	147,149

I

I don't know how to break this to you	I don't know how to tell this to you	66,68
in check	under control	19,21
in mint condition	in perfect condition	66,69
in no time	quickly, soon	3,5
in the buff	in the nude, in the raw, in one's birthday suit, naked	67,69
in the long run	in the long term, over a long period of time	67,69
in the same boat	in the same situation	210,212
in the sticks	in the countryside	195,197
into something	enjoy something	179,181

J

jack-of-all-trades (a)	a multitalented laborer	66,68
jammed-packed	crowded, mobbed	82,84
jerk	terrible man	162,164
jetlag	fatigue caused by air travel	3,5
john (the)	the bathroom/washroom	99,101
just between you and me	confidentially, privately	146,148

K

keep one's fingers crossed (to)	hope for a positive result	34,36
keep up with someone (to)	progress at the same speed as someone else	227,229
keyed up	very nervous	18,20
kick back (to)	relax, take it easy	114,116
kick off (to)	begin, start	130,132
kick oneself (to)	regret doing something	18,20
kick the bucket (to)	die, pass away	227,229

GLOSSARY

WORD/IDIOM	DEFINITION	PAGE
kick the habit (to)	break the habit	146,148
kill time (to)	waste time	98,100
kitty-corner	diagonal in location	19,21
knock around somewhere (to)	travel around somewhere	242,244
knock it off (to)	stop it	115,117
knot in one's stomach (a)	a nervous feeling in the stomach	18,20
know one's way around (to)	be familiar with a particular area	18,20
know like the back of one's hand (to)	be very familiar with something	19,21
knuckle down (to)	become serious about one's work	34,36

L

WORD/IDIOM	DEFINITION	PAGE
lady's man (a)	lady killer, playboy, stud	162,164
last resort (a)	a final option	83,85
leery	apprehensive, wary	163,165
let someone down (to)	disappoint someone	66,68
let someone off the hook (to)	let someone avoid punishment	66,68
light as a feather	very light	147,149
like crazy	actively, fast, very much	114,116
like it or lump it (to)	something must be accepted, like it or not	211,213
like night and day	totally different	162,165
limp (to)	walk in an awkward manner due to an injury to the leg	147,149
live out of one's suitcase (to)	stay in different places briefly, never unpacking	242,244
load (a)	a bunch, a lot, a pile, a stack, a ton	114,116
long gone	bought/left/taken a long time ago	83,85
look forward to doing something (to)	excited about doing something in the future	242,244
look into something (to)	investigate something	34,36
lose sleep over something (to)	worry about something	34,36
luck out (to)	lucky	98,100
lug something (to)	carry something heavy	242,244

M

WORD/IDIOM	DEFINITION	PAGE
make a dent in something (to)	make little progress in something	51,53
make a fuss over something (to)	overreact, go over the top	35,37
make a killing (to)	make a lot of money	131,133
make do (to)	do one's best with something that is sub-standard	227,229
make great time (to)	arrive somewhere faster than expected	98,100
make one's blood boil (to)	make someone very angry	194,197
make something from scratch (to)	make something by oneself, not store bought	66,68
mark down (to)	reduce in price	82,84
melt in one's mouth (to)	food that easily dissolves in one's mouth	83,85
mind/memory like a steel trap (a)	a great memory	50,52
miss the boat (to)	miss an opportunity or chance	242,244
mixed emotions	both positive and negative feelings	210,212
moan (to)	express pain, groan	226,229
mobbed	crowded, jam-packed	130,132
mope around (to)	move around in a sad manner	162,164
movie buff	movie fan	179,181
muggy	hot and humid	115,117
mull something over (to)	consider, think something over	50,52
munchies	snack food	178,180
muscle-bound	very muscular	162,164

N

WORD/IDIOM	DEFINITION	PAGE
never let someone live something down (to)	never let someone forget about something	66,68
new flame	new lover	51,53
nominate (to)	select for a possible award/position	179,181

O

WORD/IDIOM	DEFINITION	PAGE
old flame	ex-lover	243,245

GLOSSARY

thaw something out (to)	defrost something	66,68
there's no accounting for taste	there's no explaining someone's style	83,85
time flies	time passes quickly	210,212
time to spare	extra time	98,100
tip the scales at (to)	weigh	147,149
ton (a)	a bunch, a load, a lot, a pile, a stack	242,244
toss one's cookies (to)	barf, puke, throw up, vomit	163,165
touching	heartbreaking, moving, stirring	178,180
touchy	sensitive	195,197
tuck under/into something (to)	place under/into something	195,197
tuckered out	exhausted, pooped, tired, wiped out, worn out	146,148
turn beet red (to)	blush	67,69
turn on the charm (to)	become charming	162,164
turn up (to)	show up	242,244
twists and turns	changes in the plot	178,181
two-piece (a)	a bikini, a swimsuit that has two pieces	115,117
two thumbs up	excellent, highly recommended	179,181
two's company, three's a crowd	a third person isn't welcome	35,37

U

under the weather	ill, sick	226,228
unwind (to)	relax	195,197
up to	doing, occupied with	34,37
up to doing something	able to do something, ready to do something	226,228

V

verge (on the)	close to doing or experiencing	131,133
vivid	colorful, dramatic, vibrant	51,53

W

wander (to)	walk slowly, saunter, stroll	18,20
weigh on one's mind (to)	worry someone	243,245
weight off one's shoulders (a)	a relief	51,53
what's-(his/her)-face	used when a person's name can't be remembered	50,52
wimp	chicken, coward, sissy, wuss	179,181
wipe out (to)	fall	226,228
wipe out something (to)	destroy something	19,21
wiped out	exhausted, pooped, tired, tuckered out, worn out	194,196
work one's butt off (to)	work very hard	211,213
work out (to)	exercise	67,69,146,148
wouldn't miss something for the world	would never miss something	243,245
wrong side of the tracks (the)	the bad section of the city	18,20

X

– –	– –	– –

Y

you bet	absolutely, of course	99,101
you can say that again	I agree with you	211,213
young at heart	have a youthful attitude	35,37

Z

– –	– –	– –

ISBN 141202003-4